2009 SUPPLEMENT to

CASES AND MAT...

ON

TRADE REGULATION

By

ROBERT PITOFSKY
Sheehy Professor of Law,
Georgetown University Law Center

HARVEY J. GOLDSCHMID
Dwight Professor of Law,
Columbia University School of Law

DIANE P. WOOD
Circuit Judge, U.S. Court of Appeals,
Seventh Circuit;
Senior Lecturer in Law,
University of Chicago Law School

FIFTH EDITION

New York, New York
FOUNDATION PRESS
2009

© 2005, 2006, 2007 THOMSON REUTERS/FOUNDATION PRESS

© 2009 By THOMSON REUTERS/FOUNDATION PRESS

     195 Broadway, 9th Floor

     New York, NY 10007

     Phone Toll Free 1–877–888–1330

     Fax (212) 367–6799

     foundation–press.com

Printed in the United States of America

ISBN 978–1–59941–483–6

TABLE OF CONTENTS

CHAPTER 1: OBJECTIVES AND ORIGINS OF ANTITRUST LAW

Replace last paragraph, page 17, and all of pages 18 to the middle of page 21.

In order to understand the nature of European Union (EU) antitrust law, or competition law as it is referred to in Europe, it is helpful to look at the broad outline of the EU's system of governance. There are now five principal institutions in the Union: the European Parliament, the Council of the European Union,[1] the European Commission, the European Court of Justice, and the European Court of Auditors. The most important non-judicial organ is the Council of the European Union, or the Council of Ministers as it is often called. The Council, according to Article 203 (ex Article 146) of the Rome Treaty,[2] is composed of ministers representing each Member State,

---

[1] The Council of the European Union should not be confused with the European Council and the Council of Europe. The European Council brings together the European heads of state or government and the President of the European Commission but is not a legal council of the EU. See http://ue.eu.int/faqHomePage.asp nodeIDx=2&command=update. The Council of Europe is an international organization comprised of both EU and non-EU members based in Strasbourg, France. Its primary focus since its inception in 1949 has been on developing a social agenda within Europe. For more information, see http://www.coe.int.

[2] The European Economic Community was established by the Rome Treaty in 1957. The Rome Treaty has been amended several times since then, and the subsequent amendments, along with the initial text, have now been consolidated into a continuously updated version. The current version of the Rome Treaty is referred to as the "Treaty Establishing the European Community." Following a major amendment by the 1997 Treaty of Amsterdam, the previously used numbering of treaty provisions has been changed as well. To avoid confusion, we will refer to both the former and the new article references, as is customarily done.

including representatives from each of the ten new Member States.[3] If the question before the Council is a general one, it is usually composed of the foreign ministers of the twenty-seven Member States, but if it is a specialized question, such as agriculture or finance, the ministers with the relevant portfolios will be in attendance. So constituted, the Council functions both as a head of state for the Union and as its chief legislative body.

The Commission in Brussels is the Union's administrative and executive arm. It now has 30 members,[4] which, according to Article 213 (ex Article 157) of the Treaty of Rome, are chosen on the grounds of general competence and independence (although in practice are also allocated carefully among Member States). The Commission is divided into various Directorates-General with responsibility for substantive areas within the Union's competence. The Competition Directorate General, or DG Comp, is responsible for competition policy and enforcement.

The European Court of Justice (ECJ) and the Court of First Instance (CFI), both located in Luxembourg, constitute the Union's judicial branch. The ECJ's function is to review formal decisions of the Commission and to review questions of EC law referred to it by the national courts of the Member States. Since 1988, the ECJ has been assisted by the Court of First Instance, which was established by the Council pursuant to authority granted under Article 225 (ex

---

[3] On May 1, 2004, the European Union underwent the largest expansion in history. There were fifteen Member States prior to the enlargement: Austria, Belgium, Denmark, Finland, France, Germany, Greece, Ireland, Italy, Luxembourg, the Netherlands, Portugal, Spain, Sweden, and the United Kingdom. The enlargement brought ten new countries into the EU: Cyprus, Czech Republic, Estonia, Hungary, Latvia, Lithuania, Malta, Poland, Slovakia, and Slovenia. In 2007, Bulgaria, and Romania were added to the EU. Turkey, Croatia and Macedonia are on the list of candidates to join. See http://europa.eu.int/comm/enlargement/enlargement.htm.

[4] See http://europa.eu.int/comm/commissioners/index_en.htm.

Article 168a) of the Treaty of Rome.[5]   The CFI has always had
jurisdiction over competition cases.   Over time, its authority has
expanded. It currently also has jurisdiction to rule in the first instance
on (1) all actions for annulment, for failure to act, and for damages
brought by natural or legal persons against the Community, (2)
actions brought against the Commission under the ECSC Treaty by
business firms or associations, and (3) disputes between the
Community and its officials and employees.   The Treaty of
Amsterdam, which entered into force on May 1, 1999, contemplates
that the Court of First Instance may eventually have jurisdiction over
all categories of cases now within the jurisdiction of the Court of
Justice except for preliminary references from the national courts
made pursuant to Article 234 (ex Article 177) of the Treaty.

Two principles developed by the ECJ make EU competition
law of particular importance: first, the Court has held that it has
"direct effect" on individuals and companies, which means that
violations can be prosecuted without regard to any measures in
national law that may apply; second, the Court has developed an
equivalent to the Supremacy Clause of the U.S. Constitution, under
which EU competition law has primacy over conflicting Member
State legislation.

The European Parliament has been gaining power over the
years, but it is still misleading to think of it as the counterpart to the
British Parliament, the French Assemblé Nationale, or the German
Bundestag. Since 1979, members of the Parliament have been elected
directly by European voters.   The Parliament sits in Strasbourg,
France. Its most important role now is to review legislative proposals
from the Council and the Commission. If it approves such a proposal,
the Council may then enact the proposal by qualified majority; if it
does not, or if it is not consulted, then the Council must act
unanimously. The Parliament also has the power to put questions to
the Commission, which must be answered, and it reviews the
Commission's annual general report.

---

[5]   Article 225 (ex Article 168a) was added by the Single European
Act of 1987, which amended the Rome Treaty in a number of
significant respects.

3

The last institution, the Court of Auditors, was introduced by the Maastricht Treaty. It is responsible for examining the accounts of all revenue and expenditure of the Union and its various constituent bodies, and reporting to both the Parliament and the Council.

Through this elaborate set of institutions, the Union has developed one of the most sophisticated bodies of competition law in the world. When the original Treaty of Rome, which established the European Economic Community, was signed on March 25, 1957, it included as one of its fundamental goals "the institution of a system ensuring that competition in the common market is not distorted."[6] Part Three, Title I, Chapter 1 of the Treaty implemented that goal by setting forth rules on competition that would apply to "undertakings" (Eurospeak for business entities and governments).[7] Article 81 (ex Article 85 – a point not repeated further in this note) of the Rome Treaty prohibits agreements and other concerted practices that have as their object or effect the prevention, restriction, or distortion of competition, unless the European Commission finds that the particular agreement should be exempted from the prohibition because of its beneficial effects. (You should note that the extent to which the beneficial effects must relate to efficiencies, as contrasted with effects on employment, regional development, or other industrial policy goals, has been debated for years within European circles.) Article 82 (ex Article 86) of the Treaty prohibits abuses of a dominant position. Article 86 (ex Article 90) seeks to place state operated monopolies or enterprises with special privileges under the competition regime, to the greatest extent possible. Finally, Article 87 (ex Article 92) declares that governmental subsidies that distort or threaten to distort

---

[6]   298 UNTS 11.

[7]   More specifically, "undertakings" as used by Article 81 and 82 refers to "every entity engaged in an economic activity, regardless of the legal status of the entity and the way it is financed." Case C-41/90, Höfner & Elser v. Macrotron, 1991, ECR I-1979, at para 17. This broad definition includes business entities, governmental entities, individuals, and even Member States. Robert Lane, Current Developments – European Union Law, 53 Int'l & Comp. L.Q. 465 (2004).

competition within the common market are incompatible with it. The Commission is responsible for reviewing state aids, as they are called, and it has the power to require that incompatible aids must be discontinued.

EU competition law underwent significant changes though two sets of regulations and notices that went into effect on May 1, 2004, on the same date as the accession of the ten new Member States. The first set consists of regulations and guidelines that affect the handling of competition claims in the EU, and is commonly referred to as the "modernisation package."[8] The second set, referred to as the "merger review package," incorporates regulations, guidelines and internal reforms to change the process of merger review.[9] Both packages are primarily procedural reforms and, with exception of an important definitional change in the new merger regulation, have little effect on the substantive law.

On December 16, 2002, the member states of the EU agreed on fundamental reforms of Council Regulation 17 and enacted Regulation 1/2003, the first regulation of the modernisation package.[10] Before this regulation went into force on May 1, 2004, the Commission maintained sole discretion over all exemption determinations under Article 81(3). In some cases, the Commission granted individual exemptions, which often were accompanied by significant conditions, and in other cases it issued so-called "block exemptions," which exempted certain classes of agreements, determinations and procedures that the Commission deemed consistent with Article 81. In order to make this centralized system

---

[8] Commission Finalizes Modernization of the EU Antitrust Enforcement Rules, IP/04/411, at http://europa.eu.int/rapid/pressReleasesAction.do?reference=IP/04/41 1&format=HTML&aged=0&language=EN&guiLanguage=en.

[9] Merger Control: Merger Review Package in a Nutshell, at http://europa.eu.int/comm/competition/publications/special/3_merger. pdf.

[10] Council Reg. (EC) 1/2003, 2003 O.J. (L 1) 1.

work, the Commission required undertakings to file "notifications" with it, pursuant to Article 81(1) and Regulation 17. Those notifications included extensive information from undertakings about pending agreements, decisions and practices.[11] Under the Regulation 17 system, undertakings were permitted to request an advance opinion from the Commission about whether these agreements, decisions and practices were lawful under Article 81(1).[12] Companies that believed their actions to be consistent with Article 81 often chose not to notify (although this was a bit risky, since a wrong guess led to a finding that their agreement was void under Article 81(2), but if an undertaking wanted an exemption under Article 81(3), it had no choice but to notify.[13]

Regulation 1/2003 now grants national competition authorities of Member States ("NCAs")[14] the authority to apply Articles 81 and 82 in full. In practical terms, this means that the Commission no longer has a monopoly over exemption determinations under Article 81(3). The Commission will continue to issue block exemptions, but neither the Commission nor the NCAs are required to uphold block exemptions when they lead to effects that are incompatible with Article 81(3).[15] National courts will now make Article 81(3) exemption determinations on a case-by-case basis. This system is

---

[11] See Council Reg. (EEC) 17/62. See generally Barry Hawk, Common Market and International Antitrust—A Comparative Guide (ed.); Richard Whish, Competition Law, ch. 9 (3d ed. 1993); Leonard Ritter, Francis Rawlinson, and W. David Braun, EC Competition Law—A Practitioner's Guide (Kluwer 1991).

[12] Council Reg. (EEC) 17, art. 2, 1962 O.J. P 13.

[13] Council Reg. (EEC) 17, arts. 4-5, 1962 O.J. P 13.

[14] Commission Notice on Cooperation Within the Network of Competition Authorities, at para 1, 2004 O.J. (C 101) 03, 43.

[15] Council Reg. (EC) 1/2003, "Whereas", para 10, 2003 O.J. (L 1) 1; id., art. 29(1); see Robert Lane, Current Developments – European Union Law, 53 Int'l & Comp. L.Q. 465 (2004).

expected to increase the number of private EU competition law actions in national courts, because undertakings can no longer use as a delay tactic Article 81(3) defenses that required the Commission's involvement.[16] Regulation 1/2003 also abolishes the centralized notification system, recognizing that this system imposed considerable cost on undertakings and detracted from the Commission's ability to focus on more serious infringements. [17]

NCAs may bring actions against undertakings when the NCAs are "well placed" to deal with competition law cases.[18] Single NCAs are normally well placed when the challenged practice substantially affects competition predominately in the Member State's territory.[19] NCAs may undertake parallel actions against an agreement or practice when it substantially affects competition within the territories of each respective Member State and an action by one NCA is not likely to bring about an end to the offense.[20] As before, NCAs are prohibited from applying national competition laws that conflict with Articles 81 and 82, unless applying national merger control laws or national law that falls entirely outside the domain of competition law as reflected

---

[16] See Opinion: Rhodri Thompson Q and Kieron Beal, Matrix Chambers, The Lawyer, May 3, 2004, at 17; Donncadh Woods, The Growth of Private Rights of Action Outside the U.S.: Private Enforcement of Antitrust Rules – Modernization of the EU Rules and the Road Ahead, 16 Loy. Consumer L. Rev. 431, 433 (2004).

[17] Council Reg. (EC) 1/2003, "Whereas," paras 1-4, 2003 O.J. (L 1) 1.

[18] Commission Notice on Cooperation Within the Network of Competition Authorities, at paras 8-10, 2004 O.J. (C 101) 03, 43.

[19] Council Reg. (EC) 1/2003, art. 6, 2003 O.J. (L 1) 1; Commission Notice on Cooperation Within the Network of Competition Authorities, at para 10, 2004 O.J. (C 101) 03, 43.

[20] Commission Notice on Cooperation Within the Network of Competition Authorities, at para 12, 2004 O.J. (C 101) 03, 43.

in Articles 81 and 82.[21] Under this system of parallel competences, the Commission retains jurisdiction over all EU competition law cases and a decision by the Commission to initiate proceedings destroys the competence of Member States to apply Articles 81 and 82 unless the case is in the process of appellate review at a national court.[22]

Everyone involved in these reforms recognizes that to allow multiple competition authorities to investigate and instigate proceedings against an undertaking is at the same time to run the risk of wasteful or harassing multiple investigations and actions against an undertaking for the same offense. To guard against this possibility and to decrease duplication and waste in multiple enforcement, the regulations and guidelines provide that when one NCA is dealing with an Article 81 or 82 case, other NCAs may suspend the proceedings before them or reject the complaint and the Commission may refuse to initiate proceedings.[23] The regulations and guidelines also protect the information collected from undertakings. The Commission and NCAs are under an obligation not to disclose (other than in accordance with the rules of the proceeding) information "covered by the obligation of professional secrecy," which includes business secrets and other confidential information.[24] Information exchanged between NCAs and the Commission may be used only for applying Articles 81 and 82 and parallel national competition law so long as the national competition law does not lead to an outcome inconsistent with Articles 81 and 82.[25] The information exchanged among NCAs

---

[21]   Council Reg. (EC) 1/2003, art. 3(1-3), 2003 O.J. (L 1) 1

[22]   Council Reg. (EC) 1/2003, art. 11(6), 2003 O.J. (L 1) 1; id., art. 35(3).

[23]   Council Reg. (EC) 1/2003, art. 13, 2003 O.J. (L 1) 1.

[24]   Council Reg. (EC) 1/2003, art. 28, 2003 O.J. (L 1) 1; Commission Notice on Cooperation Within the Network of Competition Authorities, at para 28(a), 2004 O.J. (C 101) 03, 43.

[25]   Council Reg. (EC) 1/2003, art. 12(2), 2003 O.J. (L 1) 1; Commission Notice on Cooperation Within the Network of Competition Authorities, at para 28(b), 2004 O.J. (C 101) 03, 43.

and the Commission also may not be used to impose sanctions greater than permissible under the laws of the Member State of the transferring authority.[26]

While the procedural reform package decentralizes the adjudication of competition law claims, it would be a mistake to think that this necessarily means that, from a procedural standpoint, EU competition law will now evolve into something resembling the law of the United States. First, the Commission will continue to handle infringements involving Community-wide effects on competition by virtue of being well placed to handle such cases. The Commission has gone so far as to issue a notice announcing that it is best placed to initiate proceedings when agreements or practices have effects on competition in more than three Member States.[27] Second, and more importantly, the new regulations and guidelines actively seek to minimize the number of conflicting decisions. The courts of Member States may not decide an Article 81 or 82 case in a way that runs counter to a decision adopted by the Commission on the same subject.[28] At least 30 days prior to the adoption of a decision by a national court, the NCA of that Member State must inform the

---

[26] Council Reg. (EC) 1/2003, art. 12(3), 2003 O.J. (L 1) 1; Commission Notice on Cooperation Within the Network of Competition Authorities, at para 28(c), 2004 O.J. (C 101) 03, 43.

[27] Commission Notice on Cooperation Within the Network of Competition Authorities, at para 14, 2004 O.J. (C 101) 03, 43.

[28] Council Reg. (EC) 1/2003, art. 16, 2003 O.J. (L 1) 1; Commission Notice on Cooperation Within the Network of Competition Authorities, at para 43, 2004 O.J. (C 101) 03, 43. (It remains to be seen how tightly the European courts and the Commission will construe this obligation. One could imagine a rule in which the national authorities are bound only if a new case has arisen out of the very same subject matter of the previous case. Alternatively, and perhaps more likely in view of the need to develop a consistent body of law, the rule might be construed to require national courts to follow Commission decisions applicable to a class of agreements, decisions or practices.)

Commission and provide a summary of the case and the proposed decision.[29]   This period will allow the Commission to assess the proposed decision and, in the process, the Commission may communicate with the NCA to ensure consistent application of Community law.[30]   So long as the Commission does not institute proceedings, the decision will become adopted after the expiration of the 30-day period.[31]

A more recent push in EU competition law has resulted in the replacement of the original merger regulation[32] with a new one (the "EC Merger Regulation").[33]   The new regulation came into force on May 1, 2004. Like the previous merger regulation, the new regulation requires undertakings to notify the Commission pending certain combinations and joint ventures, or "concentrations," having "Community dimension."[34]   A concentration results when two previously independent undertakings combine or when a person who controls one undertaking acquires another undertaking.[35]   These concentrations have community dimension when they involve a worldwide turnover of 5 billion Euros and for which the intra-Community turnover is 250 million Euros for each of at least two participants, as long as more than two-thirds of the intra-Community

---

[29]   Council Reg. (EC) 1/2003, art. 11(4), 2003 O.J. (L 1) 1; Commission Notice on Cooperation Within the Network of Competition Authorities, at para 46, 2004 O.J. (C 101) 03, 43.

[30]   Commission Notice on Cooperation Within the Network of Competition Authorities, at para 46, 2004 O.J. (C 101) 03, 43.

[31]   Commission Notice on Cooperation Within the Network of Competition Authorities, at para 1, 2004 O.J. (C 101) 03, 46.

[32]   Council Reg. (EEC) 4064/89, 1989 O.J. (L 395).

[33]   Council Reg. (EC) 139/2004, 2004 O.J. (L 24) 1.

[34]   Council Reg. (EC) 139/2004, art. 1(1), 2004 O.J. (L 24) 1.

[35]   Council Reg. (EC) 139/2004, art. 3(1), 2004 O.J. (L 24) 1.

turnover is not in one and the same Member State.[36] Concentrations may also have a community dimension when they involve worldwide turnover of 2.5 billion Euros, turnover of more than 100 million Euros in each of at least three Member States and more than 25 million in at least two of those three, and at least two undertakings each having turnover of at least 100 million Euros, so long as more than two-thirds of aggregate intra-Community turnover is not within one Member State.[37] Other concentrations are reviewed at the Member State level, subject to the possibility of centralized review as discussed below.

Compared to modernisation package, the merger control package makes modest, but important substantive, jurisdictional, and structural modifications to the merger control system.[38] Article 82 prohibits any abuse by a single undertaking or a group of undertakings holding a "dominant position" in a market of the European Community. The EC Merger Regulation changes the emphasis of the substantive test used to determine whether an undertaking or a group of undertakings holds a dominant position. While the substantive test remains largely the same, the new test focuses on the effects a concentration has on competition instead of focusing on the creation or strengthening of a dominant position of one or more undertakings.[39] The new regulation also adds a reference

---

[36] Council Reg. (EC) 139/2004, art. 1(2), 2004 O.J. (L 24) 1.
[37] Council Reg. (EC) 139/2004, art. 1(3), 2004 O.J. (L 24) 1.

[38] Merger Control: Merger Review Package in a Nutshell, at http://europa.eu.int/comm/competition/publications/special/3_merger.pdf.

[39] Compare Council Reg. (EEC) 4064/89, art. 2(3), 1989 O.J. (L 395) ("A concentration which creates or strengthens a dominant position as a result of which effective competition would be significantly impeded in the common market or in a substantial part of it shall be declared incompatible with the common market.") with Council Reg. (EC) 139/2004, art. 2(3), 2004 O.J. (L 24) 1. ("A concentration which would significantly impede effective competition, in the common market or in a substantial part of it, in particular as a result of the creation or strengthening of a dominant position, shall be declared incompatible with the common market.").

to oligopolies in the preamble to make clear that oligopolies are indeed covered by the regulation.[40] The Commission expects that these two modifications will end a long-standing debate over whether oligopolies (or coordinated effects cases, as they are sometimes called, as opposed to unilateral effects cases) are covered under the "dominant position" language of Article 82.[41]

The EC Merger Regulation increases the time period within which merger review may take place, in order to add more flexibility to the system. The new time periods ensure that mergers are not blocked because undertakings do not have sufficient time to discuss remedies with the Commission.[42] Under the new regulation, the deadline for the end of the first phase of a merger review was increased from one month to twenty-five working days, with an

---

See Merger Control: Merger Review Package in a Nutshell, at http://europa.eu.int/comm/competition/publications/special/3_merger.pdf.

[40] Council Reg. (EC) 139/2004, "Whereas," para 25, 2004 O.J. (L 24) 1; Robert Lane, Current Developments – European Union Law, 53.2 Int'l & Comp. L.Q. 465 (2004).

[41] Merger Control: Merger Review Package in a Nutshell, at http://europa.eu.int/comm/competition/publications/special/3_merger.pdf; New Merger Reg. Frequently Asked Questions, MEMO/04/9, at http://europa.eu.int/rapid/pressReleasesAction.do?reference=IP/04/70&format=HTML&aged=0&language=EN&guiLanguage=en.
Oligopolies have historically posed a special problem to the Commission's application of Article 82 because oligopolies are not "dominant" in the sense that they are much larger than competitors. By adjusting the definition of dominance to focus on the concentrations that threaten competition and including a reference to oligopolies in the preamble, the new regulation sweeps oligopolies under the purview of the merger control system.

[42] New Merger Reg. Frequently Asked Questions, MEMO/04/9, at http://europa.eu.int/rapid/pressReleasesAction.do?reference=IP/04/70&format=HTML&aged=0&language=EN&guiLanguage=en.

extension of an additional ten working days for referral requests.[43] The deadline for the end of the second phase was increased from four months to ninety working days, again with the possibility of extension.[44]

While the modernisation package decentralizes the adjudication of competition claims, the merger control package reinforces a "one-stop shop" concept for reviewing concentrations lacking Community dimension. The former merger regulation was introduced after years of debate, in order to give exclusive competence to Brussels over very large concentrations. The thresholds were so high, however, that multiple filings were common, and as more countries enacted their own merger control laws and the Community itself became larger, the problems associated with multiple filings also grew. The new regulation is intended to reduce the number of multiple filings even further by allowing undertakings that would otherwise have to notify at least three Member States to petition the Commission for a centralized merger review.[45] The Commission will then inform the Member States of the petition and, so long as no member state objects within fifteen days, the Commission will examine the concentration.[46] An undertaking may now petition the Commission to notify a Member State instead of the Commission about a concentration having Community dimension when the concentration will significantly affect competition in a the

---

[43]   Council Reg. (EC) 139/2004, art. 10(1), 2004 O.J. (L 24) 1; see New Merger Reg. Frequently Asked Questions, MEMO/04/9, http://europa.eu.int/rapid/pressReleasesAction.do?reference=IP/04/70 &format=HTML&aged=0&language=EN&guiLanguage=en.

[44]   Council Reg. (EC) 139/2004, art. 10(3), 2004 O.J. (L 24) 1; see New Merger Reg. Frequently Asked Questions, MEMO/04/9, at http://europa.eu.int/rapid/pressReleasesAction.do?reference=IP/04/70 &format=HTML&aged=0&language=EN&guiLanguage=en.

[45]   Council Reg. (EC) 139/2004, art. 4(5), 2004 O.J. (L 24) 1.

[46]   Council Reg. (EC) 139/2004, art. 4(5), 2004 O.J. (L 24) 1.

Member State.[47] These reforms were highly anticipated by the business community because they are expected to reduce costs associated with filing to authorities who would not ultimately perform the review. In addition, undertakings now can notify the Commission when they have a good faith intent to conclude an agreement instead of needing to wait until after they conclude a binding agreement.[48]

Much of the near-explosive spread of competition laws around the world in more recent years reflects both the success and the strong influence of the European Union's competition laws, both taken alone and in combination with those in the Americas and the Asia–Pacific region. Throughout Central and Eastern Europe, countries eager to join the EU one day have modeled their new competition laws on those of the EU, in recognition of the fact that accession would mean the acceptance of the full *acquis communautaire* of competition laws, regulations, and court precedents. In addition, the administrative approach taken by the EC appeals to countries that do not share the Anglo–American common-law tradition. For that reason, we allude from time to time throughout this casebook to European rules, both by way of comparison and contrast. The extent to which European law follows efficiency principles, the extent to which it continues to reflect its roots by giving primacy to intra-European market integration goals, and the extent to which it displays more concern for equitable market behavior, all provide a useful perspective for our consideration of U.S. law.

As noted above, the central competition provisions of EC law are Articles 81 and 82 of the Rome Treaty. These provisions are set forth below. At this point, please compare Articles 81 and 82 with the provisions of Sections 1 and 2 of the Sherman Act, pp. 14-15 *supra*.

---

[47] Council Reg. (EC) 139/2004, art. 4(4), 2004 O.J. (L 24) 1.

[48] Council Reg. (EC) 139/2004, art. 4(1), 2004 O.J. (L 24) 1.

CHAPTER 2: FRAMEWORK OF ANTITRUST POLICY

Replace paragraph 2, page 71, with the following:

In 2004, Congress passed and the President signed the Antitrust Criminal Penalty Enforcement and Reform Act. The statute substantially increased civil and criminal penalties for antitrust violations. Congress' purpose was to make criminal penalties for antitrust offenses more consistent with the harsh penalties for white collar crime established in recent legislation. Criminal proceedings can result in imprisonment of individuals for a maximum of ten years (up from three years previously). Criminal fines for corporations were increased from $10 million to $100 million and criminal fines for individuals were increased from $350,000 to $1 million.

Insert before "INTERVENTION," page 89.

Largely in response to the 1995 Circuit Court decision in *Microsoft* criticizing a district judge for refusing to enter a proposed settlement, discussed in the text at pages 88 and 89, and the 2003 district court confirmation of a proposed settlement, Congress sought to clarify that district courts are to undertake a more thorough and independent determination of whether a proposed consent decree is adequate. Congress also changed the directive to the courts from the language that they "may" consider certain factors to "shall" consider those factors. It also changed slightly the language of the Tunney Act mandate (language changes are underscored):

> (a)   The competitive impact of such judgment, including termination of alleged violations, provisions for enforcement and modification, duration or relief sought, anticipated effects of alternative remedies actually considered, <u>whether its terms are ambiguous</u> and other competitive considerations bearing on the adequacy of such judgment <u>that the court deems necessary to a determination of whether</u>

the consent judgment is in the public interest, and

(b)   The impact of entry of such judgment upon competition in the relevant market or markets, upon the public generally and individuals alleging specific injury from the violations set forth in the complaint including consideration of the public benefit, if any, to be derived from a determination of the issues at trial.

Insert before "CLASS ACTIONS," page 106.

On April 2, 2007, a bipartisan Antitrust Modernization Commission, created by Congress in 2002, issued its final Report and Recommendations. The Commission generally approved of current antitrust law and policy. It recommended, however, a number of significant modifications, including that Congress enact legislation overruling both *Hanover Shoe* and *Illinois Brick*. The Commission reasoned that different federal and state standards have resulted in "wasteful, duplicative litigation," involving potentially duplicative damage recoveries and inconsistent decisions.

CHAPTER 4: COMPETITOR COLLABORATION ON
PRICE FIXING AND DIVISION OF
MARKETS

Insert after *California Dental*, page 296.

TEXACO INC. v. DAGHER

SUPREME COURT OF THE UNITED STATES, 2006

547 U.S. 1, 126 S. CT. 1276, 164 L. ED 2D 1

THOMAS, J. From 1998 until 2002, petitioners Texaco Inc. and Shell Oil Co. collaborated in a joint venture, Equilon Enterprises, to refine and sell gasoline in the western United States under the original Texaco and Shell Oil brand names. Respondents, a class of Texaco and Shell Oil service station owners, allege that petitioners engaged in unlawful price fixing when Equilon set a single price for both Texaco and Shell Oil brand gasoline. We granted certiorari to determine whether it is *per se* illegal under §1of the Sherman Act, 15 U. S. C. §1, for a lawful, economically integrated joint venture to set the prices at which the joint venture sells its products. We conclude that it is not, and accordingly we reverse the contrary judgment of the Court of Appeals.

I

Historically, Texaco and Shell Oil have competed with one another in the national and international oil and gasoline markets. Their business activities include refining crude oil into gasoline, as well as marketing gasoline to downstream purchasers, such as the service stations represented in respondents' class action.

In 1998, Texaco and Shell Oil formed a joint venture, Equilon, to consolidate their operations in the western United States, thereby ending competition between the two companies in the domestic refining and marketing of gasoline. Under the joint venture agreement, Texaco and Shell Oil agreed to pool their resources and share the risks of and profits from Equilon's activities. Equilon's board of directors would comprise

17

representatives of Texaco and Shell Oil, and Equilon gasoline would be sold to downstream purchasers under the original Texaco and Shell Oil brand names. The formation of Equilon was approved by consent decree, subject to certain divestments and other modifications, by the Federal Trade Commission, see *In re Shell Oil Co.*, 125 F. T. C. 769 (1998), as well as by the state attorneys general of California, Hawaii, Oregon, and Washington. Notably, the decrees imposed no restrictions on the pricing of Equilon gasoline.

After the joint venture began to operate, respondents brought suit in district court, alleging that, by unifying gasoline prices under the two brands, petitioners had violated the *per se* rule against price fixing that this Court has long recognized under §1 of the Sherman Act. See, *e.g.*, *Catalano, Inc.* v. *Target Sales, Inc.*, 446 U. S. 643, 647 (1980) *(per curiam)*. The District Court awarded summary judgment to Texaco and Shell Oil. It determined that the rule of reason, rather than a *per se* rule or the quick look doctrine, governs respondents' claim, and that, by eschewing rule of reason analysis, respondents had failed to raise a triable issue of fact. The Ninth Circuit reversed, characterizing petitioners' position as a request for an "exception to the *per se* prohibition on price fixing," and rejecting that request. *Dagher* v. *Saudi Refining, Inc.*, 369 F. 3d 1108, 1116 (2004). We consolidated Texaco's and Shell Oil's separate petitions and granted certiorari to determine the extent to which the *per se* rule against price fixing applies to an important and increasingly popular form of business organization, the joint venture.

II

Section 1 of the Sherman Act prohibits "[e]very contract, combination in the form of trust or otherwise, or conspiracy, in restraint of trade or commerce among the several States." 15 U. S. C. §1. This Court has not taken a literal approach to this language, however. See, *e.g.*, *State Oil Co.* v. *Khan*, 522 U. S. 3, 10 (1997) ("[T]his Court has long recognized that Congress intended to outlaw only *unreasonable* restraints" (emphasis added)). Instead, this Court presumptively applies rule of reason analysis, under which antitrust plaintiffs must demonstrate that a particular

18

contract or combination is in fact unreasonable and anticompetitive before it will be found unlawful. See, *e.g.*, *id.*, at 10–19 (concluding that vertical price-fixing arrangements are subject to the rule of reason, not *per se* liability). *Per se* liability is reserved for only those agreements that are "so plainly anticompetitive that no elaborate study of the industry is needed to establish their illegality." *National Soc. of Professional Engineers* v. *United States,* 435 U. S. 679, 692 (1978). Accordingly, "we have expressed reluctance to adopt *per se* rules . . . 'where the economic impact of certain practices is not immediately obvious.' " *State Oil, supra,* at 10 (quoting *FTC* v. *Indiana Federation of Dentists,* 476 U. S. 447, 458–459 (1986)).

Price-fixing agreements between two or more competitors, otherwise known as horizontal price-fixing agreements, fall into the category of arrangements that are *per se* unlawful. See, *e.g., Catalano, supra,* at 647. These cases do not present such an agreement, however, because Texaco and Shell Oil did not compete with one another in the relevant market—namely, the sale of gasoline to service stations in the western United States—but instead participated in that market jointly through their investments in Equilon.[1] In other words, the pricing policy challenged here amounts to little more than price setting by a single entity—albeit within the context of a joint venture—and not a pricing

---

[1] We presume for purposes of these cases that Equilon is a lawful joint venture. Its formation has been approved by federal and state regulators, and there is no contention here that it is a sham. As the court below noted: "There is a voluminous record documenting the economic justifications for creating the joint ventures. [T]he defendants concluded that numerous synergies and cost efficiencies would result" by creating Equilon as well as a parallel venture, Motiva Enterprises, in the eastern United States, and "that nationwide there would be up to $800 million in cost savings annually." 369 F. 3d 1108, 1111 (CA9 2004). Had respondents challenged Equilon itself, they would have been required to show that its creation was anticompetitive under the rule of reason. See *Copperweld Corp.* v. *Independence Tube Corp.,* 467 U. S. 752, 768 (1984).

agreement between competing entities with respect to their competing products. Throughout Equilon's existence, Texaco and Shell Oil shared in the profits of Equilon's activities in their role as investors, not competitors. When "persons who would otherwise be competitors pool their capital and share the risks of loss as well as the opportunities fo*r profit . . . such joint ventures [are] regarded as a single firm competing with other sellers in the market." *Arizona* v. *Maricopa County Medical Soc.*, 457 U. S. 332, 356 (1982). As such, though Equilon's pricing policy may be price fixing in a literal sense, it is not price fixing in the antitrust sense. See *Broadcast Music, Inc.* v. *Columbia Broadcasting System, Inc.*, 441 U. S. 1, 9 (1979) ("When two partners set the price of their goods or services they are literally 'price fixing,' but they are not *per se* in violation of the Sherman Act").

This conclusion is confirmed by respondents' apparent concession that there would be no *per se* liability had Equilon simply chosen to sell its gasoline under a single brand. We see no reason to treat Equilon differently just because it chose to sell gasoline under two distinct brands at a single price. As a single entity, a joint venture, like any other firm, must have the discretion to determine the prices of the products that it sells, including the discretion to sell a product under two different brands at a single, unified price. If Equilon's price unification policy is anticompetitive, then respondents should have challenged it pursuant to the rule of reason.[2] But it would be inconsistent with this Court's antitrust precedents to condemn the internal pricing decisions of a legitimate joint venture as *per se* unlawful.[3]

---

[2] Respondents have not put forth a rule of reason claim. 369 F. 3d, at 1113. Accordingly, we need not address petitioners' alternative argument that §1 of the Sherman Act is inapplicable to joint ventures.

[3] Respondents alternatively contend that petitioners should be held liable under the quick look doctrine. To be sure, we have applied the quick look doctrine to business activities that are so plainly anticompetitive that courts need undertake only a cursory examination before imposing antitrust liability. See *California Dental Assn.* v. *FTC,* 526 U. S. 756, 770 (1999). But for the same reasons that *per se* liability is

The court below reached the opposite conclusion by invoking the ancillary restraints doctrine. 369 F. 3d, at 1118–1124. That doctrine governs the validity of restrictions imposed by a legitimate business collaboration, such as a business association or joint venture, on nonventure activities. See, *e.g.*, *National Collegiate Athletic Assn.* v. *Board of Regents of Univ. of Okla.*, 468 U. S. 85, 113–115 (1984); *Citizen Publishing Co.* v. *United States*, 394 U. S. 131, 135–136 (1969). Under the doctrine, courts must determine whether the nonventure restriction is a naked restraint on trade, and thus invalid, or one that is ancillary to the legitimate and competitive purposes of the business association, and thus valid. We agree with petitioners that the ancillary restraints doctrine has no application here, where the business practice being challenged involves the core activity of the joint venture itself—namely, the pricing of the very goods produced and sold by Equilon. And even if we were to invoke the doctrine in these cases, Equilon's pricing policy is clearly ancillary to the sale of its own products. Judge Fernandez, dissenting from the ruling of the court below, put it well:

> "In this case, nothing more radical is afoot than the fact that an entity, which now owns all of the production, transportation, research, storage, sales and distribution facilities for engaging in the gasoline business, also prices its own products. It decided to price them the same, as any other entity could. What could be more integral to the running of a business than setting a price for its goods and services?" 369 F. 3d, at 1127.

See also *Broadcast Music, supra*, at 23 ("Joint ventures and other cooperative arrangements are . . . not usually unlawful, at least not as price-fixing schemes, where the agreement on price is necessary to market the product at all").

* * *

---

unwarranted here, we conclude that petitioners cannot be held liable under the quick look doctrine.

Because the pricing decisions of a legitimate joint venture do not fall within the narrow category of activity that is *per se* unlawful under §1 of the Sherman Act, respondents' antitrust claim cannot prevail. Accordingly, the judgment of the Court of Appeals is reversed.

Insert following Note 8, page 325.

Note on Agreements Between Holders of Patented
Pharmaceutical Products and Generic Challengers

In recent years, a considerable number of cases have been brought by the Federal Trade Commission (and occasionally by private parties) challenging payments arising out of patent litigation between a pioneer (or "branded") patent holder of a drug and a challenging generic drug. The cases arise because of an extraordinarily complicated provision in the Hatch-Waxman Act[4] whereby generic drug companies were given incentives to announce their intention to enter a market, the brand name patent holder had the right to sue the generic for patent infringement, the branded drug producer often paid the first generic to stay out of the market, and achieved an effect whereby if the "first-filed" generic stayed out of the market, it would prevent any other generics from entering the market. If the generic could successfully challenge the legitimacy of the original patent, it would have the result of curtailing the period in which the original patent could be enforced.

The first round of cases reached inconsistent results. For example, in *Cardizem CD Antitrust Litigation*, 332 F.3d 896 (6th Cir. 2003), *cert. denied*, 543 U.S. 939 (2004) the payment to the generic for the generic's commitment to stay out of the market was found to be a division of markets and illegal *per se*. In a similar case, *Valley Drug Co.,* v. *Geneva Pharmaceuticals,* 344 F.3d 1294 (11th Cir. 2003), *cert. denied*, 543 U.S. 939 (2004), the Court of Appeals required a full-blown rule of reason analysis.

At first, most agency and court decisions went against the brand-name patent holder, but in the last few years, courts of appeals have found in favor of the brand-name drug company. In *Schering-Plough Corp.* v. *Federal Trade Commission*, 402 F.3d 1056 (11th Cir. 2005), the Court of Appeals held that a payment to the generic drug challenger was consistent with rights accorded by patent, and that a

---

[4]   Drug Price Competition and Patent Term Restoration Act, pub. L. No. 98-417, 98 Stat. 1585 (1984).

contrary decision would undermine the useful procedure of negotiating patent settlements. *In re Tamoxifen Citrate Antitrust Litigation*, 466 F. 3d 187 (2ᵈ Cir. 2006), consumers and consumer groups filed some 30 lawsuits challenging the legality of a 1993 settlement between Zeneca, the holder of a patent on the most widely used cancer drug, and Barr Laboratories, a generic manufacturer who claimed that the Zeneca patent was invalid. The settlement occurred after the Zeneca patent was found by the district court to be invalid, and constituted a payment by Zeneca to Barr of $27 million on condition that Barr not introduce its low-price generic brand into the market. The Court of Appeals rejected a *per se* approach and concluded that the circumstances favored the defendants. In a two-to-one decision, it found that the Zeneca-Barr agreement was not an antitrust violation, largely on grounds that the agreement, unlike other branded drug-generic arrangements, did not bar other generic manufacturers from subsequently challenging Zeneca's patent in order to enter the market, and because, taking a broad variety of factors into account, the payment to Barr did not appear to be excessive.

The Supreme Court was asked to review the *Schering-Plough* and *Tamoxifen Citrate* decisions. Consistent with the recommendation of the Solicitor General's office, the Supreme Court rejected the Federal Trade Commission's request for review in *Schering-Plough*. In the *Tamoxifen Citrate* case, the Solicitor General's office recommended that the Supreme Court decline review even though its brief noted: "The petition presents an important and difficult question, and the Court of Appeals adopted an incorrect standard . . . ." The standard adopted by the majority in the Second Circuit held that a settlement would be valid unless (1) the settlement extended the monopoly beyond the patent scope, (2) the settlement involved fraud, or (3) the underlying lawsuit was "objectively baseless in the sense that no reasonable litigant could realistically expect success on the merits." The Solicitor General's office thought a full rule-of-reason was a better approach, but recommended denial of review on grounds that the claims in the case appeared to be moot (the patent had expired), the factual setting was atypical and unlikely to recur, and subsequent regulatory changes may have undercut one of the theories of competitive harm advanced by petitioners. In June 2007, the Supreme Court denied certiorari.

24

The FTC and private litigants have continued bringing cases challenging patent holder payments. See, e.g., *Ciprofloxacin Hydrochloride Antitrust Litig.*, 544 F.3d 1323 (Fed. Cir. 2008) (antitrust claim rejected where $398 million payment to delay entry until patent expiration); Hemphill, An Aggregate Approach to Antitrust: Using New Data and Rulemaking to Preserve Drug Competition, 109 Colum. L. Rev. 629 (2009); Hemphill, Paying for Delay: Pharmaceutical Patent Settlement as a Regulatory Design Problem, 81 N.Y.U. L.Rev. 1553 (2006).

CHAPTER 5: GROUP REFUSALS TO DEAL AND JOINT
VENTURES

Insert as Note 4, page 354.

An August 2006 decision of the Federal Trade Commission
involving Rambus demonstrates that standard setting remains, in the
view of antitrust enforcement authorities, an important and useful
element in a competitive market, and that abuse of the standard-
setting process will be the subject of enforcement. But the FTC's
decision was then reversed -- because the Commission had failed to
prove exclusionary conduct -- by the D.C. Circuit.

In re Rambus, FTC Docket No. 9302 (August 2, 2006), the
Joint Electron Device Engineering Council (JEDEC) was a standard-
setting organization committed to developing an industry standard for
various dynamic random access memory chips (DRAM) and other
devices used in personal computers, servers, printers, and cameras.
The JEDEC was committed to avoiding, where possible, the
incorporation of patented technologies into the standards that it
adopts, or if incorporated in the standards, insuring the technology
would be available to be licensed royalty-free, or on reasonable and
non-discriminatory terms, to parties who adopt the standard. Rambus
participated in DRAM standard-setting activities, but did not disclose
to other members, as required by JEDEC rules and prior practice, that
it held patents on relevant technology, had applied for additional
patents in the area, and was in the process of developing relevant
patent applications involving technology that would be incorporated
in the standard. There was also evidence that Rambus used what it
learned when it was at JEDEC meetings to amend some of its patent
applications to ensure that they covered the standard ultimately
adopted.

After the standard was adopted and published, and after the
market was committed to those technologies, Rambus brought patent
infringement lawsuits against private parties who practiced the
standard. In a unanimous vote, the Commission found that Rambus'
conduct was deceptive and an act of monopolization under Section 2
of the Sherman Act. The Commission concluded:

JEDEC expressly sought information about patents to enable its members to make informed decisions about which technologies to adopt, and JEDEC members viewed early knowledge of potential patent consequences as vital for avoiding patent hold-up. Rambus understood that knowledge of its evolving patent position would be material to JEDEC's choices, and avoided disclosure for that very reason.

In *Rambus Inc. v. FTC*, 522 F.3d 456 (D.C. Cir. 2008), the D.C. Circuit, reversing the FTC, held that the Commission failed to sustain its allegation of monopolization because a deception "merely enabling a monopolist to charge higher prices than it could have charged" would not violate Section 2 of the Sherman Act. The Court reasoned:

> Had Rambus fully disclosed its intellectual property, "JEDEC either would have excluded Rambus's patented technologies from the JEDEC DRAM standards, or would have demanded RAND assurances, with an opportunity for *ex ante* licensing negotiations." But the Commission did not determine that one or the other of these two possible outcomes was the more likely....
>
> We assume without deciding that avoidance of the first of these possible outcomes was indeed anticompetitive; that is, that if Rambus's more complete disclosure would have caused JEDEC to adopt a different (open, non-proprietary) standard, then its failure to disclose harmed

competition and would support a monopolization claim. But while we can assume that Rambus's non-disclosure made the adoption of its technologies somewhat more likely than broad disclosure would have, the Commission made clear in its remedial opinion that there was insufficient evidence that JEDEC would have standardized other technologies had it known the full scope of Rambus's intellectual property....

Thus, if JEDEC, in the world that would have existed but for Rambus's deception, would have standardized the very same technologies, Rambus's alleged deception cannot be said to have had an effect on competition in violation of the antitrust laws; JEDEC's loss of an opportunity to seek favorable licensing terms is not as such an antitrust harm. Yet the Commission did not reject this as being a possible perhaps even the more probable-effect of Rambus's conduct.

Insert after Note 1, page 398.

In 2003, a unanimous Court of Appeals for the Second Circuit affirmed the district court opinion. *United States* v. *VISA USA, Inc.*, and *MasterCard International*, 344 F.3d 229 (2d Cir. 2003). The United States had not appealed its loss in the court below on its challenge to the dual governance market structure. With respect to rules adopted by VISA and MasterCard, and applied to its 20,000 bank members - that a bank could belong to the VISA and MasterCard system but not to other competitive systems (specifically American Express and Discover) - the Second Circuit found an adverse effect on competition in violation of Section 1. In response to the VISA/MasterCard argument that the arrangement with the banks was like a vertical distributorship that has been seen in other contexts as virtually *per se* legal (*see* Casebook, *infra*, at page 931), the Court concluded that might be a valid argument if the arrangement was entered into by a single seller. The Court concluded, however, that the 20,000-member banks in effect had entered into a horizontal agreement to exclude American Express and Discover, and that agreement injured not just those two competitors but competition in general.

> The fact that they harm competitors does not, however, mean they do not also harm competition. . . . VISA USA and MasterCard would be impelled to design and market their products more competitively if the banks to which they sell their services were free to purchase network services from AmEx and Discover. 344 F.3d at 243.

CHAPTER 6:   MARKET CONCENTRATION,
             CONSPIRACY, AND THE ANTITRUST
             LAWS

Insert after *Toys "R" Us*, page 518.

Note on *Bell Atlantic Corp. v. Twombly*, 127 S.Ct. 1955
(2007). The Supreme Court returned to the issue of parallel conduct in
Twombly. That case involved an alleged agreement among the so-
called "incumbent local exchange carriers," or ILECs – essentially the
local telecommunications companies that emerged after the break-up
of the old AT&T firm – to restrain trade in two ways. Plaintiffs were
two individuals seeking to represent a putative class consisting of all
"subscribers of local telephone and/or high speed internet services ...
from February 8, 1996 to present." Defendants were the four
remaining ILECs in the market. Plaintiffs first alleged that the ILECs
allegedly acted to impair access to their markets by rival firms, called
"competitive local exchange carriers" or CLECs, through actions like
provision of inferior connections, overcharges, and billing in ways
designed to sabotage the CLECs' relations with their own customers.
Second, the ILECs allegedly had agreements among themselves to
refrain from competing in the markets of other ILECs. The district
court dismissed the complaint for failure to state a claim, but the
Second Circuit reversed, finding that it could imagine a set of facts
that the plaintiff class could prove, consistent with the complaint, that
would entitle the class to recover. In an opinion authored by Justice
Souter (in a decision where the Court split 7-2), the Supreme Court
reversed the Court of Appeals and reinstated the dismissal, finding
that even under the notice pleading regime of Rule 8, an antitrust
plaintiff in a Section 1 case must allege enough facts to show what
agreement is being attacked and why that agreement (if proven)
would be illegal.

Earlier decisions of the Supreme Court had focused on the
level of proof necessary at the summary judgment stage (*Matsushita
Elec. Indus. Co. v. Zenith Radio Corp.*, 475 U.S. 574 (1986)), the
directed verdict stage (*Theatre Enterprises v. Paramount Film*

Distrib. Corp., 346 U.S. 537(1954)), and the jury instruction stage (*Monsanto Co. v. Spray-Rite Service Corp.,* 465 U.S. 752 (1984). This time, the Court addressed the threshold standard for pleading a complaint that can survive a motion to dismiss for failure to state a claim on which relief can be granted under Fed. R. Civ. P. 12(b)(6). In so doing, it expressed great concern about the potential expense and burden that an antitrust claim can place on a defendant:

> [I]t is one thing to be cautious before dismissing an antitrust complaint in advance of discovery, ... but quite another to forget that proceeding to antitrust discovery can be expensive. As we indicated over 20 years ago ... "a district court must retain the power to insist upon some specificity in pleading before allowing a potentially massive factual controversy to proceed." ... That potential expense is obvious enough in the present case: plaintiffs represent a putative class of at least 90 percent of all subscribers to local telephone or high-speed Internet service in the continental United States, in an action against America's largest telecommunications firms (with many thousands of employees generating reams and gigabytes of business records) for unspecified (if any) instances of antitrust violations that allegedly occurred over a period of seven years.
>
> It is no answer to say [as the dissent does] that a claim just shy of a plausible entitlement to relief can, if groundless, be weeded out early in the discovery process through "careful case management,"... given the common lament that the success of judicial supervision in checking discovery abuse has been on the modest side. ... And it is self-evident that the problem of discovery abuse cannot be solved by "careful scrutiny of evidence at the summary judgment stage," much less "lucid instructions to juries," [quoting the dissent]; the threat of discovery expense will push cost-conscious defendants to settle even anemic cases before reaching those proceedings. Probably,

31

then, it is only by taking care to require allegations that reach the level suggesting conspiracy that we can hope to avoid the potentially enormous expense of discovery in cases with no "'reasonably founded hope that the [discovery] process will reveal relevant evidence'" to support a § 1 claim.

127 S. Ct. at 1967. The Court's solution to this problem was to reject a broad reading of one of its oldest cases setting forth the rules for pleading under Fed. R. Civ. P. 8, *Conley v. Gibson*, 355 U.S. 41 (1957), and to hold that a Section 1 complaint must provide "more than labels and conclusions." Instead, the Court held,

stating [a § 1] claim requires a complaint with enough factual matter (taken as true) to suggest that an agreement was made. Asking for plausible grounds to infer an agreement does not impose a probability requirement at the pleading stage; it simply calls for enough fact to raise a reasonable expectation that discovery will reveal evidence of illegal agreement. And, of course, a well-pleaded complaint may proceed even if it strikes a savvy judge that actual proof of those facts is improbable, and "that a recovery is very remote and unlikely." *Ibid.* In identifying facts that are suggestive enough to render a § 1 conspiracy plausible, we have the benefit of the prior rulings and considered views of leading commentators ... that lawful parallel conduct fails to bespeak unlawful agreement. It makes sense to say, therefore, that an allegation of parallel conduct and a bare assertion of conspiracy will not suffice. Without more, parallel conduct does not suggest conspiracy, and a conclusory allegation of agreement at some unidentified point does not supply facts adequate to show illegality. Hence, when allegations of parallel conduct are set out in order to make a § 1 claim, they must be placed in a context that raises a suggestion of a preceding agreement, not merely parallel conduct that could just as well be independent action.

32

127 S.Ct. at 1965-66.

From a substantive point of view, the Court reiterated its concern about the ambiguity of parallel or interdependent conduct, which it described as "consistent with conspiracy, but just as much in line with a wide swath of rational and competitive business strategy unilaterally prompted by common perceptions of the market." *Id.* at 1964. The heart of its reasoning upholding the dismissal of the complaint is reflected in the following passage:

> When we look for plausibility in this complaint, we agree with the District Court that plaintiffs' claim of conspiracy in restraint of trade comes up short. To begin with, the complaint leaves no doubt that plaintiffs rest their § 1 claim on descriptions of parallel conduct and not on any independent allegation of actual agreement among the ILECs. ... Although in form a few stray statements speak directly of agreement, on fair reading these are merely legal conclusions resting on the prior allegations. Thus, the complaint first takes account of the alleged "absence of any meaningful competition between [the ILECs] in one another's markets," "the parallel course of conduct that each [ILEC] engaged in to prevent competition from CLECs," "and the other facts and market circumstances alleged [earlier]"; "in light of" these, the complaint concludes "that [the ILECs] have entered into a contract, combination or conspiracy to prevent competitive entry into their ... markets and have agreed not to compete with one another." ... The nub of the complaint, then, is the ILECs' parallel behavior, consisting of steps to keep the CLECs out and manifest disinterest in becoming CLECs themselves, and its sufficiency turns on the suggestions raised by this conduct when viewed in light of common economic experience.

We think that nothing contained in the complaint

33

invests either the action or inaction alleged with a plausible suggestion of conspiracy. As to the ILECs' supposed agreement to disobey the 1996 Act and thwart the CLECs' attempts to compete, we agree with the District Court that nothing in the complaint intimates that the resistance to the upstarts was anything more than the natural, unilateral reaction of each ILEC intent on keeping its regional dominance. The 1996 Act did more than just subject the ILECs to competition; it obliged them to subsidize their competitors with their own equipment at wholesale rates. The economic incentive to resist was powerful, but resisting competition is routine market conduct, and even if the ILECs flouted the 1996 Act in all the ways the plaintiffs allege, … there is no reason to infer that the companies had agreed among themselves to do what was only natural anyway; so natural, in fact, that if alleging parallel decisions to resist competition were enough to imply an antitrust conspiracy, pleading a § 1 violation against almost any group of competing businesses would be a sure thing.

The complaint makes its closest pass at a predicate for conspiracy with the claim that collusion was necessary because success by even one CLEC in an ILEC's territory "would have revealed the degree to which competitive entry by CLECs would have been successful in the other territories." … But, its logic aside, this general premise still fails to answer the point that there was just no need for joint encouragement to resist the 1996 Act; as the District Court said, "each ILEC has reason to want to avoid dealing with CLECs" and "each ILEC would attempt to keep CLECs out, regardless of the actions of the other ILECs." …

Plaintiffs' second conspiracy theory rests on the competitive reticence among the ILECs themselves in the wake of the 1996 Act, which was supposedly passed in the "'hop[e] that the large incumbent local monopoly companies ... might attack their neighbors' service areas, as they are the best situated to do so.'" ... Contrary to hope, the ILECs declined "'to enter each other's service territories in any significant way,'" ... , and the local telephone and high speed Internet market remains highly compartmentalized geographically, with minimal competition. Based on this state of affairs, and perceiving the ILECs to be blessed with "especially attractive business opportunities" in surrounding markets dominated by other ILECs, the plaintiffs assert that the ILECs' parallel conduct was "strongly suggestive of conspiracy." ...

But it was not suggestive of conspiracy, not if history teaches anything. In a traditionally unregulated industry with low barriers to entry, sparse competition among large firms dominating separate geographical segments of the market could very well signify illegal agreement, but here we have an obvious alternative explanation. In the decade preceding the 1996 Act and well before that, monopoly was the norm in telecommunications, not the exception. ... The ILECs were born in that world, doubtless liked the world the way it was, and surely knew the adage about him who lives by the sword. Hence, a natural explanation for the noncompetition alleged is that the former Government-sanctioned monopolists were sitting tight, expecting their neighbors to do the same thing.

In fact, the complaint itself gives reasons to believe that the ILECs would see their best interests in keeping to their old turf. Although the complaint says generally that the ILECs passed up "especially attractive business opportunit[ies]" by declining to compete as CLECs against other ILECs, ... it does

35

not allege that competition as CLECs was potentially any more lucrative than other opportunities being pursued by the ILECs during the same period, and the complaint is replete with indications that any CLEC faced nearly insurmountable barriers to profitability owing to the ILECs' flagrant resistance to the network sharing requirements of the 1996 Act.... . Not only that, but even without a monopolistic tradition and the peculiar difficulty of mandating shared networks, "[f]irms do not expand without limit and none of them enters every market that an outside observer might regard as profitable, or even a small portion of such markets." Areeda & Hovenkamp ¶ 307d, at 155 (Supp.2006) (commenting on the case at bar). The upshot is that Congress may have expected some ILECs to become CLECs in the legacy territories of other ILECs, but the disappointment does not make conspiracy plausible. We agree with the District Court's assessment that antitrust conspiracy was not suggested by the facts adduced under either theory of the complaint, which thus fails to state a valid § 1 claim.

127 S.Ct. at 1970-73. *Twombly* thus stands as a powerful reaffirmation of *Theatre Enterprises*, and a caution to future plaintiffs to provide the "who, what, when, where, and why" details of any alleged conspiracies, whether explicit or implicit, in their complaints.

CHAPTER 7: VERTICAL RESTRAINTS ON COMPEITION

Insert after *State Oil Co. v. Khan*, page 643.

LEEGIN CREATIVE LEATHER PRODUCTS, INC. V. PSKS, INC.

SUPREME COURT OF THE UNITED STATES, 2007

551 U.S. 877, 127 S. CT. 2705, 168 L. ED. 623

KENNEDY, J. *In Dr. Miles Medical Co. v. John D. Park & Sons Co.*, 220 U.S. 373 (1911), the Court established the rule that it is *per se* illegal under § 1 of the Sherman Act, for a manufacturer to agree with its distributor to set the minimum price the distributor can charge for the manufacturer's goods. The question presented by the instant case is whether the Court should overrule the *per se* rule and allow resale price maintenance agreements to be judged by the rule of reason, the usual standard applied to determine if there is a violation of § 1. The Court has abandoned the rule of *per se* illegality for other vertical restraints a manufacturer imposes on its distributors. Respected economic analysts, furthermore, conclude that vertical price restraints can have procompetitive effects. We now hold that *Dr. Miles* should be overruled and that vertical price restraints are to be judged by the rule of reason.

I

Petitioner, Leegin Creative Leather Products, Inc. (Leegin), designs, manufactures, and distributes leather goods and accessories. In 1991, Leegin began to sell belts under the brand name "Brighton." The Brighton brand has now expanded into a variety of women's fashion accessories. It is sold across the United States in over 5,000 retail establishments, for the most part independent, small boutiques and specialty stores. Leegin's president, Jerry Kohl, also has an interest in about 70 stores that sell Brighton products. Leegin asserts that, at least for its products, small retailers treat customers better, provide customers more services, and make their shopping experience more satisfactory than do larger, often impersonal retailers. Kohl explained: "[W]e want the consumers to get a different experience than they get in Sam's Club or in Wal-Mart. And you can't get that kind of experience or support or customer service from a store like Wal-Mart."

Respondent, PSKS, Inc. (PSKS), operates Kay's Kloset, a women's apparel store in Lewisville, Texas. Kay's Kloset buys from about 75 different manufacturers and at one time sold the Brighton brand. It first started purchasing Brighton goods from Leegin in 1995. Once it began selling the brand, the store promoted Brighton. For example, it ran Brighton advertisements and had Brighton days in the store. Kay's Kloset became the destination retailer in the area to buy Brighton products. Brighton was the store's most important brand and once accounted for 40 to 50 percent of its profits.

In 1997, Leegin instituted the "Brighton Retail Pricing and Promotion Policy." Following the policy, Leegin refused to sell to retailers that discounted Brighton goods below suggested prices. The policy contained an exception for products not selling well that the retailer did not plan on reordering. In the letter to retailers establishing the policy, Leegin stated:

"In this age of mega stores like Macy's, Bloomingdales, May Co. and others, consumers are perplexed by promises of product quality and support of product which we believe is lacking in these large stores. Consumers are further confused by the ever popular sale, sale, sale, etc."

"We, at Leegin, choose to break away from the pack by selling [at] specialty stores; specialty stores that can offer the customer great quality merchandise, superb service, and support the Brighton product 365 days a year on a consistent basis."

"We realize that half the equation is Leegin producing great Brighton product and the other half is you, our retailer, creating great looking stores selling our products in a quality manner." *Ibid.*

Leegin adopted the policy to give its retailers sufficient margins to provide customers the service central to its distribution strategy. It also expressed concern that discounting harmed Brighton's brand image and reputation.

A year after instituting the pricing policy Leegin introduced a marketing strategy known as the "Heart Store Program." It offered retailers incentives to become Heart Stores, and, in exchange, retailers pledged, among other things, to sell at Leegin's suggested prices. Kay's Kloset became a Heart Store soon after Leegin created the program. After a Leegin employee visited the store and found it unattractive, the parties appear to have agreed that Kay's Kloset would not be a Heart Store beyond 1998. Despite losing this status, Kay's Kloset continued to increase its Brighton sales.

In December 2002, Leegin discovered Kay's Kloset had been marking down Brighton's entire line by 20 percent. Kay's Kloset contended it placed Brighton products on sale to compete with nearby retailers who also were undercutting Leegin's suggested prices. Leegin, nonetheless, requested that Kay's Kloset cease discounting. Its request refused, Leegin stopped selling to the store. The loss of the Brighton brand had a considerable negative impact on the store's revenue from sales.

PSKS sued Leegin in the United States District Court for the Eastern District of Texas. It alleged, among other claims, that Leegin had violated the antitrust laws by "enter[ing] into agreements with retailers to charge only those prices fixed by Leegin." *Id.*, at 1236. Leegin planned to introduce expert testimony describing the procompetitive effects of its pricing policy. The District Court excluded the testimony, relying on the *per se* rule established by *Dr. Miles*. At trial PSKS argued that the Heart Store program, among other things, demonstrated Leegin and its retailers had agreed to fix prices. Leegin responded that it had established a unilateral pricing policy lawful under §1, which applies only to concerted action. See *United States v. Colgate & Co.*, 250 U.S. 300 (1919). The jury agreed with PSKS and awarded it $1.2 million. Pursuant to 15 U.S.C. §15(a), the District Court trebled the damages and reimbursed PSKS for its attorney's fees and costs. It entered judgment against Leegin in the amount of $3,975,000.80.

The Court of Appeals for the Fifth Circuit affirmed (*per curiam*). On appeal Leegin did not dispute that it had entered into vertical price-fixing agreements with its retailers. Rather, it contended that the rule of reason should have applied to those agreements. The Court of Appeals rejected this argument. *Id.*, at 466-467. It was correct to explain that it remained bound by *Dr. Miles* "[b]ecause [the Supreme] Court has consistently applied the *per se* rule to [vertical minimum price-fixing] agreements." On this premise the Court of Appeals held that the District Court did not abuse its discretion in excluding the testimony of Leegin's economic expert, for the *per se* rule rendered irrelevant any procompetitive justifications for Leegin's pricing policy. *Id.*, at 467. We granted certiorari to determine whether vertical minimum resale price maintenance agreements should continue to be treated as *per se* unlawful.

II

Section 1 of the Sherman Act prohibits "[e]very contract, combination in the form of trust or otherwise, or conspiracy, in restraint of trade or commerce among the several States." While §1 could be interpreted to proscribe all contracts, see, *e.g., Board of Trade of Chicago v. United States*, 246 U.S. 231, 238 (1918), the Court has never "taken a literal approach to [its] language," *Texaco Inc. v. Dagher*, 547 U.S. 1, 5 (2006). Rather, the Court has repeated time and again that §1 "outlaw[s] only unreasonable restraints." *State Oil Co. v. Khan*, 522 U.S. 3, 10 (1997).

The rule of reason is the accepted standard for testing whether a practice restrains trade in violation of § 1. See *Texaco, supra*, at 5. "Under this rule, the factfinder weighs all of the circumstances of a case in deciding whether a restrictive practice should be prohibited as imposing an unreasonable restraint on competition." *Continental T. V., Inc. v. GTE Sylvania Inc.*, 433 U.S. 36, 49 (1977). Appropriate factors to take into account include "specific information about the relevant business" and "the restraint's history, nature, and effect." *Khan, supra*, at 10. Whether the businesses involved have market power is a further, significant consideration. See, *e.g., Copperweld Corp. v. Independence Tube Corp.*, 467 U.S. 752, 768 (1984) (equating the rule of reason with "an inquiry into market power and

40

market structure designed to assess [a restraint's] actual effect"); see also *Illinois Tool Works Inc. v. Independent Ink, Inc.*, 547 U.S. 28, 45-46 (2006). In its design and function the rule distinguishes between restraints with anticompetitive effect that are harmful to the consumer and restraints stimulating competition that are in the consumer's best interest.

The rule of reason does not govern all restraints. Some types "are deemed unlawful per se." *Khan, supra*, at 10. The *per se* rule, treating categories of restraints as necessarily illegal, eliminates the need to study the reasonableness of an individual restraint in light of the real market forces at work, *Business Electronics Corp. v. Sharp Electronics Corp.*, 485 U.S. 717, 723 (1988); and, it must be acknowledged, the *per se* rule can give clear guidance for certain conduct. Restraints that are *per se* unlawful include horizontal agreements among competitors to fix prices, see *Texaco, supra*, at 5, 126 or to divide markets, see *Palmer v. BRG of Ga., Inc.*, 498 U.S. 46, 49-50 (1990) (*per curiam*).

Resort to *per se* rules is confined to restraints, like those mentioned, "that would always or almost always tend to restrict competition and decrease output." *Business Electronics, supra*, at 723 (internal quotation marks omitted). To justify a *per se* prohibition a restraint must have "manifestly anticompetitive" effects, *GTE Sylvania, supra*, at 50, and "lack ... any redeeming virtue," *Northwest Wholesale Stationers, Inc. v. Pacific Stationery & Printing Co.*, 472 U.S. 284, 289 (1985) (internal quotation marks omitted).

As a consequence, the *per se* rule is appropriate only after courts have had considerable experience with the type of restraint at issue, see *Broadcast Music, Inc. v. Columbia Broadcasting System, Inc.*, 441 U.S. 1, 9 (1979), and only if courts can predict with confidence that it would be invalidated in all or almost all instances under the rule of reason, see *Arizona v. Maricopa County Medical Soc.*, 457 U.S. 332, 344 (1982). It should come as no surprise, then, that "we have expressed reluctance to adopt *per se* rules with regard to restraints imposed in the context of business relationships where the economic impact of certain practices is not immediately obvious." Khan, supra, at 10, (internal quotation marks omitted); see also *White*

Motor Co. v. United States, 372 U.S. 253, 263 (1963) (refusing to adopt a *per se* rule for a vertical nonprice restraint because of the uncertainty concerning whether this type of restraint satisfied the demanding standards necessary to apply a *per se* rule). And, as we have stated, a "departure from the rule-of-reason standard must be based upon demonstrable economic effect rather than ... upon formalistic line drawing." *GTE Sylvania, supra*, at 58-59.

III

The Court has interpreted *Dr. Miles Medical Co. v. John D. Park & Sons Co.*, 220 U.S. 373 (1911), as establishing a *per se* rule against a vertical agreement between a manufacturer and its distributor to set minimum resale prices. See, e.g., *Monsanto Co. v. Spray-Rite Service Corp.*, 465 U.S. 752, 761 (1984). In *Dr. Miles* the plaintiff, a manufacturer of medicines, sold its products only to distributors who agreed to resell them at set prices. The Court found the manufacturer's control of resale prices to be unlawful. It relied on the common-law rule that "a general restraint upon alienation is ordinarily invalid." 220 U.S., at 404-405. The Court then explained that the agreements would advantage the distributors, not the manufacturer, and were analogous to a combination among competing distributors, which the law treated as void. *Id.*, at 407-408.

The reasoning of the Court's more recent jurisprudence has rejected the rationales on which *Dr. Miles* was based. By relying on the common-law rule against restraints on alienation, *id.*, at 404-405, the Court justified its decision based on "formalistic" legal doctrine rather than "demonstrable economic effect," *GTE Sylvania, supra*, at 58-59. The Court in *Dr. Miles* relied on a treatise published in 1628, but failed to discuss in detail the business reasons that would motivate a manufacturer situated in 1911 to make use of vertical price restraints. Yet the Sherman Act's use of "restraint of trade" "invokes the common law itself, ... not merely the static content that the common law had assigned to the term in 1890." *Business Electronics, supra*, at 732. The general restraint on alienation, especially in the age when then-Justice Hughes used the term, tended to evoke policy concerns extraneous to the question that controls here. Usually associated with land, not chattels, the rule arose from restrictions removing real property from the stream of commerce for generations. The Court should be cautious about putting dispositive weight on doctrines from antiquity but of slight relevance. We reaffirm that "the state of the common law 400 or even 100 years ago is irrelevant to the issue before us: the effect of the antitrust laws upon vertical distributional restraints in the American economy today." *GTE Sylvania*, 433 U.S., at 53, n. 21 (internal quotation marks omitted).

Dr. Miles, furthermore, treated vertical agreements a manufacturer makes with its distributors as analogous to a horizontal combination among competing distributors. See 220 U.S., at 407-408. In later cases, however, the Court rejected the approach of reliance on rules governing horizontal restraints when defining rules applicable to vertical ones. See, *e.g.*, *Business Electronics, supra*, at 734 (disclaiming the "notion of equivalence between the scope of horizontal *per se* illegality and that of vertical *per se* illegality"); *Maricopa County*, supra, at 348, n. 18, 102 S.Ct. 2466 (noting that "horizontal restraints are generally less defensible than vertical restraints"). Our recent cases formulate antitrust principles in accordance with the appreciated differences in economic effect between vertical and horizontal agreements, differences the *Dr. Miles* Court failed to consider.

The reasons upon which *Dr. Miles* relied do not justify *a per se rule*. As a consequence, it is necessary to examine, in the first instance, the economic effects of vertical agreements to fix minimum resale prices, and to determine whether the *per se* rule is nonetheless appropriate. See *Business Electronics*, 485 U.S., at 726.

A

Though each side of the debate can find sources to support its position, it suffices to say here that economics literature is replete with procompetitive justifications for a manufacturer's use of resale price maintenance. See, *e.g.*, Brief for Economists as *Amici Curiae* 16 ("In the theoretical literature, it is essentially undisputed that minimum [resale price maintenance] can have procompetitive effects and that under a variety of market conditions it is unlikely to have anticompetitive effects"); Brief for United States as Amicus Curiae 9 ("[T]here is a widespread consensus that permitting a manufacturer to control the price at which its goods are sold may promote inter brand

43

competition and consumer welfare in a variety of ways"); ABA Section of Antitrust Law, Antitrust Law and Economics of Product Distribution 76 (2006) ("[T]he bulk of the economic literature on [resale price maintenance] suggests that [it] is more likely to be used to enhance efficiency than for anticompetitive purposes"); see also H. Hovenkamp, The Antitrust Enterprise: Principle and Execution 184-191 (2005) (hereinafter Hovenkamp); R. Bork, The Antitrust Paradox 288-291 (1978) (hereinafter Bork). Even those more skeptical of resale price maintenance acknowledge it can have procompetitive effects. See, e.g., Brief for William S. Comanor et al. as *Amici Curiae* 3 ("[G]iven [the] diversity of effects [of resale price maintenance], one could reasonably take the position that a *rule of reason* rather than a *per se* approach is warranted"); F.M. Scherer & D. Ross, Industrial Market Structure and Economic Performance 558 (3d ed.1990) (hereinafter Scherer & Ross) ("The overall balance between benefits and costs [of resale price maintenance] is probably close").

The few recent studies documenting the competitive effects of resale price maintenance also cast doubt on the conclusion that the practice meets the criteria for a *per se* rule. See T. Overstreet, Resale Price Maintenance: Economic Theories and Empirical Evidence 170 (1983) (hereinafter Overstreet) (noting that "[e]fficient uses of [resale price maintenance] are evidently not unusual or rare"); see also Ippolito, Resale Price Maintenance: Empirical Evidence From Litigation, 34 J. Law & Econ. 263, 292-293 (1991) (hereinafter Ippolito).

The justifications for vertical price restraints are similar to those for other vertical restraints. See GTE Sylvania, 433 U.S., at 54-57. Minimum resale price maintenance can stimulate interbrand competition-the competition among manufacturers selling different brands of the same type of product-by reducing intrabrand competition-the competition among retailers selling the same brand. The promotion of interbrand competition is important because "the primary purpose of the antitrust laws is to protect [this type of] competition." *Khan*, 522 U.S., at 15. A single manufacturer's use of vertical price restraints tends to eliminate intrabrand price competition; this in turn encourages retailers to invest in tangible or intangible services or promotional efforts that aid the manufacturer's position as against rival manufacturers. Resale price maintenance also has the potential to give consumers more options so that they can choose among low-price, low-service brands; high-price, high-service brands; and brands that fall in between.

Absent vertical price restraints, the retail services that enhance interbrand competition might be underprovided. This is because discounting retailers can free ride on retailers who furnish services and then capture some of the increased demand those services generate. *GTE Sylvania, supra*, at 55. Consumers might learn, for example, about the benefits of a manufacturer's product from a retailer that invests in fine showrooms, offers product demonstrations, or hires and trains knowledgeable employees. R. Posner, Antitrust Law 172-173 (2d ed.2001) (hereinafter Posner). Or consumers might decide to buy the product because they see it in a retail establishment that has a reputation for selling high-quality merchandise. Marvel & McCafferty, Resale Price Maintenance and Quality Certification, 15 Rand J. Econ. 346, 347-349 (1984) (hereinafter Marvel & McCafferty). If the consumer can then buy the product from a retailer that discounts because it has not spent capital providing services or developing a quality reputation, the high-service retailer will lose sales to the discounter, forcing it to cut back its services to a level lower than consumers would otherwise prefer. Minimum resale price maintenance alleviates the problem because it prevents the discounter from undercutting the service provider. With price competition decreased, the manufacturer's retailers compete among themselves over services.

Resale price maintenance, in addition, can increase interbrand competition by facilitating market entry for new firms and brands. "[N]ew manufacturers and manufacturers entering new markets can use the restrictions in order to induce competent and aggressive retailers to make the kind of investment of capital and labor that is often required in the distribution of products unknown to the consumer." *GTE Sylvania, supra*, at 55; see Marvel & McCafferty 349 (noting that reliance on a retailer's reputation "will decline as the manufacturer's brand becomes better known, so that [resale price maintenance] may be particularly important as a competitive device for new entrants"). New products and new brands are essential to a

45

dynamic economy, and if markets can be penetrated by using resale price maintenance there is a procompetitive effect.

Resale price maintenance can also increase interbrand competition by encouraging retailer services that would not be provided even absent free riding. It may be difficult and inefficient for a manufacturer to make and enforce a contract with a retailer specifying the different services the retailer must perform. Offering the retailer a guaranteed margin and threatening termination if it does not live up to expectations may be the most efficient way to expand the manufacturer's market share by inducing the retailer's performance and allowing it to use its own initiative and experience in providing valuable services. See Mathewson & Winter, The Law and Economics of Resale Price Maintenance, 13 Rev. Indus. Org. 57, 74-75 (1998) (hereinafter Mathewson & Winter); Klein & Murphy, Vertical Restraints as Contract Enforcement Mechanisms, 31 J. Law & Econ. 265, 295 (1988); see also Deneckere, Marvel, & Peck, Demand Uncertainty, Inventories, and Resale Price Maintenance, 111 Q.J. Econ. 885, 911 (1996) (noting that resale price maintenance may be beneficial to motivate retailers to stock adequate inventories of a manufacturer's goods in the face of uncertain consumer demand).

B

While vertical agreements setting minimum resale prices can have procompetitive justifications, they may have anticompetitive effects in other cases; and unlawful price fixing, designed solely to obtain monopoly profits, is an ever present temptation. Resale price maintenance may, for example, facilitate a manufacturer cartel. See *Business Electronics*, 485 U.S., at 725. An unlawful cartel will seek to discover if some manufacturers are undercutting the cartel's fixed prices. Resale price maintenance could assist the cartel in identifying price-cutting manufacturers who benefit from the lower prices they offer. Resale price maintenance, furthermore, could discourage a manufacturer from cutting prices to retailers with the concomitant benefit of cheaper prices to consumers. See *ibid.*; see also Posner 172; Overstreet 19-23.

Vertical price restraints also "might be used to organize cartels at the retailer level." *Business Electronics*, *supra*, at 725-726. A group of retailers might collude to fix prices to consumers and then compel a manufacturer to aid the unlawful arrangement with resale price maintenance. In that instance the manufacturer does not establish the practice to stimulate services or to promote its brand but to give inefficient retailers higher profits. Retailers with better distribution systems and lower cost structures would be prevented from charging lower prices by the agreement. See Posner 172; Overstreet 13-19. Historical examples suggest this possibility is a legitimate concern. See, *e.g.*, Marvel & McCafferty, The Welfare Effects of Resale Price Maintenance, 28 J. Law & Econ. 363, 373 (1985) (hereinafter Marvel) (providing an example of the power of the National Association of Retail Druggists to compel manufacturers to use resale price maintenance); Hovenkamp 186 (suggesting that the retail druggists in *Dr. Miles* formed a cartel and used manufacturers to enforce it).

A horizontal cartel among competing manufacturers or competing retailers that decreases output or reduces competition in order to increase price is, and ought to be, *per se* unlawful. See *Texaco*, 547 U.S., at 5; *GTE Sylvania*, 433 U.S., at 58, n. 28. To the extent a vertical agreement setting minimum resale prices is entered upon to facilitate either type of cartel, it, too, would need to be held unlawful under the rule of reason. This type of agreement may also be useful evidence for a plaintiff attempting to prove the existence of a horizontal cartel.

Resale price maintenance, furthermore, can be abused by a powerful manufacturer or retailer. A dominant retailer, for example, might request resale price maintenance to forestall innovation in distribution that decreases costs. A manufacturer might consider it has little choice but to accommodate the retailer's demands for vertical price restraints if the manufacturer believes it needs access to the retailer's distribution network. See Overstreet 31; 8 P. Areeda & H. Hovenkamp, Antitrust Law 47 (2d ed.2004) (hereinafter Areeda & Hovenkamp); cf. *Toys "R" Us, Inc. v. FTC*, 221 F.3d 928, 937-938 (CA7 2000). A manufacturer with market power, by comparison, might use resale price maintenance to give retailers an incentive not to sell the products of smaller rivals or new entrants. See, e.g., Marvel 366-368. As should be evident, the potential anticompetitive consequences of vertical price restraints must not be ignored or underestimated.

C

Notwithstanding the risks of unlawful conduct, it cannot be stated with any degree of confidence that resale price maintenance "always or almost always tend[s] to restrict competition and decrease output." *Business Electronics, supra*, at 723, 108 S.Ct. 1515 (internal quotation marks omitted). Vertical agreements establishing minimum resale prices can have either procompetitive or anticompetitive effects, depending upon the circumstances in which they are formed. And although the empirical evidence on the topic is limited, it does not suggest efficient uses of the agreements are infrequent or hypothetical. See Overstreet 170; see also *id.*, at 80 (noting that for the majority of enforcement actions brought by the Federal Trade Commission between 1965 and 1982, "the use of [resale price maintenance] was not likely motivated by collusive dealers who had successfully coerced their suppliers"); Ippolito 292 (reaching a similar conclusion). As the rule would proscribe a significant amount of procompetitive conduct, these agreements appear ill suited for *per se* condemnation.

Respondent contends, nonetheless, that vertical price restraints should be *per se* unlawful because of the administrative convenience of *per se* rules. See, *e.g.*, *GTE Sylvania, supra*, at 50, n. 16 (noting "*per se* rules tend to provide guidance to the business community and to minimize the burdens on litigants and the judicial system"). That argument suggests *per se* illegality is the rule rather than the exception. This misinterprets our antitrust law. *Per se* rules may decrease administrative costs, but that is only part of the equation. Those rules can be counterproductive. They can increase the total cost of the antitrust system by prohibiting procompetitive conduct the antitrust laws should encourage. See Easterbrook, Vertical Arrangements and the Rule of Reason, 53 Antitrust L.J. 135, 158 (1984) (hereinafter Easterbrook). They also may increase litigation costs by promoting frivolous suits against legitimate practices. The Court has thus explained that administrative "advantages are not sufficient in themselves to justify the creation of *per se* rules," *GTE Sylvania*, 433 U.S., at 50, n. 16, and has relegated their use to restraints that are "manifestly anticompetitive," *id.*, at 49-50. Were the Court now to conclude that vertical price restraints should be *per se* illegal based on administrative costs, we would undermine, if not overrule, the traditional "demanding standards" for adopting *per se* rules. *Id.*, at 50. Any possible reduction in administrative costs cannot alone justify the *Dr. Miles* rule.

Respondent also argues the *per se* rule is justified because a vertical price restraint can lead to higher prices for the manufacturer's goods. See also Overstreet 160 (noting that "price surveys indicate that [resale price maintenance] in most cases increased the prices of products sold"). Respondent is mistaken in relying on pricing effects absent a further showing of anticompetitive conduct. *Cf. id.*, at 106 (explaining that price surveys "do not necessarily tell us anything conclusive about the welfare effects of [resale price maintenance] because the results are generally consistent with both procompetitive and anticompetitive theories"). For, as has been indicated already, the antitrust laws are designed primarily to protect interbrand competition, from which lower prices can later result. See *Khan*, 522 U.S., at 15. The Court, moreover, has evaluated other vertical restraints under the rule of reason even though prices can be increased in the course of promoting procompetitive effects. See, *e.g.*, *Business Electronics*, 485 U.S., at 728. And resale price maintenance may reduce prices if manufacturers have resorted to costlier alternatives of controlling resale prices that are not per se unlawful.

Respondent's argument, furthermore, overlooks that, in general, the interests of manufacturers and consumers are aligned with respect to retailer profit margins. The difference between the price a manufacturer charges retailers and the price retailers charge consumers represents part of the manufacturer's cost of distribution, which, like any other cost, the manufacturer usually desires to minimize. See *GTE Sylvania*, 433 U.S., at 56, n. 24; see also *id.*, at 56 ("Economists ... have argued that manufacturers have an economic interest in maintaining as much intrabrand competition as is consistent with the efficient distribution of their products"). A manufacturer has no incentive to overcompensate retailers with unjustified margins. The retailers, not the manufacturer, gain from higher retail prices. The manufacturer often loses; interbrand competition reduces its competitiveness and market share because consumers will "substitute a different brand of the same product." *Id.*, at 52, n. 19; see *Business Electronics, supra*, at 725. As a general matter, therefore, a single manufacturer will desire to set minimum resale prices only if the "increase in demand resulting from enhanced service ... will more than offset a negative impact on demand of a higher retail price." Mathewson & Winter 67.

The implications of respondent's position are far reaching. Many decisions a manufacturer makes and carries out through concerted action can lead to higher prices. A manufacturer might, for example, contract with different suppliers to obtain better inputs that improve product quality. Or it might hire an advertising agency to promote awareness of its goods. Yet no one would think these actions violate the Sherman Act because they lead to higher prices. The antitrust laws do not require manufacturers to produce generic goods that consumers do not know about or want. The manufacturer strives to improve its product quality or to promote its brand because it believes this conduct will lead to increased demand despite higher prices. The same can hold true for resale price maintenance.

Resale price maintenance, it is true, does have economic dangers. If the rule of reason were to apply to vertical price restraints, courts would have to be diligent in eliminating their anticompetitive uses from the market. This is a realistic objective, and certain factors are relevant to the inquiry. For example, the number of manufacturers that make use of the practice in a given industry can provide important instruction. When only a few manufacturers lacking market power adopt the practice, there is little likelihood it is facilitating a manufacturer cartel, for a cartel then can be undercut by rival manufacturers. See Overstreet 22; Bork 294. Likewise, a retailer cartel is unlikely when only a single manufacturer in a competitive market uses resale price maintenance. Interbrand competition would divert consumers to lower priced substitutes and eliminate any gains to retailers from their price-fixing agreement over a single brand. See Posner 172; Bork 292. Resale price maintenance should be subject to more careful scrutiny, by contrast, if many competing manufacturers adopt the practice. Cf. Scherer & Ross 558 (noting that "except when [resale price maintenance] spreads to cover the bulk of an industry's output, depriving consumers of a meaningful choice between high-service and low-price outlets, most [resale price maintenance arrangements] are probably innocuous"); Easterbrook 162 (suggesting that "every one of the potentially-anticompetitive outcomes of vertical arrangements depends on the uniformity of the practice").

The source of the restraint may also be an important consideration. If there is evidence retailers were the impetus for a vertical price restraint, there is a greater likelihood that the restraint facilitates a retailer cartel or supports a dominant, inefficient retailer. See Brief for William S. Comanor et al. as *Amici Curiae* 7-8. If, by contrast, a manufacturer adopted the policy independent of retailer pressure, the restraint is less likely to promote anticompetitive conduct. Cf. Posner 177 ("It makes all the difference whether minimum retail prices are imposed by the manufacturer in order to evoke point-of-sale services or by the dealers in order to obtain monopoly profits"). A manufacturer also has an incentive to protest inefficient retailer-induced price restraints because they can harm its competitive position.

As a final matter, that a dominant manufacturer or retailer can abuse resale price maintenance for anticompetitive purposes may not be a serious concern unless the relevant entity has market power. If a retailer lacks market power, manufacturers likely can sell their goods through rival retailers. See also *Business Electronics*, *supra*, at 727, n. 2 (noting "[r]etail market power is rare, because of the usual presence of interbrand competition and other dealers"). And if a manufacturer lacks market power, there is less likelihood it can use the practice to keep competitors away from distribution outlets.

The rule of reason is designed and used to eliminate anticompetitive transactions from the market. This standard principle applies to vertical price restraints. A party alleging injury from a vertical agreement setting minimum resale prices will have, as a general matter, the information and resources available to show the existence of the agreement and its scope of operation. As courts gain experience considering the effects of these restraints by applying the rule of reason over the course of decisions, they can establish the litigation structure to ensure the rule operates to eliminate anticompetitive restraints from the market and to provide more guidance to businesses. Courts can, for example, devise rules over

51

time for offering proof, or even presumptions where justified, to make the rule of reason a fair and efficient way to prohibit anticompetitive restraints and to promote procompetitive ones.

For all of the foregoing reasons, we think that were the Court considering the issue as an original matter, the rule of reason, not a *per se* rule of unlawfulness, would be the appropriate standard to judge vertical price restraints.

IV

We do not write on a clean slate, for the decision in *Dr. Miles* is almost a century old. So there is an argument for its retention on the basis of *stare decisis* alone. Even if *Dr. Miles* established an erroneous rule, "*[s]tare decisis* reflects a policy judgment that in most matters it is more important that the applicable rule of law be settled than that it be settled right." *Khan*, 522 U.S., at 20 (internal quotation marks omitted). And concerns about maintaining settled law are strong when the question is one of statutory interpretation. See, *e.g.*, *Hohn v. United States*, 524 U.S. 236, 251 (1998).

Stare decisis is not as significant in this case, however, because the issue before us is the scope of the Sherman Act. *Khan, supra*, at 20 ("[T]he general presumption that legislative changes should be left to Congress has less force with respect to the Sherman Act"). From the beginning the Court has treated the Sherman Act as a common-law statute. See *National Soc. of Professional Engineers v. United States*, 435 U.S. 679, 688 (1978); see also *Northwest Airlines, Inc. v. Transport Workers*, 451 U.S. 77, 98, n. 42 (1981) ("In antitrust, the federal courts ... act more as common-law courts than in other areas governed by federal statute"). Just as the common law adapts to modern understanding and greater experience, so too does the Sherman Act's prohibition on "restraint[s] of trade" evolve to meet the dynamics of present economic conditions. The case-by-case adjudication contemplated by the rule of reason has implemented this common-law approach. See *National Soc. of Professional Engineers*, supra, at 688. Likewise, the boundaries of the doctrine of *per se* illegality should not be immovable. For "[i]t would make no sense to create out of the single term 'restraint of trade' a chronologically schizoid statute, in which a ' rule of reason' evolves with new circumstance and new wisdom, but a line of *per se* illegality remains forever fixed where it was." *Business Electronics*, 485 U.S., at 732.

A

Stare decisis, we conclude, does not compel our continued adherence to the *per se* rule against vertical price restraints. As discussed earlier, respected authorities in the economics literature suggest the *per se* rule is inappropriate, and there is now widespread agreement that resale price maintenance can have procompetitive effects. See, e.g., Brief for Economists as *Amici Curiae* 16. It is also significant that both the Department of Justice and the Federal Trade Commission-the antitrust enforcement agencies with the ability to assess the long-term impacts of resale price maintenance-have recommended that this Court replace the per se rule with the traditional rule of reason. See Brief for United States as *Amicus Curiae 6*. In the antitrust context the fact that a decision has been "called into serious question" justifies our reevaluation of it. *Khan, supra*, at 21.

Other considerations reinforce the conclusion that *Dr. Miles* should be overturned. Of most relevance, "we have overruled our precedents when subsequent cases have undermined their doctrinal underpinnings." *Dickerson v. United States*, 530 U.S. 428, 443, (2000). The Court's treatment of vertical restraints has progressed away from Dr. Miles 'strict approach. We have distanced ourselves from the opinion's rationales. See *supra*, at7-8; see also *Khan, supra*, at 21 (overruling a case when "the views underlying [it had been] eroded by this Court's precedent"); *Rodriguez de Quijas v. Shearson/American Express, Inc.*, 490 U.S. 477, 480-481 (1989) (same). This is unsurprising, for the case was decided not long after enactment of the Sherman Act when the Court had little experience with antitrust analysis. Only eight years after *Dr. Miles*, moreover, the Court reined in the decision by holding that a manufacturer can announce suggested resale prices and refuse to deal with distributors who do not follow them. Colgate, 250 U.S., at 307-308.

In more recent cases the Court, following a common-law approach, has continued to temper, limit, or overrule once strict

53

prohibitions on vertical restraints. In 1977, the Court overturned the per se rule for vertical nonprice restraints, adopting the rule of reason in its stead. *GTE Sylvania*, 433 U.S., at 57-59 (overruling *United States v. Arnold, Schwinn & Co.*, 388 U.S. 365 (1967)); see also 433 U.S., at 58, n. 29, 97 S.Ct. 2549 (noting "that the advantages of vertical restrictions should not be limited to the categories of new entrants and failing firms"). While the Court in a footnote in *GTE Sylvania* suggested that differences between vertical price and nonprice restraints could support different legal treatment, see 433 U.S., at 51, n. 18, the central part of the opinion relied on authorities and arguments that find unequal treatment "difficult to justify," *id.*, at 69-70 (White, J., concurring in judgment).

Continuing in this direction, in two cases in the 1980's the Court defined legal rules to limit the reach of *Dr. Miles* and to accommodate the doctrines enunciated in *GTE Sylvania and Colgate.* See *Business Electronics, supra*, at 726-728, *Monsanto*, 465 U.S., at 763-764. In *Monsanto*, the Court required that antitrust plaintiffs alleging a §1 price-fixing conspiracy must present evidence tending to exclude the possibility a manufacturer and its distributors acted in an independent manner. *Id.*, at 764. Unlike Justice Brennan's concurrence, which rejected arguments that *Dr. Miles* should be overruled, see 465 U.S., at 769, the Court "decline[d] to reach the question" whether vertical agreements fixing resale prices always should be unlawful because neither party suggested otherwise, *id.*, at 761-762, n. 7. In *Business Electronics* the Court further narrowed the scope of Dr. Miles. It held that the per se rule applied only to specific agreements over price levels and not to an agreement between a manufacturer and a distributor to terminate a price-cutting distributor. 485 U.S., at 726-727, 735-736.

Most recently, in 1997, after examining the issue of vertical maximum price-fixing agreements in light of commentary and real experience, the Court overruled a 29-year-old precedent treating those agreements as *per se* illegal. *Khan*, 522 U.S., at 22 (overruling *Albrecht v. Herald Co.*, 390 U.S. 145 (1968)). It held instead that they should be evaluated under the traditional rule of reason. 522 U.S., at 22. Our continued limiting of the reach of the decision in *Dr. Miles* and our recent treatment of other vertical restraints justify the conclusion that *Dr. Miles* should not be retained.

The *Dr. Miles* rule is also inconsistent with a principled framework, for it makes little economic sense when analyzed with our other cases on vertical restraints. If we were to decide the procompetitive effects of resale price maintenance were insufficient to overrule *Dr. Miles*, then cases such as *Colgate* and *GTE Sylvania* themselves would be called into question. These later decisions, while they may result in less intrabrand competition, can be justified because they permit manufacturers to secure the procompetitive benefits associated with vertical price restraints through other methods. The other methods, however, could be less efficient for a particular manufacturer to establish and sustain. The end result hinders competition and consumer welfare because manufacturers are forced to engage in second-best alternatives and because consumers are required to shoulder the increased expense of the inferior practices.

The manufacturer has a number of legitimate options to achieve benefits similar to those provided by vertical price restraints. A manufacturer can exercise its Colgate right to refuse to deal with retailers that do not follow its suggested prices. See 250 U.S., at 307. The economic effects of unilateral and concerted price setting are in general the same. See, *e.g.*, *Monsanto*, 465 U.S., at 762-764. The problem for the manufacturer is that a jury might conclude its unilateral policy was really a vertical agreement, subjecting it to treble damages and potential criminal liability. *Ibid.*; *Business Electronics*, supra, at 728. Even with the stringent standards in *Monsanto* and *Business Electronics*, this danger can lead, and has led, rational manufacturers to take wasteful measures. See, *e.g.*, Brief for PING, Inc., as *Amicus Curiae* 9-18. A manufacturer might refuse to discuss its pricing policy with its distributors except through counsel knowledgeable of the subtle intricacies of the law. Or it might terminate longstanding distributors for minor violations without seeking an explanation. See *ibid.* The increased costs these burdensome measures generate flow to consumers in the form of higher prices.

Furthermore, depending on the type of product it sells, a manufacturer might be able to achieve the procompetitive benefits of resale price maintenance by integrating downstream and selling its

55

products directly to consumers. *Dr. Miles* tilts the relative costs of vertical integration and vertical agreement by making the former more attractive based on the per se rule, not on real market conditions. See *Business Electronics*, *supra*, at 725; see generally Coase, The Nature of the Firm, 4 Economica, New Series 386 (1937). This distortion might lead to inefficient integration that would not otherwise take place, so that consumers must again suffer the consequences of the suboptimal distribution strategy. And integration, unlike vertical price restraints, eliminates all intrabrand competition. See, *e.g.*, *GTE Sylvania*, 433 U.S., at 57, n. 26.

There is yet another consideration. A manufacturer can impose territorial restrictions on distributors and allow only one distributor to sell its goods in a given region. Our cases have recognized, and the economics literature confirms, that these vertical nonprice restraints have impacts similar to those of vertical price restraints; both reduce intrabrand competition and can stimulate retailer services. See, *e.g.*, *Business Electronics*, *supra*, at 728; *Monsanto*, *supra*, at 762-763; see also Brief for Economists as *Amici Curiae* 17-18. Cf. Scherer & Ross 560 (noting that vertical nonprice restraints "can engender inefficiencies at least as serious as those imposed upon the consumer by resale price maintenance"); Steiner, How Manufacturers Deal with the Price-Cutting Retailer: When Are Vertical Restraints Efficient?, 65 Antitrust L.J. 407, 446-447 (1997) (indicating that "antitrust law should recognize that the consumer interest is often better served by [resale price maintenance]-contrary to its per se illegality and the rule-of-reason status of vertical nonprice restraints"). The same legal standard (*per se* unlawfulness) applies to horizontal market division and horizontal price fixing because both have similar economic effect. There is likewise little economic justification for the current differential treatment of vertical price and nonprice restraints. Furthermore, vertical nonprice restraints may prove less efficient for inducing desired services, and they reduce intrabrand competition more than vertical price restraints by eliminating both price and service competition. See Brief for Economists as *Amici Curiae* 17-18.

In sum, it is a flawed antitrust doctrine that serves the interests of lawyers-by creating legal distinctions that operate as traps for the unwary-more than the interests of consumers-by requiring manufacturers to choose second-best options to achieve sound business objectives.

B

Respondent's arguments for reaffirming Dr. Miles on the basis of *stare decisis* do not require a different result. Respondent looks to congressional action concerning vertical price restraints. In 1937, Congress passed the Miller-Tydings Fair Trade Act, 50 Stat. 693, which made vertical price restraints legal if authorized by a fair trade law enacted by a State. Fifteen years later, Congress expanded the exemption to permit vertical price-setting agreements between a manufacturer and a distributor to be enforced against other distributors not involved in the agreement. McGuire Act, 66 Stat. 632. In 1975, however, Congress repealed both Acts. Consumer Goods Pricing Act, 89 Stat. 801. That the *Dr. Miles* rule applied to vertical price restraints in 1975, according to respondent, shows Congress ratified the rule.

This is not so. The text of the Consumer Goods Pricing Act did not codify the rule of *per se* illegality for vertical price restraints. It rescinded statutory provisions that made them *per se* legal. Congress once again placed these restraints within the ambit of §1 of the Sherman Act. And, as has been discussed, Congress intended §1 to give courts the ability "to develop governing principles of law" in the common-law tradition. *Texas Industries, Inc. v. Radcliff Materials, Inc.*, 451 U.S. 630, 643, (1981); see *Business Electronics*, 485 U.S., at 731 ("The changing content of the term 'restraint of trade' was well recognized at the time the Sherman Act was enacted"). Congress could have set the Dr. Miles rule in stone, but it chose a more flexible option. We respect its decision by analyzing vertical price restraints, like all restraints, in conformance with traditional § 1 principles, including the principle that our antitrust doctrines "evolv[e] with new circumstances and new wisdom." Business Electronics, supra, at 732, 108 S.Ct. 1515; see also Easterbrook 139.

The rule of reason, furthermore, is not inconsistent with the Consumer Goods Pricing Act. Unlike the earlier congressional exemption, it does not treat vertical price restraints as per se legal. In

57

this respect, the justifications for the prior exemption are illuminating. Its goal "was to allow the States to protect small retail establishments that Congress thought might otherwise be driven from the marketplace by large-volume discounters." *California Retail Liquor Dealers Assn. v. Midcal Aluminum, Inc.*, 445 U.S. 97, 102 (1980). The state fair trade laws also appear to have been justified on similar grounds. See Areeda & Hovenkamp 298. The rationales for these provisions are foreign to the Sherman Act. Divorced from competition and consumer welfare, they were designed to save inefficient small retailers from their inability to compete. The purpose of the antitrust laws, by contrast, is "the protection of *competition*, not *competitors*." *Atlantic Richfield Co. v. USA Petroleum Co.*, 495 U.S. 328, 338 (1990) (internal quotation marks omitted). To the extent Congress repealed the exemption for some vertical price restraints to end its prior practice of encouraging anticompetitive conduct, the rule of reason promotes the same objective.

Respondent also relies on several congressional appropriations in the mid-1980's in which Congress did not permit the Department of Justice or the Federal Trade Commission to use funds to advocate overturning *Dr. Miles*. See, *e.g.*, 97 Stat. 1071. We need not pause long in addressing this argument. The conditions on funding are no longer in place, see, *e.g.*, Brief for United States as *Amicus Curiae 21*, and they were ambiguous at best. As much as they might show congressional approval for *Dr. Miles*, they might demonstrate a different proposition: that Congress could not pass legislation codifying the rule and reached a short-term compromise instead.

Reliance interests do not require us to reaffirm *Dr. Miles*. To be sure, reliance on a judicial opinion is a significant reason to adhere to it, *Payne v. Tennessee*, 501 U.S. 808, (1991), especially "in cases involving property and contract rights," *Khan*, 522 U.S., at 20. The reliance interests here, however, like the reliance interests in *Khan*, cannot justify an inefficient rule, especially because the narrowness of the rule has allowed manufacturers to set minimum resale prices in other ways. And while the *Dr. Miles* rule is longstanding, resale price maintenance was legal under fair trade laws in a majority of States for a large part of the past century up until 1975.

It is also of note that during this time "when the legal environment in the [United States] was most favorable for [resale price maintenance], no more than a tiny fraction of manufacturers ever employed [resale price maintenance] contracts." Overstreet 6; see also *id.*, at 169 (noting that "no more than one percent of manufacturers, accounting for no more than ten percent of consumer goods purchases, ever employed [resale price maintenance] in any single year in the [United States]"); Scherer & Ross 549 (noting that "[t]he fraction of U.S. retail sales covered by [resale price maintenance] in its heyday has been variously estimated at from 4 to 10 percent"). To the extent consumers demand cheap goods, judging vertical price restraints under the rule of reason will not prevent the market from providing them. Cf. Easterbrook 152-153 (noting that "S.S. Kresge (the old K-Mart) flourished during the days of manufacturers' greatest freedom" because "discount stores offer a combination of price and service that many customers value" and that "[n]othing in restricted dealing threatens the ability of consumers to find low prices"); Scherer & Ross 557 (noting that "for the most part, the effects of the [Consumer Goods Pricing Act] were imperceptible because the forces of competition had already repealed the [previous antitrust exemption] in their own quiet way").

For these reasons the Court's decision in *Dr. Miles Medical Co. v. John D. Park & Sons Co.*, 220 U.S. 373 (1911), is now overruled. Vertical price restraints are to be judged according to the rule of reason.

V

Noting that Leegin's president has an ownership interest in retail stores that sell Brighton, respondent claims Leegin participated in an unlawful horizontal cartel with competing retailers. Respondent did not make this allegation in the lower courts, and we do not consider it here.

The judgment of the Court of Appeals is reversed, and the case is remanded for proceedings consistent with this opinion.

Breyer, J., with whom Stevens, Souter, and Ginsburg, JJ., join, dissenting. In *Dr. Miles Medical Co. v. John D. Park & Sons Co.*,

220 U.S. 373, 394, 408-409 (1911), this Court held that an agreement between a manufacturer of proprietary medicines and its dealers to fix the minimum price at which its medicines could be sold was "invalid ... under the [Sherman Act, 15 U.S.C. §1]." This Court has consistently read *Dr. Miles* as establishing a bright-line rule that agreements fixing minimum resale prices are *per se* illegal. See, *e.g.*, *United States v. Trenton Potteries Co.*, 273 U.S. 392, 399-401, (1927); *NYNEX Corp. v. Discon, Inc.*, 525 U.S. 128, 133 (1998). That *per se* rule is one upon which the legal profession, business, and the public have relied for close to a century. Today the Court holds that courts must determine the lawfulness of minimum resale price maintenance by applying, not a bright-line *per se* rule, but a circumstance-specific "rule of reason." And in doing so it overturns Dr. Miles.

The Court justifies its departure from ordinary considerations of *stare decisis* by pointing to a set of arguments well known in the antitrust literature for close to half a century. Congress has repeatedly found in these arguments insufficient grounds for overturning the *per se* rule. See, *e.g.*, Hearings on H.R. 10527 et al. before the Subcommittee on Commerce and Finance of the House Committee on Interstate and Foreign Commerce, 85th Cong., 2d Sess., 74-76, 89, 99, 101-102, 192-195, 261-262 (1958). And, in my view, they do not warrant the Court's now overturning so well-established a legal precedent.

I

The Sherman Act seeks to maintain a marketplace free of anticompetitive practices, in particular those enforced by agreement among private firms. The law assumes that such a marketplace, free of private restrictions, will tend to bring about the lower prices, better products, and more efficient production processes that consumers typically desire. In determining the lawfulness of particular practices, courts often apply a "rule of reason." They examine both a practice's likely anticompetitive effects and its beneficial business justifications. See, *e.g.*, *National Collegiate Athletic Assn. v. Board of Regents of Univ. of Okla.*, 468 U.S. 85, 109-110, and n. 39 (1984); *National Soc. of Professional Engineers v. United States*,

435 U.S. 679, 688-691 (1978); *Board of Trade of Chicago v. United States*, 246 U.S. 231, 238 (1918).

Nonetheless, sometimes the likely anticompetitive consequences of a particular practice are so serious and the potential justifications so few (or, e.g., so difficult to prove) that courts have departed from a pure "rule of reason" approach. And sometimes this Court has imposed a rule of *per se* unlawfulness-a rule that instructs courts to find the practice unlawful all (or nearly all) the time. See, *e.g.*, *NYNEX*, *supra*, at 133; *Arizona v. Maricopa County Medical Soc.*, 457 U.S. 332, 343-344, and n. 16 (1982); *Continental T. V., Inc. v. GTE Sylvania Inc.*, 433 U.S. 36, 50, n. 16, (1977); *United States v. Topco Associates, Inc.*, 405 U.S. 596, 609-611 (1972); *United States v. Socony-Vacuum Oil Co.*, 310 U.S. 150, 213-214 (1940) (citing and quoting Trenton Potteries, supra, at 397-398.

The case before us asks which kind of approach the courts should follow where minimum resale price maintenance is at issue. Should they apply a *per se* rule (or a variation) that would make minimum resale price maintenance always (or almost always) unlawful? Should they apply a "rule of reason"? Were the Court writing on a blank slate, I would find these questions difficult. But, of course, the Court is not writing on a blank slate, and that fact makes a considerable legal difference.

To best explain why the question would be difficult were we deciding it afresh, I briefly summarize several classical arguments for and against the use of a per se rule. The arguments focus on three sets of considerations, those involving: (1) potential anticompetitive effects, (2) potential benefits, and (3) administration. The difficulty arises out of the fact that the different sets of considerations point in different directions. See, *e.g.*, 8 P. Areeda, Antitrust Law ¶¶1628-1633, pp. 330-392 (1st ed.1989) (hereinafter Areeda); 8 P. Areeda & H. Hovenkamp, Antitrust Law ¶¶1628-1633, pp. 288-339 (2d ed.2004) (hereinafter Areeda & Hovenkamp); Easterbrook, Vertical Arrangements and the Rule of Reason, 53 Antitrust L.J. 135, 146-152 (1984) (hereinafter Easterbrook); Pitofsky, In Defense of Discounters: The No-Frills Case for a Per Se Rule Against Vertical Price Fixing, 71 Geo. L.J. 1487 (1983) (hereinafter Pitofsky); Scherer, The Economics of Vertical Restraints, 52 Antitrust L.J. 687, 706-707

(1983) (hereinafter Scherer); Posner, The Next Step in the Antitrust Treatment of Restricted Distribution: Per Se Legality, 48 U. Chi. L.Rev. 6, 22-26 (1981); Brief for William S. Comanor and Frederic M. Scherer as *Amici Curiae* 7-10.

On the one hand, agreements setting minimum resale prices may have serious anticompetitive consequences. *In respect to dealers*: Resale price maintenance agreements, rather like horizontal price agreements, can diminish or eliminate price competition among dealers of a single brand or (if practiced generally by manufacturers) among multibrand dealers. In doing so, they can prevent dealers from offering customers the lower prices that many customers prefer; they can prevent dealers from responding to changes in demand, say falling demand, by cutting prices; they can encourage dealers to substitute service, for price, competition, thereby threatening wastefully to attract too many resources into that portion of the industry; they can inhibit expansion by more efficient dealers whose lower prices might otherwise attract more customers, stifling the development of new, more efficient modes of retailing; and so forth. See, *e.g.*, 8 Areeda & Hovenkamp ¶1632c, at 319-321; Steiner, The Evolution and Applications of Dual-Stage Thinking, 49 The Antitrust Bulletin 877, 899-900 (2004); Comanor, Vertical Price-Fixing, Vertical Market Restrictions, and the New Antitrust Policy, 98 Harv. L.Rev. 983, 990-1000 (1985).

In respect to producers: Resale price maintenance agreements can help to reinforce the competition-inhibiting behavior of firms in concentrated industries. In such industries firms may tacitly collude, i.e., observe each other's pricing behavior, each understanding that price cutting by one firm is likely to trigger price competition by all. See 8 Areeda & Hovenkamp ¶1632d, at 321-323; P. Areeda & L. Kaplow, Antitrust Analysis ¶¶231-233, pp. 276-283 (4th ed.1988) (hereinafter Areeda & Kaplow). Cf. *United States v. Container Corp. of America*, 393 U.S. 333 (1969); Areeda & Kaplow ¶¶247-253, at 327-348. Where that is so, resale price maintenance can make it easier for each producer to identify (by observing retail markets) when a competitor has begun to cut prices. And a producer who cuts wholesale prices without lowering the minimum resale price will stand to gain little, if anything, in increased profits, because the dealer will be unable to stimulate increased consumer demand by passing along the producer's price cut to consumers. In either case, resale price maintenance agreements will tend to prevent price competition from "breaking out"; and they will thereby tend to stabilize producer prices. See Pitofsky 1490-1491. Cf., *e.g.*, *Container Corp.*, *supra*, at 336-337, 89 S.Ct. 510.

Those who express concern about the potential anticompetitive effects find empirical support in the behavior of prices before, and then after, Congress in 1975 repealed the Miller-Tydings Fair Trade Act, 50 Stat. 693, and the McGuire Act, 66 Stat. 631. Those Acts had permitted (but not required) individual States to enact "fair trade" laws authorizing minimum resale price maintenance. At the time of repeal minimum resale price maintenance was lawful in 36 States; it was unlawful in 14 States. See Hearings on S. 408 before the Subcommittee on Antitrust and Monopoly of the Senate Committee on the Judiciary, 94th Cong., 1st Sess., 173 (1975) (hereinafter Hearings on S. 408) (statement of Thomas E. Kauper, Assistant Attorney General, Antitrust Division). Comparing prices in the former States with prices in the latter States, the Department of Justice argued that minimum resale price maintenance had raised prices by 19% to 27%. See Hearings on H.R. 2384 before the Subcommittee on Monopolies and Commercial Law of the House Committee on the Judiciary, 94th Cong., 1st Sess., 122 (1975) (hereinafter Hearings on H.R. 2384) (statement of Keith I. Clearwaters, Deputy Assistant Attorney General, Antitrust Division).

After repeal, minimum resale price maintenance agreements were unlawful per se in every State. The Federal Trade Commission (FTC) staff, after studying numerous price surveys, wrote that collectively the surveys "indicate[d] that [resale price maintenance] in most cases increased the prices of products sold with [resale price maintenance]." Bureau of Economics Staff Report to the FTC, T. Overstreet, Resale Price Maintenance: Economic Theories and Empirical Evidence, 160 (1983) (hereinafter Overstreet). Most economists today agree that, in the words of a prominent antitrust treatise, "resale price maintenance tends to produce higher consumer prices than would otherwise be the case." 8 Areeda & Hovenkamp ¶1604b, at 40 (finding "[t]he evidence ... persuasive on this point"). See also Brief for William S. Comanor and Frederic M. Scherer as *Amici Curiae* 4 ("It is uniformly acknowledged that [resale price

63

maintenance] and other vertical restraints lead to higher consumer prices").

On the other hand, those favoring resale price maintenance have long argued that resale price maintenance agreements can provide important consumer benefits. The majority lists two: First, such agreements can facilitate new entry. *Ante*, at 11-12. For example, a newly entering producer wishing to build a product name might be able to convince dealers to help it do so-if, but only if, the producer can assure those dealers that they will later recoup their investment. Without resale price maintenance, late-entering dealers might take advantage of the earlier investment and, through price competition, drive prices down to the point where the early dealers cannot recover what they spent. By assuring the initial dealers that such later price competition will not occur, resale price maintenance can encourage them to carry the new product, thereby helping the new producer succeed. See 8 Areeda & Hovenkamp ¶¶1617a, 1631b, at 193-196, 308. The result might be increased competition at the producer level, i.e., greater inter-brand competition, that brings with it net consumer benefits.

Second, without resale price maintenance a producer might find its efforts to sell a product undermined by what resale price maintenance advocates call "free riding." *Ante*, at 10-11. Suppose a producer concludes that it can succeed only if dealers provide certain services, say, product demonstrations, high quality shops, advertising that creates a certain product image, and so forth. Without resale price maintenance, some dealers might take a "free ride" on the investment that others make in providing those services. Such a dealer would save money by not paying for those services and could consequently cut its own price and increase its own sales. Under these circumstances, dealers might prove unwilling to invest in the provision of necessary services. See, *e.g.*, 8 Areeda & Hovenkamp ¶¶ 1611-1613, 1631c, at 126-165, 309-313; R. Posner, Antitrust Law 172-173 (2d ed.2001); R. Bork, The Antitrust Paradox 290-291 (1978) (hereinafter Bork); Easterbrook 146-149.

Moreover, where a producer and not a group of dealers seeks a resale price maintenance agreement, there is a special reason to believe some such benefits exist. That is because, other things being equal, producers should want to encourage price competition among their dealers. By doing so they will often increase profits by selling more of their product. See *Sylvania*, 433 U.S., at 56, n. 24; Bork 290. And that is so, even if the producer possesses sufficient market power to earn a super-normal profit. That is to say, other things being equal, the producer will benefit by charging his dealers a competitive (or even a higher-than-competitive) wholesale price while encouraging price competition among them. Hence, if the producer is the moving force, the producer must have some special reason for wanting resale price maintenance; and in the absence of, say, concentrated producer markets (where that special reason might consist of a desire to stabilize wholesale prices), that special reason may well reflect the special circumstances just described: new entry, "free riding," or variations on those themes.

The upshot is, as many economists suggest, sometimes resale price maintenance can prove harmful; sometimes it can bring benefits. See, *e.g.*, Brief for Economists as *Amici Curiae* 16; 8 Areeda & Hovenkamp ¶¶1631-1632, at 306-328; Pitofsky 1495; Scherer 706-707. But before concluding that courts should consequently apply a rule of reason, I would ask such questions as, how often are harms or benefits likely to occur? How easy is it to separate the beneficial sheep from the antitrust goats?

Economic discussion, such as the studies the Court relies upon, can help provide answers to these questions, and in doing so, economics can, and should, inform antitrust law. But antitrust law cannot, and should not, precisely replicate economists' (sometimes conflicting) views. That is because law, unlike economics, is an administrative system the effects of which depend upon the content of rules and precedents only as they are applied by judges and juries in courts and by lawyers advising their clients. And that fact means that courts will often bring their own administrative judgment to bear, sometimes applying rules of per se unlawfulness to business practices even when those practices sometimes produce benefits. See, *e.g.*, F.M. Scherer & D. Ross, Industrial Market Structure and Economic Performance 335-339 (3d ed.1990) (hereinafter Scherer & Ross) (describing some circumstances under which price-fixing agreements could be more beneficial than "unfettered competition," but also noting potential costs of moving from a per se ban to a rule of reasonableness assessment of such agreements).

I have already described studies and analyses that suggest (though they cannot prove) that resale price maintenance can cause harms with some regularity-and certainly when dealers are the driving force. But what about benefits? How often, for example, will the benefits to which the Court points occur in practice? I can find no economic consensus on this point. There is a consensus in the literature that "free riding" takes place. But "free riding" often takes place in the economy without any legal effort to stop it. Many visitors to California take free rides on the Pacific Coast Highway. We all benefit freely from ideas, such as that of creating the first supermarket. Dealers often take a "free ride" on investments that others have made in building a product's name and reputation. The question is how often the "free riding" problem is serious enough significantly to deter dealer investment.

To be more specific, one can easily *imagine* a dealer who refuses to provide important presale services, say a detailed explanation of how a product works (or who fails to provide a proper atmosphere in which to sell expensive perfume or alligator billfolds), lest customers use that "free" service (or enjoy the psychological benefit arising when a high-priced retailer stocks a particular brand of billfold or handbag) and then buy from another dealer at a lower price. Sometimes this must happen in reality. But does it happen often? We do, after all, live in an economy where firms, despite *Dr. Mile' per se* rule, still sell complex technical equipment (as well as expensive perfume and alligator billfolds) to consumers.

All this is to say that the ultimate question is not whether, but *how much*, "free riding" of this sort takes place. And, after reading the briefs, I must answer that question with an uncertain "sometimes." See, *e.g.*, Brief for William S. Comanor and Frederic M. Scherer as *Amici Curiae* 6-7 (noting "skepticism in the economic literature about how often [free riding] actually occurs"); Scherer & Ross 551-555 (explaining the "severe limitations" of the free-rider justification for resale price maintenance); Pitofsky, Why Dr. Miles Was Right, 8 Regulation, No. 1, pp. 27, 29-30 (Jan./Feb.1984) (similar analysis).

How easily can courts identify instances in which the benefits are likely to outweigh potential harms? My own answer is, *not very easily*. For one thing, it is often difficult to identify who-producer or dealer-is the moving force behind any given resale price maintenance agreement. Suppose, for example, several large multibrand retailers all sell resale-price-maintained products. Suppose further that small producers set retail prices because they fear that, otherwise, the large retailers will favor (say, by allocating better shelf-space) the goods of other producers who practice resale price maintenance. Who " initiated" this practice, the retailers hoping for considerable insulation from retail competition, or the producers, who simply seek to deal best with the circumstances they find? For another thing, as I just said, it is difficult to determine just when, and where, the "free riding" problem is serious enough to warrant legal protection.

I recognize that scholars have sought to develop check lists and sets of questions that will help courts separate instances where anticompetitive harms are more likely from instances where only benefits are likely to be found. See, *e.g.*, 8 Areeda & Hovenkamp ¶¶ 1633c-1633e, at 330-339. See also Brief for William S. Comanor and Frederic M. Scherer as Amici Curiae 8-10. But applying these criteria in court is often easier said than done. The Court's invitation to consider the existence of "market power," for example, ante, at ---- 18, invites lengthy time-consuming argument among competing experts, as they seek to apply abstract, highly technical, criteria to often ill-defined markets. And resale price maintenance cases, unlike a major merger or monopoly case, are likely to prove numerous and involve only private parties. One cannot fairly expect judges and juries in such cases to apply complex economic criteria without making a considerable number of mistakes, which themselves may impose serious costs. See, *e.g.*, H. Hovenkamp, The Antitrust Enterprise 105 (2005) (litigating a rule of reason case is "one of the most costly procedures in antitrust practice"). See also Bok, Section 7 of the Clayton Act and the Merging of Law and Economics, 74 Harv. L.Rev. 226, 238-247 (1960) (describing lengthy FTC efforts to apply complex criteria in a merger case).

Are there special advantages to a bright-line rule? Without such a rule, it is often unfair, and consequently impractical, for enforcement officials to bring criminal proceedings. And since enforcement resources are limited, that loss may tempt some producers or dealers to enter into agreements that are, on balance, anticompetitive.

Given the uncertainties that surround key items in the overall balance sheet, particularly in respect to the "administrative" questions, I can concede to the majority that the problem is difficult. And, if forced to decide now, at most I might agree that the per se rule should be slightly modified to allow an exception for the more easily identifiable and temporary condition of "new entry." See Pitofsky 1495. But I am not now forced to decide this question. The question before us is not what should be the rule, starting from scratch. We here must decide whether to change a clear and simple price-related antitrust rule that the courts have applied for nearly a century.

II

We write, not on a blank slate, but on a slate that begins with *Dr. Miles* and goes on to list a century's worth of similar cases, massive amounts of advice that lawyers have provided their clients, and untold numbers of business decisions those clients have taken in reliance upon that advice. See, *e.g.*, *United States v. Bausch & Lomb Optical Co.*, 321 U.S. 707, 721 (1944); Sylvania, 433 U.S., at 51, n. 18 ("The *per se* illegality of [vertical] price restrictions has been established firmly for many years ..."). Indeed a Westlaw search shows that *Dr. Miles* itself has been cited dozens of times in this Court and hundreds of times in lower courts. Those who wish this Court to change so well-established a legal precedent bear a heavy burden of proof. See *Illinois Brick Co. v. Illinois*, 431 U.S. 720, 736 (1977) (noting, in declining to overrule an earlier case interpreting §4 of the Clayton Act, that "considerations of stare decisis weigh heavily in the area of statutory construction, where Congress is free to change this Court's interpretation of its legislation"). I am not aware of any case in which this Court has overturned so well-established a statutory precedent. Regardless, I do not see how the Court can claim that ordinary criteria for over-ruling an earlier case have been met. See, *e.g.*, *Planned Parenthood of Southeastern Pa. v. Casey*, 505 U.S. 833, 854-855 (1992). See also *Federal Election Comm'n v. Wisconsin Right to Life, Inc.*, ante, at 19-21 (Scalia, J., concurring in part and concurring in judgment).

A

I can find no change in circumstances in the past several decades that helps the majority's position. In fact, there has been one important change that argues strongly to the contrary. In 1975, Congress repealed the McGuire and Miller-Tydings Acts. See Consumer Goods Pricing Act of 1975, 89 Stat. 801. And it thereby consciously extended *Dr. Miles' per se* rule. Indeed, at that time the Department of Justice and the FTC, then urging application of the per se rule, discussed virtually every argument presented now to this Court as well as others not here presented. And they explained to Congress why Congress should reject them. See Hearings on S. 408, at 176-177 (statement of Thomas E. Kauper, Assistant Attorney General, Antitrust Division); id., at 170-172 (testimony of Lewis A. Engman, Chairman of the FTC); Hearings on H.R. 2384, at 113-114 (testimony of Keith I. Clearwaters, Deputy Assistant Attorney General, Antitrust Division). Congress fully understood, and consequently intended, that the result of its repeal of McGuire and Miller-Tydings would be to make minimum resale price maintenance per se unlawful. See, *e.g.*, S.Rep. No. 94-466, pp. 1-3 (1975), U.S.Code Cong. & Admin.News 1975, pp. 1569, 1570-71 ("Without [the exemptions authorized by the Miller-Tydings and McGuire Acts,] the agreements they authorize would violate the antitrust laws.... [R]epeal of the fair trade laws generally will prohibit manufacturers from enforcing resale prices"). See also *Sylvania, supra*, at 51, n. 18 ("Congress recently has expressed its approval of a *per se* analysis of vertical price restrictions by repealing those provisions of the Miller-Tydings and McGuire Acts allowing fair-trade pricing at the option of the individual States").

Congress did not prohibit this Court from reconsidering the per se rule. But enacting major legislation premised upon the existence of that rule constitutes important public reliance upon that rule. And doing so aware of the relevant arguments constitutes even stronger reliance upon the Court's keeping the rule, at least in the absence of some significant change in respect to those arguments.

Have there been any such changes? There have been a few economic studies, described in some of the briefs, that argue, contrary to the testimony of the Justice Department and FTC to Congress in 1975, that resale price maintenance is not harmful. One study, relying on an analysis of litigated resale price maintenance cases from 1975 to 1982, concludes that resale price maintenance does not ordinarily involve producer or dealer collusion. See Ippolito, Resale Price Maintenance: Empirical Evidence from Litigation, 34 J. Law & Econ. 263, 281-282, 292 (1991). But this study equates the failure of plaintiffs to *allege* collusion with the *absence* of collusion-an equation that overlooks the superfluous nature of allegations of horizontal collusion in a resale price maintenance case and the tacit form that such collusion might take. See H. Hovenkamp, Federal Antitrust Policy §11.3c, p. 464, n. 19 (3d ed.2005); *supra*, at 4-5.

The other study provides a theoretical basis for concluding that resale price maintenance "need not lead to higher retail prices." Marvel & McCafferty, The Political Economy of Resale Price Maintenance, 94 J. Pol. Econ. 1074, 1075 (1986). But this study develops a theoretical model "under the assumption that [resale price maintenance] is efficiency-enhancing." *Ibid.* Its only empirical support is a 1940 study that the authors acknowledge is much criticized. See *id.*, at 1091. And many other economists take a different view. See Brief for William S. Comanor and Frederic M. Scherer as Amici Curiae 4.

Regardless, taken together, these studies at most may offer some mild support for the majority's position. But they cannot constitute a major change in circumstances.

Petitioner and some *amici* have also presented us with newer studies that show that resale price maintenance sometimes brings consumer benefits. Overstreet 119-129 (describing numerous case studies). But the proponents of a *per se* rule have always conceded as much. What is remarkable about the majority's arguments is that *nothing* in this respect is new. See supra, at ----3, ----12 (citing articles and congressional testimony going back several decades). The only new feature of these arguments lies in the fact that the most current advocates of overruling *Dr. Miles* have abandoned a host of other not-very-persuasive arguments upon which prior resale price maintenance proponents used to rely. See, *e.g.*, 8 Areeda ¶1631a, at 350-352 (listing "'[t]raditional' justifications" for resale price maintenance).

The one arguable exception consists of the majority's claim that "even absent free riding," resale price maintenance "may be the most efficient way to expand the manufacturer's market share by inducing the retailer's performance and allowing it to use its own initiative and experience in providing valuable services." *Ante*, at 12. I cannot count this as an exception, however, because I do not understand how, in the absence of free-riding (and assuming competitiveness), an established producer would need resale price maintenance. Why, on these assumptions, would a dealer not "expand" its "market share" as best that dealer sees fit, obtaining appropriate payment from consumers in the process? There may be an answer to this question. But I have not seen it. And I do not think that we should place significant weight upon justifications that the parties do not explain with sufficient clarity for a generalist judge to understand.

No one claims that the American economy has changed in ways that might support the majority. Concentration in retailing has increased. See, *e.g.*, Brief for Respondent 18 (since minimum resale price maintenance was banned nationwide in 1975, the total number of retailers has dropped while the growth in sales per store has risen); Brief for American Antitrust Institute as *Amicus Curiae* 17, n. 20 (citing private study reporting that the combined sales of the 10 largest retailers worldwide has grown to nearly 30% of total retail sales of top 250 retailers; also quoting 1999 Organisation for Economic Co-operation and Development report stating that the "'last twenty years have seen momentous changes in retail distribution including significant increases in concentration'"); Mamen, Facing Goliath: Challenging the Impacts of Supermarket Consolidation on our Local Economies, Communities, and Food Security, The Oakland Institute, 1 Policy Brief, No. 3, pp. 1, 2 (Spring 2007), http://www.oaklandinstitute.org/pdfs/facing_goliath.pdf (as visited June 25, 2007, and available in Clerks of Court's case file) (noting that "[f]or many decades, the top five food retail firms in the U.S. controlled less than 20 percent of the market"; from 1997 to 2000, "the top five firms increased their market share from 24 to 42 percent of all retail sales"; and "[b]y 2003, they controlled over half of all grocery sales"). That change, other things being equal, may enable (and motivate) more retailers, accounting for a greater percentage of total retail sales volume, to seek resale price maintenance, thereby making it more difficult for price-cutting competitors (perhaps internet retailers) to obtain market share.

Nor has anyone argued that concentration among manufacturers that might use resale price maintenance has diminished significantly. And as far as I can tell, it has not. Consider household electrical appliances, which a study from the late 1950's suggests constituted a significant portion of those products subject to resale price maintenance at that time. See Hollander, United States of America, in Resale Price Maintenance 67, 80-81 (B. Yamey ed.1966). Although it is somewhat difficult to compare census data from 2002 with that from several decades ago (because of changes in the classification system), it is clear that at least some subsets of the household electrical appliance industry are *more* concentrated, in terms of manufacturer market power, now than they were then. For instance, the top eight domestic manufacturers of household cooking appliances accounted for 68% of the domestic market (measured by value of shipments) in 1963 (the earliest date for which I was able to find data), compared with 77% in 2002. See Dept. of Commerce, Bureau of Census, 1972 Census of Manufacturers, Special Report Series, Concentration Ratios in Manufacturing, No. MC72(SR)-2, p. SR2-38 (1975) (hereinafter 1972 Census); Dept. of Commerce, Bureau of Census, 2002 Economic Census, Concentration Ratios: 2002, No. EC02-31SR-1, p. 55 (2006) (hereinafter 2002 Census). The top eight domestic manufacturers of household laundry equipment accounted for 95% of the domestic market in 1963 (90% in 1958), compared with 99% in 2002.1972 Census, at SR2-38; 2002 Census, at 55. And the top eight domestic manufacturers of household refrigerators and freezers accounted for 91% of the domestic market in 1963, compared with 95% in 2002. 1972 Census, at SR2-38; 2002 Census, at 55. Increased concentration among manufacturers increases the likelihood that producer-originated resale price maintenance will prove more prevalent today than in years past, and more harmful. At the very least, the majority has not explained how these, or other changes in the economy could help support its position.

In sum, there is no relevant change.   And without some such change, there is no ground for abandoning a well-established antitrust rule.

B

With the preceding discussion in mind, I would consult the list of factors that our case law indicates are relevant when we consider overruling an earlier case.   Justice SCALIA, writing separately in another of our cases this Term, well summarizes that law.   *See Wisconsin Right to Life, Inc.*, ante, at 19-21 (opinion concurring in part and concurring in judgment).   And every relevant factor he mentions argues against overruling *Dr. Miles* here.

First, the Court applies *stare decisis* more "rigidly" in statutory than in constitutional cases.   See *Glidden Co. v. Zdanok*, 370 U.S. 530, 543 (1962); *Illinois Brick Co.*, 431 U.S., at 736.   This is a statutory case.

Second, the Court does sometimes overrule cases that it decided wrongly only a reasonably short time ago.   As Justice SCALIA put it, "[o]verruling a constitutional case decided just a few years earlier is far from unprecedented." *Wisconsin Right to Life, ante* 19 (emphasis added).   We here overrule one statutory case, *Dr. Miles*, decided 100 years ago, and we overrule the cases that reaffirmed its *per se* rule in the intervening years.   See, *e.g., Trenton Potteries*, 273 U.S., at 399-401, *Bausch & Lomb*, 321 U.S., at 721, *United States v. Parke, Davis & Co.*, 362 U.S. 29, 45-47 (1960); *Simpson v. Union Oil Co. of Cal.*, 377 U.S. 13, 16-17 (1964).

Third, the fact that a decision creates an "unworkable" legal regime argues in favor of overruling.   See *Payne v. Tennessee*, 501 U.S. 808, 827-828 (1991); *Swift & Co. v. Wickham*, 382 U.S. 111, 116 (1965).   Implementation of the per se rule, even with the complications attendant the exception allowed for in *United States v. Colgate & Co.*, 250 U.S. 300 (1919), has proved practical over the course of the last century, particularly when compared with the many complexities of litigating a case under the "rule of reason" regime. No one has shown how moving from the *Dr. Miles* regime to "rule of

73

reason" analysis would make the legal regime governing minimum resale price maintenance more "administrable," *Wisconsin Right to Life, ante*, 20, (opinion of Scalia, J.), particularly since *Colgate* would remain good law with respect to *unreasonable* price maintenance.

Fourth, the fact that a decision "unsettles" the law may argue in favor of overruling. See *Sylvania*, 433 U.S., at 47, *Wisconsin Right to Life, ante* 20-21 (opinion of Scalia, J.). The *per se* rule is well-settled law, as the Court itself has previously recognized. *Sylvania, supra*, at 51. It is the majority's change here that will unsettle the law.

Fifth, the fact that a case involves property rights or contract rights, where reliance interests are involved, argues against overruling. *Payne, supra*, at 828. This case involves contract rights and perhaps property rights (consider shopping malls). And there has been considerable reliance upon the *per se* rule. As I have said, Congress relied upon the continued vitality of *Dr. Miles* when it repealed Miller-Tydings and McGuire. *Supra*, at 12-13. The Executive Branch argued for repeal on the assumption that *Dr. Miles* stated the law. *Ibid*. Moreover, whole sectors of the economy have come to rely upon the *per se* rule. A factory outlet store tells us that the rule "form[s] an essential part of the regulatory background against which [that firm] and many other discount retailers have financed, structured, and operated their businesses." Brief for Burlington Coat Factory Warehouse Corp. as *Amicus Curiae* 5. The Consumer Federation of America tells us that large low-price retailers would not exist without *Dr. Miles*; minimum resale price maintenance, "by stabilizing price levels and preventing low-price competition, erects a potentially insurmountable barrier to entry for such low-price innovators." Brief for Consumer Federation of America as *Amicus Curiae* 5, 7-9 (discussing, *inter alia*, comments by Wal-Mart's founder 25 years ago that relaxation of the per se ban on minimum resale price maintenance would be a "'great danger'" to Wal-Mart's then-relatively-nascent business). See also Brief for American Antitrust Institute as *Amicus Curiae* 14-15, and sources cited therein (making the same point). New distributors, including internet distributors, have similarly invested time, money, and labor in an effort to bring yet lower cost goods to Americans.

This Court's overruling of the *per se* rule jeopardizes this reliance, and more. What about malls built on the assumption that a discount distributor will remain an anchor tenant? What about home buyers who have taken a home's distance from such a mall into account? What about Americans, producers, distributors, and consumers, who have understandably assumed, at least for the last 30 years, that price competition is a legally guaranteed way of life? The majority denies none of this. It simply says that these "reliance interests ...], like the reliance interests in *Khan*, cannot justify an inefficient rule." *Ante*, at 27.

The Court minimizes the importance of this reliance, adding that it "is also of note" that at the time resale price maintenance contracts were lawful "'no more than a tiny fraction of manufacturers ever employed'" the practice. *Ibid.* (quoting Overstreet 6). By "tiny" the Court means manufacturers that accounted for up to "'ten percent of consumer goods purchases'" annually. *Ibid.* That figure in today's economy equals just over $300 billion. See Dept. of Commerce, Bureau of Census, Statistical Abstract of the United States: 2007, p. 649 (126th ed.) (over $3 trillion in U.S. retail sales in 2002). Putting the Court's estimate together with the Justice Department's early 1970's study translates a legal regime that permits all resale price maintenance into retail bills that are higher by an average of roughly $750 to $1000 annually for an American family of four. Just how much higher retail bills will be after the Court's decision today, of course, depends upon what is now unknown, namely how courts will decide future cases under a "rule of reason." But these figures indicate that the amounts involved are important to American families and cannot be dismissed as "tiny."

Sixth, the fact that a rule of law has become "embedded" in our "national culture" argues strongly against overruling. *Dickerson v. United States*, 530 U.S. 428, 443-444 (2000). The *per se* rule forbidding minimum resale price maintenance agreements has long been "embedded" in the law of antitrust. It involves price, the economy's "'central nervous system.'" *National Soc. of Professional Engineers*, 435 U.S., at 692, (quoting *Socony-Vacuum Oil*, 310 U.S., at 226, n. 59). It reflects a basic antitrust assumption (that consumers often prefer lower prices to more service). It embodies a basic antitrust objective (providing consumers with a free choice about such matters). And it creates an easily administered and enforceable bright line, "Do not agree about price," that businesses as well as lawyers have long understood.

The only contrary *stare decisis* factor that the majority mentions consists of its claim that this Court has "[f]rom the beginning ... treated the Sherman Act as a common-law statute," and has previously overruled antitrust precedent. *Ante*, at 20, 21-22. It points in support to *State Oil Co. v. Khan*, 522 U.S. 3 (1997), overruling *Albrecht v. Herald Co.*, 390 U.S. 145 (1968), in which this Court had held that maximum resale price agreements were unlawful per se, and to *Sylvania*, overruling *United States v. Arnold, Schwinn & Co.*, 388 U.S. 365 (1967), in which this Court had held that producer-imposed territorial limits were unlawful *per se*.

The Court decided *Khan*, however, 29 years after *Albrecht*- still a significant period, but nowhere close to the century *Dr. Miles* has stood. The Court specifically noted the lack of any significant reliance upon *Albrecht*. 522 U.S., at 18-19 (*Albrecht* has had "little or no relevance to ongoing enforcement of the Sherman Act"). *Albrecht* had far less support in traditional antitrust principles than did Dr. Miles. Compare, e.g., 8 Areeda & Hovenkamp ¶1632, at 316-328 (analyzing potential harms of minimum resale price maintenance), with id., ¶1637, at 352-361 (analyzing potential harms of maximum resale price maintenance). See also, *e.g.*, Pitofsky 1490, n. 17. And Congress had nowhere expressed support for *Albrecht's* rule. *Khan*, supra, at 19.

In *Sylvania*, the Court, in overruling Schwinn, explicitly distinguished *Dr. Miles* on the ground that while Congress had "recently .expressed its approval of a *per se* analysis of vertical price restrictions" by repealing the Miller-Tydings and McGuire Acts, "[n]o similar expression of congressional intent exists for nonprice restrictions." 433 U.S., at 51, n. 18. Moreover, the Court decided Sylvania only a decade after *Schwinn*. And it based its overruling on a generally perceived need to avoid "confusion" in the law, 433 U.S., at 47-49, a factor totally absent here.

The Court suggests that it is following "the common-law tradition." *Ante* at 26. But the common law would not have permitted overruling *Dr. Miles* in these circumstances. Common-law courts rarely overruled well-established earlier rules outright. Rather, they would over time issue decisions that gradually eroded the scope and effect of the rule in question, which might eventually lead the courts to put the rule to rest. One can argue that modifying the per se rule to make an exception, say, for new entry, see Pitofsky 1495, could prove consistent with this approach. To swallow up a century-old precedent, potentially affecting many billions of dollars of sales, is not. The reader should compare today's "common-law" decision with Justice Cardozo's decision in *Allegheny College v. National Chautauqua Cty. Bank of Jamestown*, 246 N.Y. 369, 159 N.E. 173 (1927), and note a gradualism that does not characterize today's decision.

Moreover, a Court that rests its decision upon economists' views of the economic merits should also take account of legal scholars' views about common-law overruling. Professors Hart and Sacks list 12 factors (similar to those I have mentioned) that support judicial "adherence to prior holdings." They all support adherence to *Dr. Miles* here. See H. Hart & A. Sacks, The Legal Process 568-569 (W. Eskridge & P. Frickey eds.1994). Karl Llewellyn has written that the common-law judge's "conscious reshaping" of prior law "must so move as to hold the degree of movement down to the degree to which need truly presses." The Bramble Bush 156 (1960). Where here is the pressing need? The Court notes that the FTC argues here in favor of a rule of reason. See *ante*, at -20-21. But both Congress and the FTC, unlike courts, are well-equipped to gather empirical evidence outside the context of a single case. As neither has done so, we cannot conclude with confidence that the gains from eliminating the per se rule will outweigh the costs.

In sum, every *stare decisis* concern this Court has ever mentioned counsels against overruling here. It is difficult for me to understand how one can believe both that (1) satisfying a set of *stare decisis* concerns justifies over-ruling a recent constitutional decision, *Wisconsin Right to Life, Inc., ante*, at 19-2 (Scalia, J., joined by Kennedy and Thomas, JJ., concurring in part and concurring in judgment), but (2) failing to satisfy any of those same concerns nonetheless permits overruling a longstanding statutory decision. Either those concerns are relevant or they are not.

The only safe predictions to make about today's decision are that it will likely raise the price of goods at retail and that it will create considerable legal turbulence as lower courts seek to develop workable principles. I do not believe that the majority has shown new or changed conditions sufficient to warrant overruling a decision of such long standing. All ordinary *stare decisis* considerations indicate the contrary. For these reasons, with respect, I dissent.

CHAPTER 8: ADDITIONAL LIMITATIONS ON A SINGLE FIRM

Insert after *Aspen Skiing*, page 750.

VERIZON COMMUNICATIONS v. LAW OFFICE OF CURTIS V. TRINKO

SUPREME COURT OF THE UNITED STATES, 2004

540 U.S. 398, 124 S. CT. 872, 159 L. ED. 2D 823

SCALIA, J. The Telecommunications Act of 1996, Pub. L. 104-104, 110 Stat. 56, imposes certain duties upon incumbent local telephone companies in order to facilitate market entry by competitors, and establishes a complex regime for monitoring and enforcement. In this case we consider whether a complaint alleging breach of the incumbent's duty under the 1996 Act to share its network with competitors states a claim under §2 of the Sherman Act, 26 Stat. 209.

I

Petitioner Verizon Communications Inc. is the incumbent local exchange carrier (LEC) serving New York State. Before the 1996 Act, Verizon,[1] like other incumbent LECs, enjoyed an exclusive franchise within its local service area. The 1996 Act sought to "uproo[t]" the incumbent LECs' monopoly and to introduce competition in its place. *Verizon Communications Inc.* v. *FCC*, 535 U.S. 467, 488 (2002). Central to the scheme of the Act is the incumbent LEC's obligation under 47 U.S.C. §251(c) to share its

---

[1] In 1996, NYNEX was the incumbent LEC for New York State. NYNEX subsequently merged with Bell Atlantic Corporation, and the merged entity retained the Bell Atlantic name; a further merger produced Verizon. We use "Verizon" to refer to NYNEX and Bell Atlantic as well.

network with competitors, see *AT&T Corp.* v. *Iowa Utilities Bd.,* 525 U.S. 366, 371 (1999), including provision of access to individual elements of the network on an "unbundled" basis. §251(c)(3). New entrants, so-called competitive LECs, resell these unbundled network elements (UNEs), recombined with each other or with elements belonging to the LECs.

Verizon, like other incumbent LECs, has taken two significant steps within the Act's framework in the direction of increased competition. First, Verizon has signed interconnection agreements with rivals such as AT&T, as it is obliged to do under §252, detailing the terms on which it will make its network elements available. (Because Verizon and AT&T could not agree upon terms, the open issues were subjected to compulsory arbitration under §§252(b) and (c).) In 1997, the state regulator, New York's Public Service Commission (PSC), approved Verizon's interconnection agreement with AT&T.

Second, Verizon has taken advantage of the opportunity provided by the 1996 Act for incumbent LECs to enter the long-distance market (from which they had long been excluded). That required Verizon to satisfy, among other things, a 14-item checklist of statutory requirements, which includes compliance with the Act's network-sharing duties. §§271(d)(3)(A) and (c)(2)(B). Checklist item two, for example, includes "nondiscriminatory access to network elements in accordance with the requirements" of §251(c)(3). §271(c)(2)(B)(ii). Whereas the state regulator approves an interconnection agreement, for long-distance approval the incumbent LEC applies to the Federal Communications Commission (FCC). In December 1999, the FCC approved Verizon's §271 application for New York.

Part of Verizon's UNE obligation under §251(c)(3) is the provision of access to operations support systems (OSS), a set of systems used by incumbent LECs to provide services to customers and ensure quality. Verizon's interconnection agreement and long-distance authorization each specified the mechanics by which its OSS obligation would be met. As relevant here, a competitive LEC sends orders for service through an electronic interface with Verizon's ordering system, and as Verizon completes certain steps in filling the order, it sends confirmation back through the same interface. Without OSS access a rival cannot fill its customers' orders.

In late 1999, competitive LECs complained to regulators that many orders were going unfilled, in violation of Verizon's obligation to provide access to OSS functions. The PSC and FCC opened parallel investigations, which led to a series of orders by the PSC and a consent decree with the FCC.[2] Under the FCC consent decree, Verizon undertook to make a "voluntary contribution" to the U.S. Treasury in the amount of $3 million, 15 FCC Rcd. 5415, 5421, 116 (2000); under the PSC orders, Verizon incurred liability to the competitive LECs in the amount of $10 million. Under the consent decree and orders, Verizon was subjected to new performance measurements and new reporting requirements to the FCC and PSC, with additional penalties for continued noncompliance. In June 2000, the FCC terminated the consent decree. Enforcement Bureau Announces that Bell Atlantic Has Satisfied Consent Decree Regarding Electronic Ordering Systems in New York (June 20, 2000), http://www.fcc.gov/eb/ News_Releases/bellatlet.html (all Internet materials as visited Dec. 12, 2003, and available in the Clerk of Court's case file). The next month the PSC relieved Verizon of the heightened reporting requirement. Order Addressing OSS Issues, *MCI Worldcom, Inc.* v. *Bell Atlantic-New York,* Nos. 00-C-0008, 00-C-0009, 99-C- 0949, 2000 WL 1531916 (N. Y. PSC, July 27, 2000).

Respondent Law Offices of *Curtis V. Trinko, LLP,* a New York City law firm, was a local telephone service customer of AT&T.

---

[2] Order Directing Improvements To Wholesale Service Performance, *MCI Worldcom, Inc.* v. *Bell Atlantic-New York,* Nos. 00-C-0008, 00-C-0009, 2000 WL 363378 (N. Y. PSC, Feb. 11, 2000); Order Directing Market Adjustments and Amending Performance Assurance Plan, *MCI Worldcom, Inc.* v. *Bell Atlantic-New York,* Nos. 00-C-0008, 00-C-0009, 99-C-0949, 2000 WL 517633 (N. Y. PSC, Mar. 23, 2000); Order Addressing OSS Issues, *MCI Worldcom, Inc.* v. *Bell Atlantic-New York,* Nos. 00-C-0008, 00-C-0009, 99-C-0949, 2000 WL 1531916 (N.Y. PSC, July 27, 2000); I*n re Bell Atlantic-New York Authorization Under Section 271 of the Communications Act to Provide In-Region, InterLATA Service in the State of New York,* 15 FCC Rcd. 5413 (2000) (Order); *id.,* at 5415 (Consent Decree).

The day after Verizon entered its consent decree with the FCC, respondent filed a complaint in the District Court for the Southern District of New York, on behalf of itself and a class of similarly situated customers, See App. 12-33. The complaint, as later amended, *id.,* at 34-50, alleged that Verizon had filled rivals' orders on a discriminatory basis as part of an anticompetitive scheme to discourage customers from becoming or remaining customers of competitive LECs, thus impeding the competitive LECs' ability to enter and compete in the market for local telephone service. See, *e.g., id.,* at 34-35, 46-47, §§1, 2, 52, 54. According to the complaint, Verizon "has filled orders of [competitive LEC] customers after filling those for its own local phone service, has failed to fill in a timely manner, or not at all, a substantial number of orders for [competitive LEC] customers . . ., and has systematically failed to inform [competitive LECs] of the status of their customers' orders." *Id.,* at 39, ¶21. The complaint set forth a single example of the alleged "failure to provide adequate access to [competitive LECs]," namely the OSS failure that resulted in the FCC consent decree and PSC orders. *Id.,* at 40, ¶22, It asserted that the result of Verizon's improper "behavior with respect to providing access to its local loop" was to "deter potential customers [of rivals] from switching." *Id.,* at 47, ¶57, 35, ¶2. The complaint sought damages and injunctive relief for violation of §2 of the Sherman Act, 15 U.S.C. §2, pursuant to the remedy provisions of §§4 and 16 of the Clayton Act, 38 Stat. 731, as amended, 15 U.S.C. §15, 26. The complaint also alleged violations of the 1996 Act, §202(a) of the Communications Act of 1934, 48 Stat. 1064, as amended, 47 U.S.C. §151 *et seq.,* and state law.

The District Court dismissed the complaint in its entirety. As to the antitrust portion, it concluded that respondent's allegations of deficient assistance to rivals failed to satisfy the requirements of §2. The Court of Appeals for the Second Circuit reinstated the complaint in part, including the antitrust claim. 305 F. 3d 89, 113 (2002). We granted certiorari, limited to the question whether the Court of Appeals erred in reversing the District Court's dismissal of respondent's antitrust claims. 538 U.S. 905 (2003).

To decide this case, we must first determine what effect (if any) the 1996 Act has upon the application of traditional antitrust principles. The Act imposes a large number of duties upon incumbent LECs — above and beyond those basic responsibilities it imposes upon all carriers, such as assuring number portability and providing access to rights-of-way, see 47 U.S.C. §§251(b)(2), (4). Under the sharing duties of §251(c), incumbent LECs are required to offer three kinds of access. Already noted, and perhaps most intrusive, is the duty to offer access to UNEs on "just, reasonable, and nondiscriminatory" terms, §251(c)(3), a phrase that the FCC has interpreted, to mean a price reflecting long-run incremental cost. See *Verizon Communications Inc.* v. *FCC,* 535 U.S., at 495-496. A rival can interconnect its own facilities with those of the incumbent LEC, or it can simply purchase services at wholesale from the incumbent and resell them to consumers. See §§251(c)(2), (4). The Act also imposes upon incumbents the duty to allow physical "collocation" - that is, to permit a competitor to locate and install its equipment on the incumbent's premises - which makes feasible interconnection and access to UNEs. See §251(c)(6).

That Congress created these duties, however, does not automatically lead to the conclusion that they can be enforced by means of an antitrust claim. Indeed, a detailed regulatory scheme such as that created by the 1996 Act ordinarily raises the question whether the regulated entities are not shielded from antitrust scrutiny altogether by the doctrine of implied immunity. See, *e.g., United States* v. *National Assn. of Securities Dealers, Inc.,* 422 U.S. 694 (1975); *Gordon* v. *New York Stock Exchange, Inc.,* 422 U.S. 659 (1975). In some respects the enforcement scheme set up by the 1996 Act is a good candidate for implication of antitrust immunity, to avoid the real possibility of judgments conflicting with the agency's regulatory scheme "that might be voiced by courts exercising jurisdiction under the antitrust laws." *United States* v. *National Assn. of Securities Dealers, Inc., supra,* at 734.

Congress, however, precluded that interpretation. Section 601(b)(l) of the 1996 Act is an antitrust-specific saving clause providing that "nothing in this Act or the amendments made by this

Act shall be construed to modify, impair, or supersede the applicability of any of the antitrust laws." 110 Stat. 143, 47 U.S.C. §152, note. This bars a finding of implied immunity. As the FCC has put the point, the saving clause preserves those "claims that satisfy established antitrust standards." Brief for United States and the Federal Communications Commission as *Amici Curiae* Supporting Neither Party in No. 0-7057, *Covad Communications Co.* v. *Bell Atlantic Corp.* (CADC), p. 8.

But just as the 1996 Act preserves claims that satisfy existing antitrust standards, it does not create new claims that go beyond existing antitrust standards; that would be equally inconsistent with the saving clause's mandate that nothing in the Act "modify, impair, or supersede the applicability" of the antitrust laws. We turn, then, to whether the activity of which respondent complains violates preexisting antitrust standards.

III

The complaint alleges that Verizon denied interconnection services to rivals in order to limit entry. If that allegation states an antitrust claim at all, it does so under §2 of the Sherman Act, 15 U.S.C. §2, which declares that a firm shall not "monopolize" or "attempt to monopolize." *Ibid.* It is settled law that this offense requires, in addition to the possession of monopoly power in the relevant market, "the willful acquisition or maintenance of that power as distinguished from growth or development as a consequence of a superior product, business acumen, or historic accident." *United States* v. *Grinnell Corp.,* 384 U.S 563, 570-571 (1966). The mere possession of monopoly power, and the concomitant charging of monopoly prices, is not only not unlawful; it is an important element of the free-market system. The opportunity to charge monopoly prices - at least for a short period - is what attracts "business acumen" in the first place; it induces risk taking that produces innovation and economic growth. To safeguard the incentive to innovate, the possession of monopoly power will not be found unlawful unless it is accompanied by an element of anticompetitive *conduct.*

Firms may acquire monopoly power by establishing an infrastructure that renders them uniquely suited to serve their

84

customers. Compelling such firms to share the source of their advantage is in some tension with the underlying purpose of antitrust law, since it may lessen the incentive for the monopolist, the rival, or both to invest in those economically beneficial facilities. Enforced sharing also requires antitrust courts to act as central planners, identifying the proper price, quantity, and other terms of dealing - a role for which they are ill-suited. Moreover, compelling negotiation between competitors may facilitate the supreme evil of antitrust: collusion. Thus, as a general matter, the Sherman Act "does not restrict the long recognized right of [a] trader or manufacturer engaged in an entirely private business, freely to exercise his own independent discretion as to parties with whom he will deal." *United States* v. *Colgate & Co.,* 250 U.S. 300, 307 (1919).

However, "[t]he high value that we have placed on the right to refuse to deal with other firms does not mean that the right is unqualified." *Aspen Skiing Co.* v. *Aspen Highlands Skiing Corp.,* 472 U.S. 585, 601 (1985). Under certain circumstances, a refusal to cooperate with rivals can constitute anticompetitive conduct and violate §2. We have been very cautious in recognizing such exceptions, because of the uncertain virtue of forced sharing and the difficulty of identifying and remedying anticompetitive conduct by a single firm. The question before us today is whether the allegations of respondent's complaint fit within existing exceptions or provide a basis, under traditional antitrust principles, for recognizing a new one.

The leading case for §2 liability based on refusal to cooperate with a rival, and the case upon which respondent understandably places greatest reliance, is *Aspen Skiing, supra.* The Aspen ski area consisted of four mountain areas. The defendant, who owned three of those areas, and the plaintiff, who owned the fourth, had cooperated for years in the issuance of a joint, multiple-day, all-area ski ticket. After repeatedly demanding an increased share of the proceeds, the defendant canceled the joint ticket. The plaintiff, concerned that skiers would bypass its mountain without some joint offering, tried a variety of increasingly desperate measures to re-create the joint ticket, even to the point of in effect offering to buy the defendant's tickets at retail price. *Id.,* at 593-594. The defendant refused even that. We upheld a jury verdict for the plaintiff, reasoning that "[t]he jury may well have concluded that [the defendant] elected to forgo these short-run benefits because it was more interested in reducing competition . . . over the long run by harming its smaller competitor." *Id.,* at 608.

Aspen Skiing is at or near the outer boundary of §2 liability. The Court there found significance in the defendant's decision to cease participation in a cooperative venture. See *id.,* at 608, 610-611. The unilateral termination of a voluntary *(and thus presumably profitable)* course of dealing suggested a willingness to forsake short-term profits to achieve an anticompetitive end. *Ibid.* Similarly, the defendant's unwillingness to renew the ticket *even if compensated at retail price* revealed a distinctly anticompetitive bent.

The refusal to deal alleged in the present case does not fit within the limited exception recognized in *Aspen Skiing.* The complaint does not allege that Verizon voluntarily engaged in a course of dealing with its rivals, or would ever have done so absent statutory compulsion. Here, therefore, the defendant's prior conduct sheds no light upon the motivation of its refusal to deal - upon whether its regulatory lapses were prompted not by competitive zeal but by anticompetitive malice. The contrast between the cases is heightened by the difference in pricing behavior. In *Aspen Skiing,* the defendant turned down a proposal to sell at its own retail price, suggesting a calculation that its future monopoly retail price would be higher. Verizon's reluctance to interconnect at the cost-based rate of compensation available under §251(c)(3) tells us nothing about dreams of monopoly.

The specific nature of what the 1996 Act compels makes this case different from *Aspen Skiing* in a more fundamental way. In *Aspen Skiing,* what the defendant refused to provide to its competitor was a product that it already sold at retail - to oversimplify slightly, lift tickets representing a bundle of services to skiers. Similarly, in *Otter Tail Power Co.* v. *United States,* 410 U.S. 366 (1973), another case relied upon by respondent, the defendant was already in the business of providing a service to certain customers (power transmission over its network), and refused to provide the same service to certain other customers. *Id.,* at 370-371, 377-378. In the present case, by contrast, the services allegedly withheld are not otherwise marketed or available to the public. The sharing obligation imposed by the 1996 Act created "something brand new" – "the

86

wholesale market for leasing network elements." *Verizon Communications Inc.* v. *FCC,* 535 U.S., at 528. The unbundled elements offered pursuant to §251(c)(3) exist only deep within the bowels of Verizon; they are brought out on compulsion of the 1996 Act and offered not to consumers but to rivals, and at considerable expense and effort. New systems must be designed and implemented simply to make that access possible - indeed, it is the failure of one of those systems that prompted the present complaint.[3]

We conclude that Verizon's alleged insufficient assistance in the provision of service to rivals is not a recognized antitrust claim under this Court's existing refusal-to-deal precedents. This conclusion would be unchanged even if we considered to be established law the "essential facilities" doctrine crafted by some lower courts, under which the Court of Appeals concluded respondent's allegations might state a claim. See generally Areeda, Essential Facilities: An Epithet in Need of Limiting Principles, 58 Antitrust L. J. 841 (1989). We have never recognized such a doctrine, see *Aspen Skiing Co.,* 472 U.S., at 611, n. 44; *AT&T Corp.* v. *Iowa Utilities Bd.,* 525 U.S., at 428 (opinion of BREYER, J.), and we find no need either to recognize it or to repudiate it here. It suffices for present purposes to note that the indispensable requirement for invoking the doctrine is the unavailability of access to the "essential facilities"; where access exists, the doctrine serves no purpose. Thus, it is said that "essential facility claims should . . . be denied where a state or federal agency has effective power to compel sharing and to regulate its scope and terms." P. Areeda & H. Hovenkamp, Antitrust Law, p. 150, ¶773e (2003 Supp,). Respondent believes that the existence of sharing duties under the 1996 Act supports its case. We think the opposite: The 1996 Act's extensive provision for access makes it unnecessary to impose a judicial doctrine of forced access.

---

[3] Respondent also relies upon *United States* v. *Terminal Railroad Assn. of St. Louis,* 224 U.S. 383 (1912), and *Associated Press* v. *United States,* 326 U.S. 1 (1945). These cases involved *concerted* action, which presents greater anticompetitive concerns and is amenable to a remedy that does not require judicial estimation of free-market forces: simply requiring that the outsider be granted nondiscriminatory admission to the club.

To the extent respondent's "essential facilities" argument is distinct from its general §2 argument, we reject it.

IV

Finally, we do not believe that traditional antitrust principles justify adding the present case to the few existing exceptions from the proposition that there is no duty to aid competitors. Antitrust analysis must always be attuned to the particular structure and circumstances of the industry at issue. Part of that attention to economic context is an awareness of the significance of regulation. As we have noted, "careful account must be taken of the pervasive federal and state regulation characteristic of the industry." *United States* v. *Citizens & Southern Nat. Bank,* 422 U.S. 86, 91(1975); see also IA P. Areeda & H. Hovenkamp, Antitrust Law, p. 12, §240c3 (2d ed. 2000). "[A]ntitrust analysis must sensitively recognize and reflect the distinctive economic and legal setting of the regulated industry to which it applies." *Concord* v. *Boston Edison Co.,* 915 F. 2d 17, 22 (CAl 1990) (Breyer, C. J.) (internal quotation marks omitted).

One factor of particular importance is the existence of a regulatory structure designed to deter and remedy anticompetitive harm. Where such a structure exists, the additional benefit to competition provided by antitrust enforcement will tend to be small, and it will be less plausible that the antitrust laws contemplate such additional scrutiny. Where, by contrast, "[t]here is nothing built into the regulatory scheme which performs the antitrust function," *Silver* v. *New York Stock Exchange,* 373 U.S. 341, 358 (1963), the benefits of antitrust are worth its sometimes considerable disadvantages. Just as regulatory context may in other cases serve as a basis for implied immunity, see, *e.g., United States* v. *National Assn. of Securities Dealers, Inc.,* 422 U.S., at 730-735, it may also be a consideration in deciding whether to recognize an expansion of the contours of §2.

The regulatory framework that exists in this case demonstrates how, in certain circumstances, "regulation significantly diminishes the likelihood of major antitrust harm." *Concord* v. *Boston Edison Co., supra,* at 25. Consider, for example, the statutory restrictions upon Verizon's entry into the potentially lucrative market for long-distance service. To be allowed to enter the long-distance market in the first place, an incumbent LEC must be on good behavior in its local market. Authorization by the FCC requires state-by-state satisfaction of §271's competitive checklist, which as we have noted includes the non-discriminatory provision of access to UNEs. Section 271 applications to provide long-distance service have now been approved for incumbent LECs in 47 States and the District of Columbia. See FCC Authorizes SBC to Provide Long Distance Service in Illinois, Indiana, Ohio and Wisconsin (Oct. 15, 2003), http://hraunfoss.fcc.gov/edocs_public/attachmatch/DOC-239978Al.pdf.

The FCC's §271 authorization order for Verizon to provide long-distance service in New York discussed at great length Verizon's commitments to provide access to UNEs, including the provision of OSS. *In re Application by Bell Atlantic New York for Authorization Under Section 271 of the Communications Act To Provide In-Region, InterLATA Service in the State of New York,* 15 FCC Rcd. 3953, 3989-4077, ¶¶82-228 (1999) (Memorandum Opinion and Order) (hereinafter *In re Application).* Those commitments are enforceable by the FCC through continuing oversight; a failure to meet an authorization condition can result in an order that the deficiency be corrected, in the imposition of penalties, or in the suspension or revocation of long-distance approval. See 47 U.S.C. §271(d)(6)(A). Verizon also subjected itself to oversight by the PSC under a so-called "Performance Assurance Plan" (PAP). See *In re New York Telephone Co.,* 197 P.U.R. 4th 266, 280-281 (N.Y. PSC, 1999) (Order Adopting the Amended PAP) (hereinafter PAP Order). The PAP, which by its terms became binding upon FCC approval, provides specific financial penalties in the event of Verizon's failure to achieve detailed performance requirements. The FCC described Verizon's having entered into a PAP as a significant factor in its §271 authorization, because that provided "a strong financial incentive for post-entry compliance with the section 271 checklist," and prevented "backsliding." *In re Application* 3958-3959, ¶¶8, 12.

The regulatory response to the OSS failure complained of in respondent's suit provides a vivid example of how the regulatory regime operates. When several competitive LECs complained about deficiencies in Verizon's servicing of orders, the FCC and PSC responded. The FCC soon concluded that Verizon was in breach of its sharing duties under §251(c), imposed a substantial fine, and set up sophisticated measurements to gauge remediation, with weekly reporting requirements and specific penalties for failure. The PSC found Verizon in violation of the PAP even earlier, and imposed additional financial penalties and measurements with *daily* reporting requirements. In short, the regime was an effective steward of the antitrust function.

Against the slight benefits of antitrust intervention here, we must weigh a realistic assessment of its costs. Under the best of circumstances, applying the requirements of §2 "can be difficult" because "the means of illicit exclusion, like the means of legitimate competition, are myriad." *United States* v. *Microsoft Corp.,* 253 F. 3d 34, 58 (CADC 2001) (en banc) *(per curiam).* Mistaken inferences and the resulting false condemnations "are especially costly, because they chill the very conduct the antitrust laws are designed to protect." *Matsushita Elec. Industrial Co.* v. *Zenith Radio Corp.,* 475 U.S. 574, 594 (1986). The cost of false positives counsels against an undue expansion of §2 liability. One false-positive risk is that an incumbent LEC's failure to provide a service with sufficient alacrity might have nothing to do with exclusion. Allegations of violations of §251(c)(3) duties are difficult for antitrust courts to evaluate, not only because they are highly technical, but, also because they are likely to be extremely numerous, given the incessant, complex, and constantly changing interaction of competitive and incumbent LECs implementing the sharing and interconnection obligations. *Amici* States have filed a brief asserting that competitive LECs are threatened with "death by a thousand cuts." Brief for New York et al. as *Amici Curiae* 10 (internal quotation marks omitted) - the identification of which would surely be a daunting task for a generalist antitrust court. Judicial oversight under the Sherman Act would seem destined to distort investment and lead to a new layer of interminable litigation, atop the variety of litigation routes already available to and actively pursued by competitive LECs.

Even if the problem of false positives did not exist, conduct consisting of anticompetitive violations of §251 may be, as we have concluded with respect to above-cost predatory pricing schemes, "beyond the practical ability of a judicial tribunal to control." *Brooke Group Ltd.* v. *Brown & Williamson Tobacco Corp.,* 509 U.S. 209,

90

223 (1993). Effective remediation of violations of regulatory sharing requirements will ordinarily require continuing supervision of a highly detailed decree. We think that Professor Areeda got it exactly right: "No court should impose a duty to deal that it cannot explain or adequately and reasonably supervise. The problem should be deemed irremedia[ble] by antitrust law when compulsory access requires the court to assume the day-to-day controls characteristic of a regulatory agency." Areeda, 58 Antitrust L.J., at 853. In this case, respondent has requested an equitable decree to "[p]reliminarily and permanently enjoi[n} [Verizon] from providing access to the local loop market ... to [rivals} on terms and conditions that are not as favorable" as those that Verizon enjoys. App. 49-50. An antitrust court is unlikely to be an effective day-to-day enforcer of these detailed sharing obligations.[4]

The 1996 Act is in an important respect much more ambitious than the antitrust laws. It attempts *to eliminate the monopolies enjoyed by the inheritors of AT&T's local franchises." Verizon Communications Inc.* v. *FCC,* 535 U.S., at 476 (emphasis added). Section 2 of the Sherman Act, by contrast, seeks merely to prevent *unlawful monopolization.* It would be a serious mistake to conflate the two goals. The Sherman Act is indeed the "Magna Carta of free enterprise," *United States* v. *Topco Associates, Inc.,* 405 U.S. 596, 610 (1972), but it does not give judges *carte blanche* to insist that a monopolist alter its way of doing business whenever some other approach might yield greater competition. We conclude that respondent's complaint fails to state a claim under the Sherman Act.[5]

---

[4]   The Court of Appeals also thought that respondent's complaint might state a claim under a 'monopoly leveraging' theory (a theory barely discussed by respondent, see Brief for Respondent 24, n. 10). We disagree. To the extent the Court of Appeals dispensed with a requirement that there be a "dangerous probability of success" in monopolizing a second market, it erred, *Spectrum Sports, Inc.* v. *McQuillan,* 506 U.S. 447, 459 (1993). In any event, leveraging presupposes anticompetitive conduct, which in this case could only be the refusal-to-deal claim we have rejected.

[5]   Our disposition makes it unnecessary to consider petitioner's alternative contention that respondent lacks antitrust standing. See *Steel Co.* v. *Citizens for Better Environment,* 523 U.S. 83, 97, and n. 2

Accordingly, the judgment of the Court of Appeals is reversed, and the case is remanded for further proceedings consistent with this opinion.

For the EU's view of the "essential facilities" doctrine, *see* Note on *IMS Health* and the European Approach to Essential Facilities, page 197 *infra*.

Note on *Credit Suisse*

In *Trinko*, Justice Scalia commented that "a detailed regulatory scheme such as that created by the 1996 Act ordinarily raises the question whether the regulated entities are not shielded from antitrust scrutiny altogether by the doctrine of implied immunity." The question in *Trinko* was answered by the 1996 Act's specific antitrust savings clause.

In June 2007, in *Credit Suisse Securities (USA) LLC v. Billing*, 551 U.S. 264 (2007), the Supreme Court addressed the issue of implied antitrust immunity. A group of buyers of newly issued securities had filed antitrust claims against underwriters that distributed so-called IPOs. The buyers alleged tying arrangements (i.e., forcing IPO buyers to commit to purchasing less attractive securities) and other potential antitrust violations.

The Supreme Court, reversing the Second Circuit, dismissed the antitrust claims because in this context there was "a 'clear repugnacy' between the securities law and the antitrust complaint." The Court reasoned:

> This Court's prior decisions. . . . have treated the following factors as critical: (1) the existence of regulatory authority under the securities law to supervise the activities in question; (2) evidence that the responsible regulatory entities exercise that authority; and (3) a resulting risk that the securities and antitrust laws, if both applicable, would

---

(1998); *National Railroad Passenger Corporation* v. *National Assn. of Railroad Passengers,* 414 U.S. 453, 456 (1974).

produce conflicting guidance, requirements, duties, privileges, or standards of conduct. We also note (4) that in *Gordon* and *NASD* the possible conflict affected practices that lie squarely within an area of financial market activity that the securities law seeks to regulate. . . .

We believe it fair to conclude that, where conduct at the core of the marketing of new securities is at issue; where securities regulators proceed with great care to distinguish the encouraged and permissible from the forbidden; where the threat of antitrust lawsuits, through error and disincentive, could seriously alter underwriter conduct in undesirable ways, to allow an antitrust lawsuit would threaten serious harm to the efficient functioning of the securities markets.

Second, any enforcement-related need for an antitrust lawsuit is unusually small. For one thing, the SEC actively enforces the rules and regulations that forbid the conduct in question. For another, as we have said, investors harmed by underwriters' unlawful practices may bring lawsuits and obtain damages under the securities law. Finally, the SEC is itself required to take account of competitive considerations when it creates securities-related policy and embodies it in rules and regulations. And that fact makes it somewhat less necessary to rely upon antitrust actions to address anticompetitive behavior.

PACIFIC BELL TELEPHONE v. LINKLINE
COMMUNICATIONS, INC.

SUPREME COURT OF THE UNITED STATES, 2009

__ U.S. __, 129 S. Ct. 1109, 172 L. ED. 2d 836

ROBERTS, C. J., The plaintiffs in this case, respondents here, allege that a competitor subjected them to a "price squeeze" in violation of § 2 of the Sherman Act. They assert that such a claim can arise when a vertically integrated firm sells inputs at wholesale and also sells finished goods or services at retail. If that firm has power in the wholesale market, it can simultaneously raise the wholesale price of inputs and cut the retail price of the finished good. This will have the effect of "squeezing" the profit margins of any competitors in the retail market. Those firms will have to pay more for the inputs they need; at the same time, they will have to cut their retail prices to match the other firm's prices. The question before us is whether such a price-squeeze claim may be brought under § 2 of the Sherman Act when the defendant is under no antitrust obligation to sell the inputs to the plaintiff in the first place. We hold that no such claim may be brought.

This case involves the market for digital subscriber line (DSL) service, which is a method of connecting to the Internet at high speeds over telephone lines. AT&T owns much of the infrastructure and facilities needed to provide DSL service in California. In particular, AT&T controls most of what is known as the "last mile" -- the lines that connect homes and businesses to the telephone network. Competing DSL providers must generally obtain access to AT&T's facilities in order to serve their customers.

Until recently, the Federal Communications Commission (FCC) required incumbent phone companies such as AT&T to sell transmission service to independent DSL providers, under the theory that this would spur competition. In 2005, the Commission largely abandoned this forced-sharing requirement in light of the emergence of a competitive market beyond DSL for high-speed Internet service; DSL now faces robust competition from cable companies and

94

wireless and satellite services. As a condition for a recent merger, however, AT&T remains bound by the mandatory interconnection requirements, and is obligated to provide wholesale "DSL transport" service to independent firms at a price no greater than the retail price of AT&T's DSL service.

The plaintiffs are four independent Internet service providers (ISPs) that compete with AT&T in the retail DSL market. Plaintiffs do not own all the facilities needed to supply their customers with this service. They instead lease DSL transport service from AT&T pursuant to the merger conditions described above. AT&T thus participates in the DSL market at both the wholesale and retail levels; it provides plaintiffs and other independent ISPs with wholesale DSL transport service, and it also sells DSL service directly to consumers at retail.

In July 2003, the plaintiffs brought suit in District Court, alleging that AT&T violated *§ 2* of the Sherman Act by monopolizing the DSL market in California. The complaint alleges that AT&T refused to deal with the plaintiffs, denied the plaintiffs access to essential facilities, and engaged in a "price squeeze." Specifically, plaintiffs contend that AT&T squeezed their profit margins by setting a high wholesale price for DSL transport and a low retail price for DSL Internet service. This maneuver allegedly "exclude[d] and unreasonably impede[d] competition," thus allowing AT&T to "preserve and maintain its monopoly control of DSL access to the Internet."

[In *Trinko*,] we held that a firm with no antitrust duty to deal with its rivals at all is under no obligation to provide those rivals with a "sufficient" level of service. Shortly after we issued that decision, AT&T moved for judgment on the pleadings, arguing that the plaintiffs' claims in this case were foreclosed by *Trinko*. The District Court held that AT&T had no antitrust duty to deal with the plaintiffs, but it denied the motion to dismiss with respect to the price-squeeze claims. The court acknowledged that AT&T's argument "has a certain logic to it," but held that *Trinko* "simply does not involve price-squeeze claims." The District Court also noted that price-squeeze claims have been recognized by several Circuits and "are cognizable under existing antitrust standards….."

On interlocutory appeal, the Court of Appeals for the Ninth Circuit affirmed the District Court's denial of AT&T's motion for judgment on the pleadings on the price-squeeze claims. The court emphasized that "*Trinko* did not involve a price squeezing theory." Because "a price squeeze theory formed part of the fabric of traditional antitrust law prior to *Trinko*," the Court of Appeals concluded that "those claims should remain viable notwithstanding either the telecommunications statutes or *Trinko.*" Based on the record before it, the court held that plaintiffs' original complaint stated a potentially valid claim under *§ 2* of the Sherman Act.

Judge Gould dissented, noting that "the notion of a 'price squeeze' is itself in a squeeze between two recent Supreme Court precedents." A price-squeeze claim involves allegations of both a high wholesale price and a low retail price, so Judge Gould analyzed each component separately. He concluded that "*Trinko* insulates from antitrust review the setting of the upstream price." With respect to the downstream price, he argued that "the retail side of a price squeeze cannot be considered to create an antitrust violation if the retail pricing does not satisfy the requirements of *Brooke Group*, which set unmistakable limits on what can be considered to be predatory within the meaning of the antitrust laws." Judge Gould concluded that the plaintiffs' complaint did not satisfy these requirements because it contained no allegations that the retail price was set below cost and that those losses could later be recouped. Judge Gould would have allowed the plaintiffs to amend their complaint if they could, in good faith, raise predatory pricing claims meeting the *Brooke Group* requirements.

We granted certiorari, to resolve a conflict over whether a plaintiff can bring price-squeeze claims under *§ 2* of the Sherman Act when the defendant has no antitrust duty to deal with the plaintiff. We reverse.

This case has assumed an unusual posture. The plaintiffs now assert that they agree with Judge Gould's dissenting position that price-squeeze claims must meet the *Brooke Groupy* requirements for predatory pricing. They ask us to vacate the decision below in their favor and remand with instructions that they be given leave to amend their complete to allege a *Brooke Group* claim. In other words, plaintiffs are no longer pleased with their initial theory....

Section 2 of the Sherman Act makes it unlawful to "monopolize, or attempt to monopolize, or combine or conspire with any other person or persons, to monopolize any part of the trade or commerce among the several States, or with foreign nations." Simply possessing monopoly power and charging monopoly prices does not violate *§ 2*; rather, the statute targets "the willful acquisition or maintenance of that power as distinguished from growth or development as a consequence of a superior product, business acumen, or historic accident." *United States v. Grinnell Corp.*, *384 U.S. 563, 570-571 (1966).*

As a general rule, businesses are free to choose the parties with whom they will deal, as well as the prices, terms, and conditions of that dealing. See *United States v. Colgate & Co., 250 U.S. 300, 307 (1919)*. But there are rare instances in which a dominant firm may incur antitrust liability for purely unilateral conduct. For example, we have ruled that firms may not charge "predatory" prices -- below-cost prices that drive rivals out of the market and allow the monopolist to raise its prices later and recoup its losses. *Brooke Group, 509 U.S., at 222-224.* Here, however, the complaint at issue does not contain allegations meeting those requirements.

There *are* also limited circumstances in which a firm's unilateral refusal to deal with its rivals can give rise to antitrust liability. See *Aspen Skiing Co.*. Here, however, the District Court held that AT&T had no such antitrust duty to deal with its competitors, and this holding was not challenged on appeal.[6]

---

[6] The Court of Appeals assumed that any duty to deal arose only from FCC regulations, and the question on which we granted certiorari made the same assumption. Even aside from the District Court's reasoning, it seems quite unlikely that AT&T would have an antitrust duty to deal with the plaintiffs. Such a duty requires a showing of monopoly power, but -- as the FCC has recognized -- the market for high-speed Internet service is now quite competitive; DSL providers face stiff competition from cable companies and wireless and satellite providers.

The challenge here focuses on retail prices -- where there is no predatory pricing -- and the terms of dealing -- where there is no duty to deal. Plaintiffs' price-squeeze claims challenge a different type of unilateral conduct in which a firm "squeezes" the profit margins of its competitors. This requires the defendant to be operating in two markets, a wholesale ("upstream") market and a retail ("downstream") market. A firm with market power in the upstream market can squeeze its downstream competitors by raising the wholesale price of inputs while cutting its own retail prices. This will raise competitors' costs (because they will have to pay more for their inputs) and lower their revenues (because they will have to match the dominant firm's low retail price). Price-squeeze plaintiffs assert that defendants must leave them a "fair" or "adequate" margin between the wholesale price and the retail price. In this case, we consider whether a plaintiff can state a price-squeeze claim when the defendant has no obligation under the antitrust laws to deal with the plaintiff at wholesale.

1. A straightforward application of our recent decision in *Trinko* forecloses any challenge to AT&T's *wholesale* prices. In *Trinko*, Verizon was required by statute to lease its network elements to competing firms at wholesale rates. The plaintiff -- a customer of one of Verizon's rivals -- asserted that Verizon denied its competitors access to interconnection support services, making it difficult for those competitors to fill their customers' orders. The complaint alleged that this conduct in the upstream market violated *§ 2* of the Sherman Act by impeding the ability of independent carriers to compete in the downstream market for local telephone service.

We held that the plaintiff's claims were not actionable under *§ 2*. Given that Verizon had no antitrust duty to deal with its rivals at all, we concluded that "Verizon's alleged insufficient assistance in the provision of service to rivals" did not violate the Sherman Act. *Trinko* thus makes clear that if a firm has no antitrust duty to deal with its competitors at wholesale, it certainly has no duty to deal under terms and conditions that the rivals find commercially advantageous.

In this case, as in *Trinko*, the defendant has no antitrust duty to deal with its rivals at wholesale; any such duty arises only from FCC regulations, not from the Sherman Act. There is no meaningful distinction between the "insufficient assistance" claims we rejected in *Trinko* and the plaintiffs' price-squeeze claims in the instant case. The *Trinko* plaintiffs challenged the quality of Verizon's interconnection service, while this case involves a challenge to AT&T's pricing structure. But for antitrust purposes, there is no reason to distinguish between price and nonprice components of a transaction.... The nub of the complaint in both *Trinko* and this case is identical -- the plaintiffs alleged that the defendants (upstream monopolists) abused their power in the wholesale market to prevent rival firms from competing effectively in the retail market. *Trinko* holds that such claims are not cognizable under the Sherman Act in the absence of an antitrust duty to deal.

The District Court and the Court of Appeals did not regard *Trinko* as controlling because that case did not directly address price-squeeze claims. This is technically true, but the reasoning of *Trinko* applies with equal force to price-squeeze claims. AT&T could have squeezed its competitors' profits just as effectively by providing poor-quality interconnection service to the plaintiffs, as Verizon allegedly did in *Trinko*. But a firm with no duty to deal in the wholesale market has no obligation to deal under terms and conditions favorable to its competitors. If AT&T had simply stopped providing DSL transport service to the plaintiffs, it would not have run afoul of the Sherman Act. Under these circumstances, AT&T was not required to offer this service at the wholesale prices the plaintiffs would have preferred.

2. The other component of a price-squeeze claim is the assertion that the defendant's *retail* prices are "too low." Here too plaintiffs' claims find no support in our existing antitrust doctrine.

"[C]utting prices in order to increase business often is the very essence of competition." *Matsushita Elec.* In cases seeking to impose antitrust liability for prices that are too low, mistaken inferences are "especially costly, because they chill the very conduct the antitrust laws are designed to protect." To avoid chilling aggressive price competition, we have carefully limited the circumstances under which plaintiffs can state a Sherman Act claim by alleging that prices are too low. Specifically, to prevail on a predatory pricing claim, a plaintiff must demonstrate that: (1) "the prices complained of are below an appropriate measure of its rival's costs"; and (2) there is a "dangerous probability" that the defendant will be able to recoup its "investment" in below-cost prices. *Brooke Group*....

In the complaint at issue in this interlocutory appeal, there is no allegation that AT&T's conduct met either of the *Brooke Group* requirements. Recognizing a price-squeeze claim where the defendant's retail price remains above cost would invite the precise harm we sought to avoid in *Brooke Group*: Firms might raise their retail prices or refrain from aggressive price competition to avoid potential antitrust liability.....

3. Plaintiffs' price-squeeze claim, looking to the relation between retail and wholesale prices, is thus nothing more than an amalgamation of a meritless claim at the retail level and a meritless claim at the wholesale level. If there is no duty to deal at the wholesale level and no predatory pricing at the retail level, then a firm is certainly not required to price *both* of these services in a manner that preserves its rivals' profit margins.[7]

Institutional concerns also counsel against recognition of such claims. We have repeatedly emphasized the importance of clear rules in antitrust law. Courts are ill suited "to act as central planners, identifying the proper price, quantity, and other terms of dealing." *Trinko*. "'No court should impose a duty to deal that it cannot explain

---

[7] Like the Court of Appeals, amici argue that price-squeeze claims have been recognized by Circuit Courts for many years, beginning with Judge Hand's opinion in *United States v. Aluminum Co. of America, 148 F.2d 416 (CA2 1945)* (*Alcoa*). In that case, the Government alleged that Alcoa was using its monopoly power in the upstream aluminum ingot market to squeeze the profits of downstream aluminum sheet fabricators. The court concluded: "That it was unlawful to set the price of 'sheet' so low and hold the price of ingot so high, seems to us unquestionable, provided, as we have held, that on this record the price of ingot must be regarded as higher than a 'fair price.'" Given developments in economic theory and antitrust jurisprudence since *Alcoa*, we find our recent decisions in *Trinko* and *Brooke Group* more pertinent to the question before us.

or adequately and reasonably supervise. The problem should be deemed irremedia[ble] by antitrust law when compulsory access requires the court to assume the day-to-day controls characteristic of a regulatory agency.'" See also *Town of Concord v. Boston Edison Co., 915 F.2d 17, 25 (CA1 1990)* (Breyer, C. J.) ("[A]ntitrust courts normally avoid direct price administration, relying on rules and remedies . . . that are easier to administer").

It is difficult enough for courts to identify and remedy an alleged anticompetitive practice at one level, such as predatory pricing in retail markets or a violation of the duty-to-deal doctrine at the wholesale level..... Recognizing price-squeeze claims would require courts simultaneously to police both the wholesale and retail prices to ensure that rival firms are not being squeezed. And courts would be aiming at a moving target, since it is the *interaction* between these two prices that may result in a squeeze.

Perhaps most troubling, firms that seek to avoid price-squeeze liability will have no safe harbor for their pricing practices. See *Town of Concord, supra, at 22* (antitrust rules "must be clear enough for lawyers to explain them to clients"). At least in the predatory pricing context, firms know they will not incur liability as long as their retail prices are above cost. No such guidance is available for price-squeeze claims. See, *e.g.*, 3B P. Areeda & H. Hovenkamp, Antitrust Law P767c, p. 138 (3d ed. 2008) ("[A]ntitrust faces a severe problem not only in recognizing any *§ 2* [price-squeeze] offense, but also in formulating a suitable remedy").

The most commonly articulated standard for price squeezes is that the defendant must leave its rivals a "fair" or "adequate" margin between the wholesale price and the retail price. One of our colleagues has highlighted the flaws of this test in Socratic fashion:

> "[H]ow is a judge or jury to determine a 'fair price?' Is it the price charged by other suppliers of the primary product? None exist. Is it the price that competition 'would have set' were the primary level not monopolized? How can the court determine this price without examining costs and demands, indeed without

acting like a rate-setting regulatory agency, the rate-setting proceedings of which often last for several years? Further, how is the court to decide the proper size of the price 'gap?' Must it be large enough for all independent competing firms to make a 'living profit,' no matter how inefficient they may be?.. And how should the court respond when costs or demands change over time, as they inevitably will?" *Town of Concord.*

Some amici respond to these concerns by proposing a "transfer price test" for identifying an unlawful price squeeze: A price squeeze should be presumed if the upstream monopolist could not have made a profit by selling at its retail rates if it purchased inputs at its own wholesale rates. Whether or not that test is administrable, it lacks any grounding in our antitrust jurisprudence. An upstream monopolist with no duty to deal is free to charge whatever wholesale price it would like; antitrust law does not forbid lawfully obtained monopolies from charging monopoly prices. *Trinko.* ("The mere possession of monopoly power, and the concomitant charging of monopoly prices, is not only not unlawful; it is an important element of the free-market system"). Similarly, the Sherman Act does not forbid -- indeed, it *encourages* -- aggressive price competition at the retail level, as long as the prices being charged are not predatory. If both the wholesale price and the retail price are independently lawful, there is no basis for imposing antitrust liability simply because a vertically integrated firm's wholesale price happens to be greater than or equal to its retail price.

Amici assert that there are circumstances in which price squeezes may harm competition. For example, they assert that price squeezes may raise entry barriers that fortify the upstream monopolist's position; they also contend that price squeezes may impair nonprice competition and innovation in the downstream market by driving independent firms out of business.

The problem, however, is that amici have not identified any independent competitive harm caused by price squeezes above and beyond the harm that would result from a duty-to-deal violation at the wholesale level or predatory pricing at the retail level…. To the extent a monopolist violates one of these doctrines, the plaintiffs have a remedy under existing law. We do not need to endorse a new theory of liability to prevent such harm.

Lastly, as mentioned above, plaintiffs have asked us for leave to amend their complaint to bring a *Brooke Group* predatory pricing claim. We need not decide whether leave to amend should be granted. Our grant of certiorari was limited to the question whether price-squeeze claims are cognizable in the absence of an antitrust duty to deal. The Court of Appeals addressed only AT&T's motion for judgment on the pleadings on the plaintiffs' *original* complaint. For the reasons stated, we hold that the price-squeeze claims set forth in that complaint are not cognizable under the Sherman Act….

It is for the District Court on remand to consider whether the amended complaint states a claim upon which relief may be granted in light of the new pleading standard we articulated in *Twombly*, whether plaintiffs should be given leave to amend their complaint to bring a claim under *Brooke Group*, and such other matters properly before it. Even if the amended complaint is further amended to add a *Brooke Group* claim, it may not survive a motion to dismiss. For if AT&T can bankrupt the plaintiffs by refusing to deal altogether, the plaintiffs must demonstrate why the law prevents AT&T from putting them out of business by pricing them out of the market. Nevertheless, such questions are for the District Court to decide in the first instance….

In this case, plaintiffs have not stated a duty-to-deal claim under *Trinko* and have not stated a predatory pricing claim under *Brooke Group*. They have nonetheless tried to join a wholesale claim that cannot succeed with a retail claim that cannot succeed, and alchemize them into a new form of antitrust liability never before recognized by this Court. We decline the invitation to recognize such claims. Two wrong claims do not make one that is right.

BREYER, J. with whom STEVENS, SOUTER, and GINSBURG, JJ., join, concurring in the judgment.

I would accept respondents' concession that the Ninth Circuit majority's "price squeeze" holding is wrong, I would vacate the Circuit's decision, and I would remand the case in order to allow the District Court to determine whether respondents may proceed with their "predatory pricing" claim as set forth in Judge Gould's dissenting Ninth Circuit opinion.

A "price squeeze" claim finds its natural home in a Sherman Act *§ 2* monopolization case where the Government as plaintiff seeks to show that a defendant's monopoly power rests, not upon "skill, foresight and industry," *United States v. Aluminum Co. of America, 148 F.2d 416, 430 (CA2 1945) (Alcoa)*, but upon exclusionary conduct. As this Court pointed out in [*Trinko*] the "'means of illicit exclusion, like the means of legitimate competition, are myriad.'" They may involve a "course of dealing" that, even if profitable, indicates a "willingness to forsake short-term profits to achieve an anticompetitive end." *Trinko*. See, *e.g., Aspen Skiing Co.;* Complaint in *United States* v. *International Business Machines Corp.*, Civil Action No. 69 Civ. 200 (SDNY, filed Jan. 17, 1969). And, as Judge Hand wrote many years ago, a "price squeeze" may fall within that latter category. *Alcoa, supra, at 437-438*. As a matter of logic, it may be that a particular price squeeze can only be exclusionary if a refusal by the monopolist to sell to the "squeezed customer" would also be exclusionary. But a court, faced with a price squeeze rather than a refusal to deal, is unlikely to find the latter (hypothetical) question any easier to answer than the former.

I would try neither to answer these hypothetical questions here nor to foreshadow their answer. We have before us a regulated firm. During the time covered by the complaint, petitioners were required to provide wholesale digital subscriber line (DSL) transport service as a common carrier, charging "just and reasonable" rates that were not "unreasonabl[y] discriminat[ory]." And, in my view, a purchaser from a regulated firm (which, if a natural monopolist, is lawfully such) cannot win an antitrust case simply by showing that it is "squeezed" between the regulated firm's wholesale price (to the plaintiff) and its retail price (to customers for whose business both firms compete). When a regulatory structure exists to deter and remedy anticompetitive harm, the costs of antitrust enforcement are likely to be greater than the benefits…..

Unlike *Town of Concord,* the regulators here controlled prices only at the wholesale level. But respondents do not claim that that regulatory fact makes any difference; and rightly so, for as far as I can tell, respondents could have gone to the regulators and asked for petitioners' wholesale prices to be lowered in light of the alleged price squeeze.

Respondents now seek to show only that the defendant engaged in predatory pricing, within the terms of this Court's decision in *Brooke Group Ltd.* The District Court can determine whether there is anything in the procedural history of this case that bars respondents from asserting their predatory pricing claim. And if not, it can decide the merits of that claim. As I said, I would remand the case so that it can do so.

Insert following Note 3, page 812.

Note on the EU *Microsoft* decision

In 2004, the European Commission (the executive arm of the European Union) issued a far-reaching decision against Microsoft, finding that the software company violated European competition rules by abusing its dominant position in the market for personal computer operating systems (OS). *Sun Microsystems* v. *Microsoft Corp.*, EC Comm 1 (Comp/C-3/37.792) (March 24, 2004) ("European Commission Decision"), *online at* http://europa.eu.int/comm/competition/antitrust/cases/decisions/37792 /en.pdf (visited July 19, 2005). Specifically, the Commission found that Microsoft illegally leveraged its dominant position in the OS market into two adjacent markets: (1) the market for work group server (WGS) operating systems, and (2) the market for media players.

In the server market, Microsoft had refused to disclose documentation that would allow its competitors to create server software that is fully compatible with PCs that use the popular Microsoft Windows OS. The Commission held that this nondisclosure put competitors at an unfair disadvantage and risked eliminating competition in the WGS market. It held that Microsoft's actions created a significant risk of eliminating competition in the WGS market and that this violated Article 82(b) of the EU Treaty, which forbids a company from abusing its dominant position by "limiting production, markets or technical development to the prejudice of consumers." Treaty Establishing the European Community ("EC Treaty"), Common Rules on Competition, Taxation and Approximation of Laws, Art. 82 (1958). The Commission ordered Microsoft to disclose the relevant information within 120 days of the decision, but it allowed Microsoft to receive reasonable compensation to the extent that the information being disclosed was entitled to protection as intellectual property.

The Commission also found that Microsoft abused its dominant position by tying its Windows Media Player (WMP) with the Windows OS by technically integrating WMP software into

Windows, a charge similar to the one the company faced in the United States relating to its web browser software. By bundling its media software with Windows, Microsoft unfairly placed its competitors in that market at a competitive disadvantage and reduced consumer choice in violation of Article 82. The Commission ordered Microsoft to offer two versions of the Windows OS without the WMP to its customers within 90 days of its decision.

The Commission concluded that Microsoft's violations were severe enough to warrant drastic penalties:

Microsoft's anti-competitive behaviour weakens effective competition on the markets for work group server operating systems and media players in an appreciable way. Microsoft's refusal to supply interface information brings about a risk of elimination of competition on the world-wide market for work group server operating systems. Microsoft's tying of WMP with Windows risks impairing the effective structure of competition in the world-wide market for media players. European Commission Decision at para. 992.

In addition to enjoining Microsoft from continuing its abusive activity, the Commission levied a record fine of over €497 million (about $603 million) in the hopes of deterring Microsoft or others from engaging in similar conduct.

Microsoft's initial reaction to the decision was twofold: first, it announced that it would comply, but second, it stated that it intended to appeal the decision to the European Court of First Instance. It took the latter step, and the Court of First Instance heard oral arguments for a week. See Hearing T-201/04, *Microsoft v. Commission*, 24-28 April 2006. In the meantime, the Commission became concerned that Microsoft was not complying properly with the terms of the 2004 decision. On July 12, 2006, it issued a Decision "fixing the definitive amount of the periodic penalty payment imposed on Microsoft Corporation by decision C(2005)4420 final and amending that Decision as regards the amount of the periodic penalty payment. (Case COMP/C-3/37.792 Microsoft). The July 2006 decision recites in detail the exchanges between Microsoft and the Commission with respect to Microsoft's disclosures of its technical documentation and protocols. On October 4, 2005, the Commission and Microsoft agreed on the appointment of Professor Neil Barrett to be the Monitoring Trustee for compliance. Later, two advisors were appointed to assist the Trustee.

As of mid-2006, the Trustee had concluded that the disclosures Microsoft had made could not be used to develop an interoperable work group server operating system. Microsoft, of course, contested that finding, but the Commission was persuaded that the Trustee had the better of the argument. It concluded, in paragraph 233 of the July 12, 2006, decision, that "Microsoft has not complied with its obligations to make Interoperability Information available to interested undertakings...." In order to assure Microsoft's future compliance, the Commission decided to impose additional fines on Microsoft, based on its turnover of US $39.7 billion in the last year available (2004-05) and its average daily turnover of US $109 million. Paragraph 246 of the decision fixes the "definitive" amount of the periodic payment Microsoft owes for failing to comply with its obligations at € 280.5 million (or $ 357 million) for the period from 16 December 2005 to 20 June 2006 inclusive. From July 31 forward, the penalty was fixed at € 3 million per day. Microsoft, while still defending the legality of its actions, filed revised documents with the Commission in late November 2006, hoping to avoid the rapidly increasing fines.

This ongoing saga is a sobering reminder of the differences in perspective and approach that continue to exist between the European Union and the United States on the topic of abuses of a dominant position (or monopolization). The parallel action that went forward in the United States has resulted in court supervision, to be sure, but the remedies look nothing like the disclosure obligations and supporting fines that Microsoft is facing in the EU. In the fall of 2007, the Court of First Instance rejected Microsoft's underlying appeal.

Replace Note 9, page 873, with the following:

UNITED STATES v. AMR CORP., AMERICAN AIRLINES INC.

United States Court of Appeals, Tenth Circuit, 2003

335 F.3d 1109

LUCERO, J. This case involves the nature of permissible competitive practices in the airline industry under the antitrust laws of this country, centered around the hub-and-spoke system of American Airlines. The United States brought this suit against AMR Corporation, American Airlines, Inc., and American Eagle Holding Corporation ("American'), alleging monopolization and attempted monopolization through predatory pricing in violation of § 2 of the Sherman Act. In essence, the government alleges that American engaged in multiple episodes of price predation in four city-pair airline markets, all connected to American's hub at Dallas/Fort Worth International Airport ("DFW"), with the ultimate purpose of using the reputation for predatory pricing it earned in those four markets to defend a monopoly at its DFW hub. At its root, the government's complaint alleges that American: (1) priced its product on the routes in question below cost; and (2) intended to recoup these losses by charging supracompetitive prices either on the four core routes themselves, or on those routes where it stands to exclude competition by means of its "reputation for predation." Finding that the government failed to demonstrate the existence of a genuine issue of material fact as to either of these allegations, the district court granted summary judgment in favor of American, from which the government now appeals. Because we agree that the record is void of evidence that rises to the level of a material conflict, we affirm.

I

Airlines are predominantly organized in a hub-and-spoke system, with traffic routed such that passengers leave their origin city for an intermediate hub airport. Passengers traveling to a concentrated hub tend of pay higher average fares than those traveling on comparable routes that do not include a concentrated hub as an endpoint. This is known as the "hub premium" and a major airline's hub is often an important profit center. Entry of low cost carriers ("LCCs") into a hub market tends to drive down the fares charged by major carriers. Consequently, major carriers generally enjoy higher margins on routes where they do not face LCC competition.

Both American and Delta Airlines ("Delta") maintain hubs at DFW, though Delta's presence is considerably smaller than American's. As of May 2000, American's share of passengers boarded at DFW was 70.2%, Delta's share was roughly 18%, and LCC share was 2.4%. As of mid-2000, there were seven low-cost airlines serving DFW. In the period between 1997 to 2000, five new low-cost airlines entered DFW: American, Trans Air, Frontier, National, Sun Country, and Ozark. DFW has more low-fare airlines than any other hub airport and the number of passengers carried by low-fare airlines increased by over 30% from May 1999 to May 2000. Nevertheless, LCCs have a significantly higher market share in some other major U.S. hubs.

LCCs generally enjoy the advantage of having lower costs than major carriers, allowing them to offer lower fares than their major-airline competitors. During the period between 1995 and 1997, a number of LCCs, including Vanguard, Western Pacific, and Sunjet, began to take advantage of these lower costs of entering certain city-pair routes serving DFW and charging lower fares than American. The instant case primarily involves DFW-Kansas City, DFW-Wichita, DFW-Colorado Springs, and DFW-Long Beach.

American responded to lower LCC fares on these routes with changes in: (1) pricing (matching LCC prices); (2) capacity (adding flights or switching to larger planes); and (3) yield management (making more seats available at the new, lower prices). By increasing capacity, American overrode its own internal capacity-planning models for each route, which had previously indicated that such increases would be unprofitable. In each instance, American's response produced the same result: the competing LCC failed to establish a presence, moved its operations, American generally resumed its prior marketing strategy, reducing flights and raising prices to levels roughly comparable to those prior to the period of low-fare competition. Capacity was reduced after LCC exit, but usually remained higher than prior to the alleged episode of predatory activity.

The government filed suit on May 13, 1999, alleging that American participated in a scheme of predatory pricing in violation of § 2 of the Sherman Act. In the government's view, American's combined response of lowering prices, increasing capacity, and altering yield management in response to LCC competition constituted an unlawful, anticompetitive response. After reviewing a voluminous record and receiving extensive briefs, the district court granted American's motion for summary judgment on all antitrust claims, concluding that the government failed to demonstrate the existence of a genuine issue of material fact as to (1) whether American had priced below costs and (2) whether American had a dangerous probability of recouping its alleged investment in below-cost prices.

. . . Monopolization claims under § 2 of the Sherman Act require proof: (1) that a firm has monopoly power in a properly defined relevant market; and (2) that it willfully acquired or maintained this power by means of anticompetitive conduct. *TV Communications Network, Inc.* v. *Turner Network Television, Inc.*, 964 F.2d 1022, 1025 (10th Cir. 1992). This is to be distinguished from a business that acquired monopoly power by greater skill, efficiency, or by "building a better mousetrap." Claims of attempted monopolization under § 2 of the Sherman Act require four elements of proof: (1) a relevant geographic and product market; (2) specific intent to monopoize the market; (3) anticompetitive conduct in furtherance of the attempt; and (4) a dangerous probability that the firm will succeed in the attempt. *Multistate Legal Studies, Inc.* v. *Harcourt Brace Jovanovich Legal and Prof'l Publ'ns, Inc.*, 63 F.3d 1540, 1550 (10th Cir. 1995).

In the instant case, the anticompetitive conduct at issue is predatory pricing. The crux of the government's argument is that the "incremental" revenues and costs specifically associated with American" capacity additions show a loss. Because American spent more to add capacity than the revenues generated by the capacity additions, such capacity additions made no economic sense unless American intended to drive LCCs out of the market. Under the government" theory, American attempted to monopolize the four city-pair routes in question in order to develop a reputation as an exceedingly aggressive competitor and set an example to all potential competitors. Fearing American's predatory response, the theory goes, future potential competitors will decline to enter other DFW market routes and compete. If American succeeds in preventing or at least forestalling the formation of an LCC hub at DFW, it will then be able to charge higher prices on other DFW routes and thereby recoup the losses it incurred from its "capacity dumping" on the four core routes.

III

Scholars from the Chicago School of economic thought have long labeled predatory pricing as implausible and irrational. Frank Easterbrook, a leader of the Chicago School, once concluded that "there is not sufficient reason for antitrust law or the courts to take predation seriously." Frank H. Easterbrook, *Predatory Strategies & Counterstrategies*, 48 U. Chi. L. Rev. 263, 264 (1981). Chicago scholars argued that lowering prices could only be pro-competitive and any prohibition on such conduct could ultimately deter firms from engaging in conduct that is socially beneficial. Richard J. Pierce, Jr., Is Post-Chicago Ready for the Courtroom? A Response to Professor Brennan, 69 Geo. Wash. L. Rev. 1103, 1106 (2001). Commentators viewed below-cost pricing as irrational largely because of the uncertainty of recouping losses through later price increases. In order for a predatory pricing scheme to be successful, two future events had to take place: first, the victim of the alleged predation would have to exist and, second, the predator would have to generate profits in excess of its initial losses. Jonathan B. Baker, Predatory Pricing after Brooke Group: An Economic Perspective, 62 Antitrust L.J. 585, 586 (1994). In two seminal antitrust opinions, the Supreme Court adopted the skepticism of Chicago scholars, observing that "there is a consensus among commentators that predatory pricing schemes are rarely tried, and even more rarely successful." *Matsushita Elec. Indus. Co.* v. *Zenith Radio Corp.*, 475 U.S. 574, 489, 106 S.Ct. 1348, 89 L.Ed.2d 528 (1986); *Brooke Group Ltd.* v. *Brown & Williamson Tobacco Corp.*, 509 U.S. 209, 226, 113 S.Ct. 2578, 125 L.Ed.2d 168 (1993). Implausibility of predatory pricing schemes was said to flow from the fact that their success is inherently uncertain. *Matsushita*, 475 U.S. at 598, 106 S.Ct. 1348. While "the short-run loss is definite . . . the long-run gain depends on successfully neutralizing the competition. *Id.* Moreover, "[t]he success of any predatory scheme depends on *maintaining* monopoly power for long enough both to recoup the pedator's losses and to harvest some additional gain." *Id.* Furthermore, caution in predatory pricing cases is the watchword as "the costs of an erroneous finding are high." *Brooke Group*, 509 U.S. at 227, 113 S.Ct. 2578. Because "the mechanism by which a firm engages in predatory pricing – lowering prices – is the same mechanism by which a firm stimulates competition," mistaken inferences may deter the very conduct the antitrust laws were created to protect. *Cargill Inc.* v. *Monfort of Colo.*, 479 U.S. 104, 122, 107 S.Ct. 484, 93 L.Ed.2d 427 (1986). Recent scholarship has challenged the notion that predatory pricing schemes are implausible and irrational. *See, e.g.*, Patrick Bolton et al., Predatory Pricing: Strategic Theory and Legal Policy, 88 Geo. L.J. 2239, 2241 (2000) ("Modern economic analysis has developed coherent theories of predation that contravene earlier economic writing claiming that predatory pricing conduct is irrational.") Post-Chicago economists have theorized that price predation is not only plausible, but profitable, especially in a multi-market coontext where predation can occur in one market and recoupment can occur rapidly in other markets. *See* Baker, *supra*, at 590.

Although this court approaches the matter with caution, we do not do so with the incredulity that once prevailed.

IV

The Supreme Court has formulated two prerequisites to recovery on a predatory pricing claim, conditions that "are not easy to establish." *Brook Group*, 509 U.S. at 227, 113 S.Ct. 2578. First, the government must prove that "the prices complained of are below an appropriate measure of [American's] costs." *Id.* at 223, 113 S.Ct. 2578. While the first element is crucial, "[t]hat below-cost pricing may impose painful losses on its target is of no moment to the antitrust laws if competition is not injured." *Id.* at 225, 113 S.Ct. 2578. Thus, the second prerequisite to recovery on a predatory pricing claim, a demonstration that American had "a dangerous probability of recouping its investment in below-cost prices," must also be met. *Id.* at 224, 113 S.Ct. 2578. Without a dangerous probability of recoupment, competition remains unharmed even if individual competitors suffer. As frequently notes, "the antitrust laws were passed for the protection of *competition*, not *competitors*." *Id.* (citing *Brown Shoe Co.* v. *United States*, 370 U.S. 294, 320, 82 S.Ct. 1502, 8 L.Ed.2d 510 (1962)).

Speaking to the first prerequisite to recovery, the Supreme Court stated that "[p]redatory pricing means pricing below some appropriate measure of cost." *Matsushita*, 475 U.S. at 584 n. 8, 106 S.Ct. 1348.[8] Despite a great deal of debate on the subject, no consensus has emerged as to what the most "appropriate" measure of cost is in predatory pricing cases. Costs can generally be divided into those that are "fixed" and do not vary with the level of output (management expenses, interest on bonded debt, property taxes, deprecation, and other irreducible overhead) and those that are "variable" and do vary with the level of output (materials, fuel, labor used to produce the product). Marginal cost, the cost that results from producing an additional increment of output, is primarily a function of variable cost because fixed costs, as the name would imply, are largely unaffected by changes in output. *See Rebel Oil Co., Inc.* v. *Atl. Richfield Co.*, 146 F.3d 1088, 1092 (9th Cir. 1998). For predatory pricing cases, especially those involving allegedly predatory production increases, the ideal measure of cost would be marginal cost because "[a]s long as a firm's prices exceed its marginal cost, each additional sale decreases losses or increases profits." *Advo*, 51 F.3d at 1198. However, marginal cost, an economic abstraction, is notoriously difficult to measure and "cannot be determined from

---

[8]   The government notes in its brief that the "gravamen of the complaint is not limited to American's pricing." Rather, the complained of behavior includes American's capacity additions. However, as the district court correctly noted, prices and productive output are "two sides of the same coin." *United States* v. *AMR Corp.*, 140 F.Supp. 2d 1141, 1194 (D. Kan. 2001). While the specific behavior complained of in the instant case is an increase in output or frequency, these actions must be analyzed in terms of their effect on price and cost. Thus, in order to succeed in the present action, the government must meet the standards of proof for predatory pricing cases established in *Brooke Group*.

conventional accounting methods." *Northeastern Tel. Co. v. AT&T*, 651 F.2d 76, 88 (2nd Cir. 1981); *Pac. Eng'g & Prod. Co. of Nev. v. Kerr-McGee Corp.*, 551 F.2d 790, 797 (10th Cir. 1977). Economists, therefore, must resort to proxies for marginal cost. A commonly accepted proxy for marginal cost in predatory pricing cases in Average Variable Cost ("AVC"), the average of those costs that vary with the level of output. *See, e.g., Stearns Airport Equip. Co. v. FMC Corp.*, 170 F.3d 518, 532 (5th Cir. 1999); *Advo*, 51 F.3d at 1198; *Arthur S. Langenderfer, Inc. v. S.E. Johnson Co.*, 729 F.2d 1050, 1056 (6th Cir. 1984); *Northeastern Tel.*, 651 F.2d at 88.

The Supreme Court has declined to state which of the various cost measures is definitive. In *Brooke Group*, the Court accepted for the purposes of the case the parties' agreement that the appropriate measure of cost was AVC, but declined to "resolve the conflict among the lower courts over the appropriate measure of cost." 509 U.S. at 223 n. 1, 113 S.Ct. 2578. In this circuit, we have spoken of both AVC and other marginal cost measures as relevant. *See, e.g., Multistate Legal Studies*, 63 F.3d at 1549 n. 5 (observing that "evidence of marginal cost or average variable cost is extremely beneficial in establishing a case of monopoization through predatory pricing" (emphasis added)); *Pac. Eng'g*, 551 F.2d at 797. Because there may be times when courts need the flexibility to examine both AVC as well as other proxies for marginal cost in order to evaluate an alleged predatory pricing scheme, we again decline to dictate a definitive cost measure for all cases. Sole reliance on AVC as the appropriate measure of cost may obscure the nature of a particular predatory scheme and, thus, contrary to what is suggested by the district court, we do not favor AVC to the exclusion of other proxies for marginal cost. Whatever the proxy used to measure marginal cost, it must be accurate and reliable in the specific circumstances of the case at bar.

Conceding that AVC is a good proxy for marginal cost in most cases, the government nevertheless argues that there may be times when looking only to a market-wide AVC test will disguise the nature of the predatory conduct at issue. Where there is a challenge to well-defined incremental conduct, and where incremental costs may be directly and confidently measured utilizing alternative proxies to

AVC, argues the government, the market-wide AVC test is inappropriate.

Considering this to be the situation in the instant case, the government proffers four tests that purport to measure reliably incremental costs – the price costs associated with the capacity additions at issue. Rather than creating independent measures of the costs associated with American's capacity additions, the government's experts rely on cost measures used in AAIMSPAN, American's internal decisional accounting system (accounting measures that are used for internal decision making, not financial reporting). The government notes that a range of tests are necessary to rule out false positives and avoid misleading indications of predation. Due to similarities among the four tests, the district court grouped them as Tests Two and Three, and Tests One and Four for purposes of analysis. We proceed to consider each test to determine whether it is valid as a matter of law.

Two of the tests grouped together by the district court, Tests Two and Three, purport to measure incremental costs by looking to whether certain of American's internal cost-accounting measures became negative following the allegedly predatory capacity additions. Both tests rely on an internal accounting measure known as FAUDNC, or "Fully Allocated earnings plus Upline/Downline contribution Net of Costs." *United States* v. *AMR Corp.*, 140 F.Supp. 2d 1141, 1175 (D. Kan. 2001). As the name would imply, FAUDNC is a fully allocated earnings measure, meaning that general operating expenses are arbitrarily allocated by American's decision accounting system to the flight or route level, and do not necessarily represent the exact costs associated with a particular flight or route. FAUDNC reflects 97-99% of American's total costs, which include fixed costs not affected by the capacity additions at issue. Thus, while FAUDNC includes some costs directly caused by a particular flight or operations on a particular route (such as fuel and landing fees), it also includes many costs that are not related to the operation of a particular flight or route (dispatch, city ticket offices, certain station expenses, certain maintenance expenses, American's flight academy, flight simulator maintenance, general sales and advertising). In other words, FAUDNC includes costs that are not entirely avoidable even if American were to abandon an entire route.

116

Because Tests Two and Three rely on fully allocated costs and include many fixed costs, the district court held that utilizing these cost measures would be the equivalent of applying an average total cost test, implicitly ruled out by *Brooke Group*'s mention of incremental costs only.[9] The district court therefore concluded that, by relying on FAUDNC, Tests Two and Three were, by definition, not measures of marginal or incremental cost. We agree with this conclusion. While we will accept alternative proxies to marginal cost beyond AVC, Tests Two and Three are simply not proxies for marginal or incremental cost. Moreover, because these tests rely on "arbitrary allocation of costs among different classes of service," they "cannot purport to identify those costs which are *caused* by a product or service, and this is fundamental to economic cost determination." *MCI Communications Corp.* v. *AT&T,* 708 F.2d 1081, 1116 (7th Cir. 1982). Thus, given that Tests Two and Three rely on cost measures that are not, in large part, variable or avoidable with respect to capacity increases, we conclude that they are invalid as a matter of law as a measure of allegedly predatory capacity increases.[10] *See Stearns,* 170 F.3d at 532 (noting that "judgment as a matter of law is appropriate when a plaintiff fails to adequately specify how the challenged pricing undercusts the defendant's variable costs").

---

[9] While the government has not completely abandoned Tests Two and Three on appeal, it has not chosen to press them beyond a statement in a footnote of their Reply Brief noting that "American's criticisms of Tests 2 and 3 are incorrect." (Appellant's Reply Br. at 12). Notably, the government has previously taken the position that utilizing fully allocated costs as a pricing standard would result in "stultification of competition" and should be rejected as "contrary to the public interest." *S. Pac. Communications Co.* v. *AT&T,* 556 F.Supp. 825, 923 n. 107 (D.D.C. 1982).

[10] In holding that Tests Two and Three are invalid as a matter of law, we consider the uncontested fact that these tests, by relying on FAUDNC, measure a significant amount of American's fixed costs. As such, Tests Two and Three are inappropriate measures of incremental costs under *Brooke Group*, as they cannot demonstrate that American priced below an "appropriate measure of cost" with respect to the challenged capacity additions.

117

As to Tests One and Four, the district court grouped them together, labeling them as short-run profit-maximization tests. Test One examines changes in profitability. It employs FAUDNC, discussed above, and an internal measure of American's variable costs known as VAUDNC, as well as a version of VAUDNC that has been modified by the government, VAUDNC-AC.[11] If these measures declined following a capacity addition, this test allegedly demonstrates that adding capacity forced American to forgo better profit performance elsewhere. Test Four relies on VAUDNC-AC to compare the supposed revenue from incremental passengers with the average avoidable cost of adding capacity. Under Test Four, if incremental revenues are below incremental costs, this is "evidence of sacrifice." *AMR Corp.*, 140 F.Supp. 2d at 1180.

In rejecting Tests One and Four, the district court concluded that they were, in essence, short-run profit-maximization tests that focus on whether a company has sacrificed some level of profit to compete more effectively. Courts and scholars have observed that such a sacrifice test would necessarily involve a great deal of speculation and often result in injury to the consumer and a chilling of competition. *See* 3 Phillip E. Areeda & Herbert Hovenkamp, *Antitrust Law* ¶ 736c2 (2d ed. 2002); *Stearns*, 170 F.3d at 533 n. 14 (nothing that theories of predation based upon the failure to maximize profits in the short run are "no longer tenable in the wake of *Brooke Group*"). Upon closer examination, it is clear that rather than

---

[11] Unlike the other costs measures, which are taken straight out of American's internal accounting system, VAUDNC-AC is a government creation. It represents VAUDNC costs plus the cost of aircraft ownership, which is traditionally considered a fixed cost in the airline industry, not an avoidable cost of changes in capacity on a route. By treating aircraft ownership as a variable expense, this measure reduces the apparent performance of the routes by increasing the costs attributed to operations on a particular flight or route. VAUDNC-AC represents over 79% of the total costs in American's decision accounting system. The district court concluded that VAUDNC-AC overstates short-run cost because it includes fixed, unavoidable aircraft-ownership costs.

determining whether the added capacity itself was priced below an appropriate measure of cost, Test One effectively treats forgone or "sacrificed" profits as costs, and condemns activity that may have been profitable as predatory.[12] Rather than isolating the costs actually associated with the capacity additions the government purports to measure directly, Test One simply performs a "before-and-after" comparison of the route as a whole, looking to whether profits on the route as a whole decline after capacity was added, not to whether the challenged capacity additions were done below cost. In the end, Test One indicates only that a company has failed to maximize short-run profits on the route as a whole. Such a pricing standard could lead to a strangling of competition, as it would condemn nearly all output expansions, and harm to consumers. We conclude that Test One is invalid as a matter of law. Test Four does not appear to suffer from this flaw, and we do not reject it for being a short-run profit-maximization test.

---

[12] For example, if an airline earned $20.6 million on a route that cost $18 million to operate, it would have $2.6 million in profit. If the airline then added a flight to the route that would cost $500,000 to operate, but brought in an additional $1 million in revenue from passengers, the airline would make $500,000 profit. If adding this extra capacity to the route reduced the profitability of other flights on that route, reducing revenue for the rest of the route by $600,000 down to $20 million, under Test One, this conduct would be considered predatory because rather than comparing the additional flight's $1 million in revenue to its $500,000 in costs, Test One looks only to the reduction in profits on the route as a whole from $2.6 million to $2.5 million. Thus, this conduct would be labeled predatory because the profits for the route as a whole declined, even though the capacity additions themselves were profitable and the route as a whole was still profitable. *See* Einer Elhauge, "Why Above-Cost Price Cuts to Drive Out Entrants are Not Predatory – and the Implications for Defining Costs and Market Power," 112 Yale L.J. 681, 694 (2003). It is clear, therefore, that, in proffering Test One, the government has not "attempted to identify the actual costs associated with the capacity additions." *AMR Corp.*, 140 F.Supp. 2d at 1202.

As with Test One, the district court noted that, in proffering Test Four, the government has not "identif[ied] the actual costs associated with the capacity additions." *AMR Corp.*, 140 F.Supp. 2d at 1202. We agree with this conclusion as well. Test Four attempts to reveal American's predatory conduct by measuring and comparing the incremental costs incurred by American when it added capacity to the city-pair routes in question to the incremental revenue it received from the additional capacity. The government's expert who developed Test Four, Steven Berry, characterized it as a comparison of the "average revenue from incremental passengers who traveled after the capacity addition with the average avoidable cost of the capacity addition" *See also* William J. Baumol, "Predation and the Logic of the Average Variable Cost Test," 39 J.L. & Econ. 49, 58 (1996) (opining that average avoidable cost is the proper cost measure for predatory pricing tests). Berry further stated that, when considering an increase in capacity, an avoidable cost test compares, "the *incremental revenue generated by the increment* of capacity to the *avoidable cost of the increment* of capacity." Therefore, the only appropriate costs included in Test Four are those costs that American could have avoided by not adding the challenged capacity to the city-pair routes. Test Four utilizes VAUDNC-AC, the cost component of which includes both aircraft ownership costs and costs characterized as variable over an eighteen-month planning period by AAIMSPAN. *See AMR Corp.*, 140 F.Supp. 2d at 1174-75. The costs included in VAUDNC-AC include variable costs American incurs with respect to all of its operations at DFW. Because some of those variable costs do not vary proportionately with the level of flight activity, they are allocated arbitrarily to a flight or route by AAIMSPAN. American identifies these variable, non-proportional common costs as: (1) airport ticket agents, (2) arrival agents, (3) ramp workers, and (4) security. Therefore, American argues that because VAUDNC-AC is an allocated variable cost measure, it cannot b used to calculate the *avoidable* cost of the added capacity.

The government first responds to American's criticism by arguing that cost allocation is a key component of managerial accounting and a relevant and sensible method by which to assign costs for decision-making purposes. While the government may be correct, this court is not presented with the question of whether cost allocation is a reasonable *accounting* method or a technique which provides businesses with reliable data to evaluate business decisions. Because the government asserts that Test Four measures average *avoidable* cost, this court must instead determine whether that assertion is correct. Thus, the government's first response is wholly irrelevant. The government also alleges that there exists a genuine issue of material fact because its expert reworked Test Four so as to omit the contested costs and the results still indicated predation. The government's expert, however, states that when he reworked the numbers in response to criticism from American's expert, he eliminated the following costs from the test: (1) CTO ticketing, (2) direct reservations, (3) reservation communications, (4) cargo reservations, (5) and dispatch. Although the propriety of including these costs in Test Four was also disputed by American, they are not the costs that American disputed on the grounds that they are allocated arbitrarily to a route of flight by AAIMSPAN. Consequently, the expert's revisions to Test Four are not responsive to American's criticism and no genuine issue of material fact exists.

Because the cost component of Test Four includes arbitrarily allocated variable costs, it does not compare incremental revenue to average avoidable cost. Instead, it compares incremental revenue to a measure of both average variable cost and average avoidable cost. Therefore, Test Four does not measure only the avoidable or incremental cost of the capacity additions and cannot be used to satisfy the government's burden in this case. We conclude that all four proxies are invalid as a matter of law, fatally flawed in their application, and fundamentally unreliable.[13] Because it is uncontested that American did not price below AVC for any route as a whole, we agree with the district court's conclusion that the government has not

---

[13] The government's four proxies are, in effect, an illustration of the long-recognized fact that "the true marginal costs of production are difficult to generate." *Stearns*, 170 F.3d at 532. The difficulty inherent in isolating the precise costs associated with production increases is precisely why most courts attempt to "estimate [marginal cost] by using average variable costs." *Id.*, *see also Morgan* v. *Ponder*, 892 F.2d 1355, 1362 n. 17 (noting that "where it is difficult to isolate variable costs . . . the plaintiff should be required to prove across-the-board predatory pricing").

succeeded in establishing the first element of *Brooke Group*, pricing below an appropriate measure of cost.[14] Our conclusion that the government has not succeeded in establishing a genuine issue of material fact as to the first prong of *Brooke Group*, pricing below an appropriate measure of cost, renders an examination of whether the government has succeeded in creating a genuine issue of material fact as to the second prong of *Brooke Group*, dangerous probability of recoupment, unnecessary. Given the exceedingly thin line between vigorous price competition and predatory pricing, *see Northeastern Telephone Co.*, 651 F.2 at 88, the balance the Supreme Court has struck in *Brooke Group*, and the fatally flawed nature of the alternative pricing proxies proffered by the government, we conclude that the summary judgment in favor of American was appropriate.

The order of the district court granting summary judgment to American is AFFIRMED.

---

[14] The district court also stated that even if American had priced below an appropriate measure of cost, it was nevertheless entitled to summary judgment because "American's prices only matched, and never undercut, the fares of the new entrant, low cost carriers on the four core routes." *AMR Corp.*, 140 F.Supp. 2d at 1204. In so concluding the district court essentially imported the statutory "meeting competition" defense from the Robinson-Patman Act, 15 U.S.C. § 13(b). While we have never applied the "meeting competition" defense in a § 2 predatory pricing case, the district court reasoned that "there is strong inferential support for the idea that the defense may be appropriate in a given case." *Id*. at 1204. There may be strong arguments for application of the meeting competition defense in the Sherman Act context by analogy to the Robinson-Patman context. However, unlike in the Robinson-Patman Act, such a defense is not expressly provided for by the terms of the Sherman Act. The Supreme Court has never mentioned the possibility of such a defense under the Sherman Act. We therefore decline to rule that the "meeting competition" defense applies in the § 2 context.

Insert after <u>AMR</u> decision *supra.*

WEYERHAEUSER CO. v. ROSS-SIMMONS HARDWOOD LUMBER CO.

Supreme Court of the United States, 2007

549 U.S. 312, 127 S. Ct. 1069, 166 L. Ed. 2d 911

THOMAS, J. Respondent Ross-Simmons, a sawmill, sued petitioner Weyerhaeuser, alleging that Weyerhaeuser drove it out of business by bidding up the price of sawlogs to a level that prevented Ross-Simmons from being profitable. A jury returned a verdict in favor of Ross-Simmons on its monopolization claim, and the Ninth Circuit affirmed. We granted certiorari to decide whether the test we applied to claims of predatory pricing in *Brooke Group Ltd. v. Brown & Williamson Tobacco Corp., 509 U.S. 209 (1993)*, also applies to claims of predatory bidding. We hold that it does. Accordingly, we vacate the judgment of the Court of Appeals.

I

This antitrust case concerns the acquisition of red alder sawlogs by the mills that process those logs in the Pacific Northwest. These hardwood-lumber mills usually acquire logs in one of three ways. Some logs are purchased on the open bidding market. Some come to the mill through standing short- and long-term agreements with timberland owners. And others are harvested from timberland owned by the sawmills themselves. The allegations relevant to our decision in this case relate to the bidding market.

Ross-Simmons began operating a hardwood-lumber sawmill in Longview, Washington, in 1962. Weyerhaeuser entered the Northwestern hardwood-lumber market in 1980 by acquiring an existing lumber company. Weyerhaeuser gradually increased the scope of its hardwood-lumber operation, and it now owns six hardwood sawmills in the region. By 2001, Weyerhaeuser's mills were acquiring approximately 65 percent of the alder logs available for sale in the region.

From 1990 to 2000, Weyerhaeuser made more than $ 75 million in capital investments in its hardwood mills in the Pacific Northwest. During this period, production increased at every Northwestern hardwood mill that Weyerhaeuser owned. In addition to increasing production, Weyerhaeuser used "state-of-the-art technology," including sawing equipment, to increase the amount of lumber recovered from every log. By contrast, Ross-Simmons appears to have engaged in little efficiency-enhancing investment.

Logs represent up to 75 percent of a sawmill's total costs. And from 1998 to 2001, the price of alder sawlogs increased while prices for finished hardwood lumber fell. These divergent trends in input and output prices cut into the mills' profit margins, and Ross-Simmons suffered heavy losses during this time. Saddled with several million dollars in debt, Ross-Simmons shut down its mill completely in May 2001.

Ross-Simmons blamed Weyerhaeuser for driving it out of business by bidding up input costs, and it filed an antitrust suit against Weyerhaeuser for monopolization and attempted monopolization under § 2 of the Sherman Act. Ross-Simmons alleged that, among other anticompetitive acts, Weyerhaeuser had used "its dominant position in the alder sawlog market to drive up the prices for alder sawlogs to levels that severely reduced or eliminated the profit margins of Weyerhaeuser's alder sawmill competition." Proceeding in part on this "predatory-bidding" theory, Ross-Simmons argued that Weyerhaeuser had overpaid for alder sawlogs to cause sawlog prices to rise to artificially high levels as part of a plan to drive Ross-Simmons out of business. As proof that this practice had occurred, Ross-Simmons pointed to Weyerhaeuser's large share of the alder purchasing market, rising alder sawlog prices during the alleged predation period, and Weyerhaeuser's declining profits during that same period.

Prior to trial, Weyerhaeuser moved for summary judgment on Ross-Simmons' predatory-bidding theory. The District Court denied the motion. At the close of the 9-day trial, Weyerhaeuser moved for judgment as a matter of law, or alternatively, for a new trial. The motions were based in part on Weyerhaeuser's argument that Ross-Simmons had not satisfied the standard this Court set forth in *Brooke*

Group, supra. The District Court denied Weyerhaeuser's motion. The District Court also rejected proposed predatory-bidding jury instructions that incorporated elements of the *Brooke Group* test. Ultimately, the District Court instructed the jury that Ross-Simmons could prove that Weyerhaeuser's bidding practices were anticompetitive acts if the jury concluded that Weyerhaeuser "purchased more logs than it needed, or paid a higher price for logs than necessary, in order to prevent [Ross-Simmons] from obtaining the logs they needed at a fair price." Finding that Ross-Simmons had proved its claim for monopolization, the jury returned a $ 26 million verdict against Weyerhaeuser. The verdict was trebled to approximately $79 million.

Weyerhaeuser appealed to the Court of Appeals for the Ninth Circuit. There, Weyerhaeuser argued that *Brooke Group*'s standard for claims of predatory pricing should also apply to claims of predatory bidding. The Ninth Circuit disagreed and affirmed the verdict against Weyerhaeuser. *Confederated Tribes of Siletz Indians of Or. v. Weyerhaeuser Co., 411 F.3d 1030, 1035-1036 (2005).*

The Court of Appeals reasoned that "buy-side predatory bidding" and "sell-side predatory pricing," though similar, are materially different in that predatory bidding does not necessarily benefit consumers or stimulate competition in the way that predatory pricing does. Concluding that "the concerns that led the *Brooke Group* Court to establish a high standard of liability in the predatory-pricing context do not carry over to this predatory bidding context with the same force," the Court of Appeals declined to apply *Brooke Group* to Ross-Simmons' claims of predatory bidding. The Court of Appeals went on to conclude that substantial evidence supported a finding of liability on the predatory-bidding theory. We granted certiorari to decide whether *Brooke Group* applies to claims of predatory bidding. We hold that it does, and we vacate the Court of Appeals' judgment.

II

In *Brooke Group*, we considered what a plaintiff must show in order to succeed on a claim of predatory pricing under *§ 2* of the Sherman Act. In a typical predatory-pricing scheme, the predator reduces the sale price of its product (its output) to below cost, hoping to drive competitors out of business. Then, with competition vanquished, the predator raises output prices to a supracompetitive level. See *Matsushita Elec. Industrial Co. v. Zenith Radio Corp., 475 U.S. 574 (1986)* (describing predatory pricing). For the scheme to make economic sense, the losses suffered from pricing goods below cost must be recouped (with interest) during the supracompetitive-pricing stage of the scheme. Recognizing this economic reality, we established two prerequisites to recovery on claims of predatory pricing. "First, a plaintiff seeking to establish competitive injury resulting from a rival's low prices must prove that the prices complained of are below an appropriate measure of its rival's costs." Second, a plaintiff must demonstrate that "the competitor had . . . a dangerous probability of recouping its investment in below-cost prices". . . .

III

Predatory bidding, which Ross-Simmons alleges in this case, involves the exercise of market power on the buy side or input side of a market. In a predatory-bidding scheme, a purchaser of inputs "bids up the market price of a critical input to such high levels that rival buyers cannot survive (or compete as vigorously) and, as a result, the predating buyer acquires (or maintains or increases its) monopsony power." Kirkwood, Buyer Power and Exclusionary Conduct, *72 Antitrust L. J. 625, 652 (2005)* (hereinafter Kirkwood). Monopsony power is market power on the buy side of the market. Blair & Harrison, Antitrust Policy and Monopsony, *76 Cornell L. Rev. 297 (1991)*. As such, a monopsony is to the buy side of the market what a monopoly is to the sell side and is sometimes colloquially called a "buyer's monopoly." See *id., at 301, 320*; Piraino, A Proposed Antitrust Approach to Buyers' Competitive Conduct, *56 Hastings L. J. 1121, 1125 (2005)*.

A predatory bidder ultimately aims to exercise the monopsony power gained from bidding up input prices. To that end, once the predatory bidder has caused competing buyers to exit the market for purchasing inputs, it will seek to "restrict its input purchases below the competitive level," thus "reducing the unit price for the remaining inputs it purchases." Salop, Anticompetitive Overbuying by Power

Buyers, *72 Antitrust L. J. 669, 672 (2005)* (hereinafter Salop). The reduction in input prices will lead to "a significant cost saving that more than offsets the profits that would have been earned on the output." *Ibid.* If all goes as planned, the predatory bidder will reap monopsonistic profits that will offset any losses suffered in bidding up input prices.[15] (In this case, the plaintiff was the defendant's competitor in the input-purchasing market. Thus, this case does not present a situation of suppliers suing a monopsonist buyer under § 2 of the Sherman Act, nor does it present a risk of significantly increased concentration in the market in which the monopsonist sells, *i.e.*, the market for finished lumber.)

IV

A

Predatory-pricing and predatory-bidding claims are analytically similar. See Hovenkamp, The Law of Exclusionary Pricing, 2 Competition Policy Int'l, No. 1, pp. 21, 35 (Spring 2006). This similarity results from the close theoretical connection between monopoly and monopsony. See Kirkwood 653 (describing monopsony as the "mirror image" of monopoly); *Khan v. State Oil Co., 93 F.3d 1358, 1361 (CA7 1996)* ("Monopsony pricing . . . is analytically the same as monopoly or cartel pricing and [is] so treated by the law"), vacated and remanded on other grounds, *522 U.S. 3.....* The kinship between monopoly and monopsony suggests that similar legal standards should apply to claims of monopolization and to claims of monopsonization. Cf. Noll, "Buyer Power" and Economic Policy, *72 Antitrust L. J. 589, 591 (2005)* ("Asymmetric treatment of monopoly and monopsony has no basis in economic analysis").

---

[15] If the predatory firm's competitors in the input market and the output market are the same, then predatory bidding can also lead to the bidder's acquisition of monopoly power in the output market. In that case, which does not appear to be present here, the monopsonist could, under certain market conditions, also recoup its losses by raising output prices to monopolistic levels. See Salop 679-682 (describing a monopsonist's predatory strategy that depends upon raising prices in the output market).

Tracking the economic similarity between monopoly and monopsony, predatory-pricing plaintiffs and predatory-bidding plaintiffs make strikingly similar allegations. A predatory-pricing plaintiff alleges that a predator cut prices to drive the plaintiff out of business and, thereby, to reap monopoly profits from the output market. In parallel fashion, a predatory-bidding plaintiff alleges that a predator raised prices for a key input to drive the plaintiff out of business and, thereby, to reap monopsony profits in the input market. Both claims involve the deliberate use of unilateral pricing measures for anticompetitive purposes.[16] And both claims logically require firms to incur short-term losses on the chance that they might reap supracompetitive profits in the future.

B

More importantly, predatory bidding mirrors predatory pricing in respects that we deemed significant to our analysis in *Brooke Group*. In *Brooke Group*, we noted that "predatory pricing schemes are rarely tried, and even more rarely successful." *509 U.S., at 226* (quoting Matsushita). Predatory pricing requires a firm to suffer certain losses in the short term on the chance of reaping supracompetitive profits in the future. A rational business will rarely make this sacrifice. The same reasoning applies to predatory bidding. A predatory-bidding scheme requires a buyer of inputs to suffer losses today on the chance that it will reap supracompetitive profits in the

---

[16] Predatory bidding on inputs is not analytically different from predatory overbuying of inputs. Both practices fall under the rubric of monopsony predation and involve an input purchaser's use of input prices in an attempt to exclude rival input purchasers. The economic effect of the practices is identical: input prices rise. In a predatory-bidding scheme, the purchaser causes prices to rise by offering to pay more for inputs. In a predatory-overbuying scheme, the purchaser causes prices to rise by demanding more of the input. Either way, input prices increase. Our use of the term "predatory bidding" is not meant to suggest that different legal treatment is appropriate for the economically identical practice of "predatory overbuying."

future. For this reason, "successful monopsony predation is probably as unlikely as successful monopoly predation." R. Blair & J. Harrison, Monopsony 66 (1993).

And like the predatory conduct alleged in *Brooke Group*, actions taken in a predatory-bidding scheme are often "the very essence of competition. *509 U.S., at 226* (quoting *Cargill*). Just as sellers use output prices to compete for purchasers, buyers use bid prices to compete for scarce inputs. There are myriad legitimate reasons -- ranging from benign to affirmatively procompetitive -- why a buyer might bid up input prices. A firm might bid up inputs as a result of miscalculation of its input needs or as a response to increased consumer demand for its outputs. A more efficient firm might bid up input prices to acquire more inputs as a part of a procompetitive strategy to gain market share in the output market. A firm that has adopted an input-intensive production process might bid up inputs to acquire the inputs necessary for its process. Or a firm might bid up input prices to acquire excess inputs as a hedge against the risk of future rises in input costs or future input shortages. See Salop 682-683; Kirkwood 655. There is nothing illicit about these bidding decisions. Indeed, this sort of high bidding is essential to competition and innovation on the buy side of the market.[17]

Brooke Group also noted that a failed predatory-pricing scheme may benefit consumers. The potential benefit results from the difficulty an aspiring predator faces in recouping losses suffered from below-cost pricing. Without successful recoupment, "predatory pricing produces lower aggregate prices in the market, and consumer welfare is enhanced." Failed predatory-bidding schemes can also, but will not necessarily, benefit consumers. See Salop 677-678. In the first stage of a predatory-bidding scheme, the predator's high bidding will likely lead to its acquisition of more inputs. Usually, the acquisition of more inputs leads to the manufacture of more outputs. And increases in output generally result in lower prices to

---

[17] Higher prices for inputs obviously benefit existing sellers of inputs and encourage new firms to enter the market for input sales as well.

consumers.[18] Thus, a failed predatory-bidding scheme can be a "boon to consumers" in the same way that we considered a predatory-pricing scheme to be. See *Brooke Group, supra, at 224.*

In addition, predatory bidding presents less of a direct threat of consumer harm than predatory pricing. A predatory-pricing scheme ultimately achieves success by charging higher prices to consumers. By contrast, a predatory-bidding scheme could succeed with little or no effect on consumer prices because a predatory bidder does not necessarily rely on raising prices in the output market to recoup its losses. Salop 676. Even if output prices remain constant, a predatory bidder can use its power as the predominant buyer of inputs to force down input prices and capture monopsony profits.

C

The general theoretical similarities of monopoly and monopsony combined with the theoretical and practical similarities of predatory pricing and predatory bidding convince us that our two-pronged *Brooke Group* test should apply to predatory-bidding claims.

The first prong of *Brooke Group*'s test requires little adaptation for the predatory-bidding context. A plaintiff must prove that the alleged predatory bidding led to below-cost pricing of the predator's outputs. That is, the predator's bidding on the buy side must have caused the cost of the relevant output to rise above the revenues generated in the sale of those outputs. As with predatory pricing, the exclusionary effect of higher bidding that does not result in below-cost output pricing "is beyond the practical ability of a judicial tribunal to control without courting intolerable risks of chilling legitimate" procompetitive conduct. *509 U.S., at 223.* Given the multitude of procompetitive ends served by higher bidding for

---

[18] Consumer benefit does not necessarily result at the first stage because the predator might not use its excess inputs to manufacture additional outputs. It might instead destroy the excess inputs. See Salop 677, n. 22. Also, if the same firms compete in the input and output markets, any increase in outputs by the predator could be offset by decreases in outputs from the predator's struggling competitors.

inputs, the risk of chilling procompetitive behavior with too lax a liability standard is as serious here as it was in *Brooke Group*. Consequently, only higher bidding that leads to below-cost pricing in the relevant output market will suffice as a basis for liability for predatory bidding.

A predatory-bidding plaintiff also must prove that the defendant has a dangerous probability of recouping the losses incurred in bidding up input prices through the exercise of monopsony power. Absent proof of likely recoupment, a strategy of predatory bidding makes no economic sense because it would involve short-term losses with no likelihood of offsetting long-term gains. As with predatory pricing, making a showing on the recoupment prong will require "a close analysis of both the scheme alleged by the plaintiff and the structure and conditions of the relevant market." *Brooke Group, supra, at 226.*

Ross-Simmons has conceded that it has not satisfied the *Brooke Group* standard. Therefore, its predatory-bidding theory of liability cannot support the jury's verdict.

QUESTIONS

1. In general, is probability for recoupment as unlikely for a monopolist or monopsonist as for an oligopolist group?

2. What theoretical or empirical basis does the Court provide for its skepticism about Weyerhaeuser's ability to recoup? What basis does Justice Thomas provide for rejecting the jury's finding that Weyerhaeuser's bidding practices were anticompetitive and aimed at driving Ross-Simmons out of business?

Insert after *Jefferson Parish*, page 903.

1.   In *Illinois Tool Works Inc. v. Independent Ink, Inc.*,
547 U.S. 28 (2006), Justice Stevens delivered the opinion for a
unanimous Supreme Court.

Tridant, a subsidiary of Illinois Tool Works, held a patent on
print-head technology to manufacture printers, usually used to place
barcodes on cartons. Tridant also manufactured and sold ink and its
standard contract provided that it would license its ink-printing device
only if used in connection with ink supplied by Tridant. Independent
Inc., a competitor of Tridant in the ink market, challenged the
licensing arrangement as a tie-in sale under Section 1 and
monopolization under Section 2.

With respect to the tie-in sale, Independent Inc. did not prove
that the patent on print-head technology conferred significant
economic power but rather relied on *International Salt* (tying the
purchase of salt to the lease of patented salt utilization machines was
a violation without inquiry into defendant's market power) and
Jefferson Parish (suggesting that when the tying product is patented,
market power can be presumed).   Justice Stevens, rejected the
presumption of market power, with the following reasoning:

> Over the years, however, this Court's strong
> disapproval of tying arrangements has substantially
> diminished. Rather than relying on assumptions, in its more
> recent opinions the Court has required a showing of market
> power in the tying product....
>
> Rather than arguing that we should retain the rule of
> *per se* illegality [suggested by *International Salt*],
> respondent contends that we should endorse a rebuttable
> presumption that patentees possess market power when
> they condition the purchase of the patented product on an
> agreement to buy unpatented goods exclusively from the
> patentee. Respondent recognizes that a large number of
> valid patents have little, if any, commercial significance,
> but submits that those that are used to impose tying

132

arrangements on unwilling purchasers likely do exert significant market power. Hence, in respondent's view, the presumption would have no impact on patents of only slight value and would be justified, subject to being rebutted by evidence offered by the patentee, in cases in which the patent has sufficient value to enable the patentee to insist on acceptance of the tie.

Respondent also offers a narrower alternative, suggesting that we differentiate between tying arrangements involving the simultaneous purchase of two products that are arguably two components of a single product—such as the provision of surgical services and anesthesiology in the same operation, *Jefferson Parish*, 466 U. S., at 43 (O'Connor, J., concurring in judgment), or the licensing of one copyrighted film on condition that the licensee take a package of several films in the same transaction, *Loew's*, 371 U. S. 38—and a tying arrangement involving the purchase of unpatented goods over a period of time, a so-called "requirements tie." According to respondent, we should recognize a presumption of market power when faced with the latter type of arrangements because they provide a means for charging large volume purchasers a higher royalty for use of the patent than small purchasers must pay, a form of discrimination that "is strong evidence of market power." Brief for Respondent 27; see generally *Jefferson Parish*, 466 U. S., at 15, n. 23 (discussing price discrimination of this sort and citing sources).

The opinion that imported the "patent equals market power" presumption into our antitrust jurisprudence, however, provides no support for respondent's proposed alternative. In *International Salt*, it was the existence of the patent on the tying product, rather than the use of a requirements tie, that led the Court to presume market power. 332 U. S., at 395 ("The appellant's patents confer a limited monopoly of the invention they reward"). Moreover, the requirements tie in that case did not involve any price discrimination between large volume and small

133

volume purchasers or evidence of noncompetitive pricing. Instead, the leases at issue provided that if any competitor offered salt, the tied product, at a lower price, "the lessee should be free to buy in the open market, unless appellant would furnish the salt at an equal price." *Id.,* at 396.

As we have already noted, the vast majority of academic literature recognizes that a patent does not necessarily confer market power. Similarly, while price discrimination may provide evidence of market power, particularly if buttressed by evidence that the patentee has charged an above-market price for the tied package, see, *e.g.,* 10 Areeda ¶1769c, it is generally recognized that it also occurs in fully competitive markets.... We are not persuaded that the combination of these two factors should give rise to a presumption of market power when neither is sufficient to do so standing alone. Rather, the lesson to be learned from *International Salt* and the academic commentary is the same: Many tying arrangements, even those involving patents and requirements ties, are fully consistent with a free, competitive market. For this reason, we reject both respondent's proposed rebuttable presumption and their narrower alternative.

It is no doubt the virtual consensus among economists that has persuaded the enforcement agencies to reject the position that the Government took when it supported the *per se* rule that the Court adopted in the 1940's. See *supra,* at 8. In antitrust guidelines issued jointly by the Department of Justice and the Federal Trade Commission in 1995, the enforcement agencies stated that in the exercise of their prosecutorial discretion they "will not presume that a patent, copyright, or trade secret necessarily confers market power upon its owner." U. S. Dept. of Justice and FTC, Antitrust Guidelines for the Licensing of Intellectual Property §2.2 (Apr. 6, 1995), available at http://www.usdoj.gov/atr/public/guidelines/0558.pdf.... While that choice is not binding on the Court, it would be unusual for the Judiciary to replace the normal rule of lenity that is applied in criminal cases with a rule of severity for a special category of antitrust cases.

Congress, the antitrust enforcement agencies, and most economists have all reached the conclusion that a patent does not necessarily confer market power upon the patentee. Today, we reach the same conclusion, and therefore hold that, in all cases involving a tying arrangement, the plaintiff must prove that the defendant has market power in the tying product.

In this case, respondent reasonably relied on our prior opinions in moving for summary judgment without offering evidence defining the relevant market or proving that petitioners possess power within it. When the case returns to the District Court, respondent should therefore be given a fair opportunity to develop and introduce evidence on that issue, as well as any other issues that are relevant to its remaining §1 claims.

2. In April 2007, the Antitrust Division and the FTC issued a joint report on "Antitrust Enforcement and Intellectual Property Rights." With respect to tying they concluded:

> Legal and policy analysis of intellectual property bundling has evolved over time. Older case law, with its *per se* rule and presumption of market power, contends with the current analysis of the Agencies and some more recent lower court decisions that embody, in essence, a rule of reason approach. Moreover, the Supreme Court recently eliminated its rule presuming market power based on intellectual property. Panelists noted that, although intellectual property bundling may have anticompetitive potential in certain circumstances, there may also be significant efficiency justifications for such bundling in some cases. Thus, as a matter of their

135

prosecutorial discretion, the Agencies will apply the rule of reason when evaluating intellectual property tying and bundling agreements. Given the ubiquitous use of these arrangements by businesses lacking in market power and the efficiencies that such arrangements can often entail, these practices usually are not anticompetitive. When the Agencies do identify anticompetitive situations, however, they will pursue them.

Insert at the end of Note 2, page 961.

UNITED STATES v. DENTSPLY INTERNATIONAL, INC.

United States Court of Appeals, Third Circuit, 2005

399 F.3d 181

WEIS, J. In this antitrust case we conclude that an exclusivity policy imposed by a manufacturer on its dealers violates Section 2 of the Sherman Act. We come to that position because of the nature of the relevant market and the established effectiveness of the restraint despite the lack of long term contracts between the manufacturer and its dealers. Accordingly, we will reverse the judgment of the District Court in favor of the defendant and remand with directions to grant the Government's request for injunctive relief.

The Government alleged that Defendant, Dentsply International, Inc., acted unlawfully to maintain a monopoly in violation of Section 2 of the Sherman Act, 15 U.S.C. § 2; entered into illegal restrictive dealing agreements prohibited by Section 3 of the Clayton Act, 15 U.S.C. § 14; and used unlawful agreements in restraint of interstate trade in violation of Section 1 of the Sherman Act, 15 U.S.C. § 1. After a bench trial, the District Court denied the injunctive relief sought by the Government and entered judgment for defendant.

In its comprehensive opinion, the District Court found the following facts. Dentsply International, Inc. is a Delaware Corporation with its principal place of business in York Pennsylvania. It manufactures artificial teeth for use in dentures and other restorative appliances and sells them to dental products dealers. The dealers, in turn, supply the teeth and various other materials to dental laboratories, which fabricate dentures for sale to dentists.

The relevant market is the sale of prefabricated artificial teeth in the United States.

Because of advances in dental medicine, artificial tooth manufacturing is marked by a low or no-growth potential. Dentsply has long dominated the industry consisting of 12-13 manufacturers and enjoys a 75%--80% market share on a revenue basis, 67% on a unit basis, and is about 15 times larger than its next closest competitor. The other significant manufacturers and their market shares are:

5%	Ivoclar Vivadent, Inc.
3%	Vita Zahnfabrik
3%	Myerson LLC
2%	[19]American Tooth Industries
1%-2%	Universal Dental Company
1%	Heraeus Kulzer GmbH
1%	Davis, Schottlander & Davis, Ltd.

Dealers sell to dental laboratories a full range of metals, porcelains, acrylics, waxes, and other materials required to fabricate fixed or removal restorations. Dealers maintain large inventories of artificial teeth and carry thousands of products, other than teeth, made by hundreds of different manufacturers. Dentsply supplies $400 million of products other than teeth to its network of 23 dealers.

There are hundreds of dealers who compete on the basis of price and service among themselves, as well as with manufacturers who sell directly to laboratories. The dealer field has experienced significant consolidation with several large national and regional firms emerging.

For more than fifteen years, Dentsply has operated under a policy that discouraged its dealers from adding competitors' teeth to their lines of products. In 1993, Dentsply adopted "Dealer Criterion 6." It provides that in order to effectively promote Dentsply-York products, authorized dealers "may not add further tooth lines to their product offering." Dentsply operates on a purchase order basis with its distributors and, therefore, the relationship is essentially terminable at will. Dealer Criterion 6 was enforced against dealers with the exception of those who had carried competing products before 1993 and were "grandfathered" for sales of those products. Dentsply

---

[19] These companies sell directly to dental laboratories as well as to dealers.

rebuffed attempts by those particular distributors to expand their lines of competing products beyond the grandfathered ones.

Dentsply's five top dealers sell competing grandfathered brands of teeth. In 2001, their share of Dentsply's overall sales were

Zahn	39%
Patterson	28%
Darby	8%
Benco	4%
DLDS	<4%
TOTAL….	83%

16,000 dental laboratories fabricate restorations and a subset of 7,000 provide dentures. The laboratories compete with each other on the basis of price and service. Patients and dentists value fast service, particularly in the case of lost or damaged dentures. When laboratories' inventories cannot supply the necessary teeth, dealers may fill orders for walk-ins or use over-night express mail as does Dentsply, which dropped-shipped some 60% of orders from dealers.

Dealers have been dissatisfied with Dealer Criterion 6, but, at least in the recent past, none of them have given up the popular Dentsply teeth to take on a competitive line. Dentsply at one time considered selling directly to the laboratories, but abandoned the concept because of fear that dealers would retaliate by refusing to buy its other dental products.

In the 1990's Dentsply implemented aggressive sales campaigns, including efforts to promote its teeth in dental schools, providing rebates for laboratories' increased usage, and deploying a sales force dedicated to teeth, rather than the entire product mix. Its chief competitors did not as actively promote their products. Foreign manufacturers were slow to alter their designs to cope with American preferences, and, in at least one instance, pursued sales of porcelain products rather than plastic teeth.

Dentsply has had a reputation for aggressive price increases in the market and has created a high price umbrella. Its artificial tooth business is characterized as a "cash cow" whose profits are diverted to other operations of the company. A report in 1996 stated its profits from teeth since 1990 had increased 32% from $16.8 million to $22.2 million.

The District Court found that Dentsply's business justification for Dealer Criterion 6 was pretextual and designed expressly to exclude its rivals from access to dealers. The Court however concluded that other dealers were available and direct sales to laboratories was a viable method of doing business. Moreover, it concluded that Dentsply had not created a market with supra competitive pricing, dealers were free to leave the network at any time, and the Government failed to prove that Dentsply's actions "have been or could be successful in preventing 'new or potential competitors from gaining a foothold in the market.'" *United States v. Dentsply Int'l, Inc.,* 277 F.Supp.2d 387, 453 (D.Del.2003) (quoting *LePage* s, *Inc. v. 3M,* 324 F.3d 141, 159 (3d Cir.2003)). Accordingly, the Court concluded that the Government had failed to establish violations of Section 3 of the Clayton Act and Sections 1 or 2 of the Sherman Act.

The Government appealed, contending that a monopolist that prevents rivals from distributing through established dealers has maintained its monopoly by acting with predatory intent and violates Section 2. Additionally, the Government asserts that the maintenance of a 75%--80% market share, establishment of a price umbrella, repeated aggressive price increases and exclusion of competitors from a major source of distribution, show that Dentsply possesses monopoly power, despite the fact that rivals are not entirely excluded from the market and some of their prices are higher. The Government did not appeal the rulings under Section 1 of the Sherman Act or Section 3 of the Clayton Act.

Dentsply argues that rivals had obtained a share of the relevant market, that there are no artificially high prices and that competitors have access to all laboratories through existing or readily convertible systems. In addition, Dentsply asserts that its success is due to its leadership in promotion and marketing and not the imposition of Dealer Criterion 6.

I. STANDARD OF REVIEW

We exercise *de novo* review over the District Court's conclusions of law. However, we will not disturb its findings of fact unless they are clearly erroneous.

II. APPLICABLE LEGAL PRINCIPLES

. . . A violation of Section 2 consists of two elements: (1) possession of monopoly power and (2) ". . . maintenance of that power as distinguished from growth or development as a consequence of a superior product, business acumen, or historic accident." *Eastman Kodak Co. v. Image Technical Servs. Inc.* 504 U.S. 451, 480 1992 (citing *United States v. Grinnell Corp.,* 384 U.S. 563, 571 (1966)). "Monopoly power under § 2 requires . . . something greater than market power under § 1" *Eastman Kodak Co.* 504 U.S. at 481.

To run afoul of Section 2, a defendant must be guilty of illegal conduct "to foreclose competition, gain a competitive advantage, or to destroy a competitor." *Id. at* 482-83. Behavior that otherwise might comply with antitrust law may be impermissibly exclusionary when practiced by a monopolist. As we said in *LePage's, Inc. v.* 3M, 324 F.3d 141, 151-52 (3d Cir.2003), "a monopolist is not free to take certain actions that a company in a competitive (or even oligopolistic) market may take, because there is no market constraint on a monopolist's behavior." 3 Areeda & Turner, *Antitrust Law* 813, at 300-02 (1978).

Although not illegal in themselves, exclusive dealing arrangements can be an improper means of maintaining a monopoly. *United States v. Grinnell Corp.,* 384 U.S. 563 (1966); *LePage* s, 324 F.3d at 157. A prerequisite for such a violation is a finding that monopoly power exists. *See, e.g., LePage's,* 324 F.3d at 146. In addition, the exclusionary conduct must have an anti-competitive effect. If those elements are established, the monopolist still retains a defense of business justification. *See id. at* 152.

Unlawful maintenance of a monopoly is demonstrated by proof that a defendant has engaged in anti-competitive conduct that reasonably appears to be a significant contribution to maintaining monopoly power. *United States v. Microsoft,* 253 F.3d 34, 79 (D.C.Cir.2001); 3 Phillip E. Areeda & Herbert Hovenkamp, *Antitrust Law,* ¶ 651c at 78 (1996). Predatory or exclusionary practices in themselves are not sufficient. There must be proof that competition, not merely competitors, has been harmed. *LePage's,* 324 F.3d at 162.

III. MONOPOLY POWER

. . . [T]he existence of monopoly power may be inferred from a predominant share of the market, *Grinnell* 384 U.S. at 571, and the size of that portion is a primary factor in determining whether power exists. *Pennsylvania Dental Assn v. Med. Serv. Assn of Pa., 745 F.2d 248, 260 (3d Cir.1984).*

A less than predominant share of the market combined with other relevant factors may suffice to demonstrate monopoly power. *Fineman v. Armstrong World Indus.,* 980 F.2d 171, 201 (3d Cir.1992). Absent other pertinent factors, a share significantly larger than 55% has been required to established prima facie market power. *Id.* at 201. Other germane factors include the size and strength of competing firms, freedom of entry, pricing trends and practices in the industry, ability of consumers to substitute comparable goods, and consumer demand.

A. The Relevant Market

Defining the relevant market is an important part of the analysis. The District Court found the market to be "the sale of prefabricated artificial teeth in the United States." *United States v. Dentply Int'l Inc.,* 277 F.Supp.2d 387, 396 (D.Del.2003). Further, the Court found that "[t]he manufacturers participating in the United States artificial tooth market historically have distributed their teeth into the market in one of three ways: (1) directly to dental labs; (2) through dental dealers; or (3) through a hybrid system combining manufacturer direct sales and dental dealers." The Court also found that the "labs are the relevant consumers for prefabricated artificial teeth."

There is no dispute that the laboratories are the ultimate consumers because they buy the teeth at the point in the process where they are incorporated into another product. Dentsply points out that its representatives concentrate their efforts at the laboratories as well as at dental schools and dentists.

During oral argument, Dentsply's counsel said, "the dealers are not the market . . . [t]he market is the dental labs that consume the product." Emphasizing the importance of end users, Dentsply argues that the District Court understood the relevant market to be the sales of artificial teeth to dental laboratories in the United States. Although the Court used the word "market" in a number of differing contexts, the findings demonstrate that the relevant market is not as narrow as Dentsply would have it. The Court said that Dentsply "has had a persistently high market share between 75% and 80% on a revenue basis, in the artificial tooth market." Dentsply sells only to dealers and the narrow definition of market that it urges upon us would be completely inconsistent with that finding of the District Court.

The Court went on to find that Ivoclar "has the second-highest share of the market, at approximately 5%." Ivoclar sells directly to the laboratories. Therefore, these two findings establish that the relevant market in this case includes sales to dealers and direct sales to the laboratories. Other findings on Dentsply's "market share" are consistent with this understanding.

These findings are persuasive that the District Court understood, as do we, the relevant market to be the total sales of artificial teeth to the laboratories and the dealers combined.

Dentsply's apparent belief that a relevant market cannot include sales both to the final consumer and a middleman is refuted in the closely analogous case of *Allen-Myland, Inc. v. IBM Corp.,* 33 F.3d 194 (3d Cir.1994). In that case, IBM sold mainframe computers directly to the ultimate consumers and also sold to companies that leased computers to ultimate users. We concluded that the relevant market encompassed the sales directly to consumers as well as those to leasing companies. ". . . to the extent that leasing companies deal in used, non-IBM mainframes that have not already been counted in the sales market, these machines belong in the relevant market for large-scale mainframe computers." *Id.* at 203.

To resolve any doubt, therefore, we hold that the relevant market here is the sale of artificial teeth in the United States both to laboratories and to the dental dealers.

B. Power to Exclude

Dentsply's share of the market is more than adequate to establish a prima facie case of power. In addition, Dentsply has held its dominant share for more than ten years and has fought aggressively to maintain that imbalance. One court has commented that, "[i]n evaluating monopoly power, it is not market share that counts, but the ability to *maintain* market share." *United States v. Syufy Enters.*, 903 F.2d 659, 665-66 (9th Cir.1990).

The District Court found that it could infer monopoly power because of the predominant market share, but despite that factor, concluded that Dentsply's tactics did not preclude competition from marketing their products directly to the dental laboratories. "Dentsply does not have the power to exclude competitors from the ultimate consumer." *United States v. Dentsply Int'l, Inc.*, 277 F.Supp.2d 387, 452 (D.Del.2003).

Moreover, the Court determined that failure of Dentsply's two main rivals, Vident and Ivoclar, to obtain significant market shares resulted from their own business decisions to concentrate on other product lines, rather than implement active sales efforts for teeth.

The District Court's evaluation of Ivoclar and Vident business practices as a cause of their failure to secure more of the market is not persuasive. The reality is that over a period of years, because of Dentsply's domination of dealers, direct sales have not been a practical alternative for most manufacturers. It has not been so much the competitors' less than enthusiastic efforts at competition that produced paltry results, as it is the blocking of access to the key dealers. This is the part of the real market that is denied to the rivals.

The apparent lack of aggressiveness by competitors is not a matter of apathy, but a reflection of the effectiveness of Dentsply's exclusionary policy. Although its rivals could theoretically convince a dealer to buy their products and drop Dentsply's line, that has not occurred. In *United States v. Visa U.S.A..* 344 F.3d at 229, 240 2d Cir.2003), the Court of Appeals held that similar evidence indicated that defendants had excluded their rivals from the marketplace and thus demonstrated monopoly power.

The Supreme Court on more than one occasion has emphasized that economic realities rather than a formalistic approach must govern review of antitrust activity. "Legal presumptions that rest on formalistic distinctions rather than actual market realities are generally disfavored in antitrust law . . . in determining the existence of market power . . . this Court has examined closely the economic reality of the market at issue." *Eastman Kodak Co. v. Image Technical Servs. Inc.* 504 U.S. 451, 466-67 (1992). "If we look at substance rather than form, there is little room for debate." *United States v. Sealy, Inc.,* 388 U.S. 350, 352 (1967). We echoed that standard in *Weiss v. York Hosp.,* 745 F.2d 786, 815 (3d Cir.1984). "Antitrust policy requires the courts to seek the economic substance of an arrangement, not merely its form." *Id.*

The realities of the artificial tooth market were candidly expressed by two former managerial employees of Dentsply when they explained their rules of engagement. One testified that Dealer Criterion 6 was designed to "block competitive distribution points." He continued, "Do not allow competition to achieve toeholds in dealers; tie up dealers; do not 'free up' key players."

Another former manager said:
You don't want your competition with your distributors, you don't want to give the distributors an opportunity to sell a competitive product. And you don't want to give your end user, the customer, meaning a laboratory and/or a dentist, a choice. He has to buy Dentsply teeth. That's the only thing that's available. The only place you can get it is through the distributor and the only one that the distributor is selling is Dentsply teeth. That's your objective.

These are clear expressions of a plan to maintain monopolistic power.

The District Court detailed some ten separate incidents in which Dentsply required agreement by new as well as long-standing dealers not to handle competitors' teeth. For example, when the DLDS firm considered adding two other tooth lines because of customers' demand, Dentsply threatened to sever access not only to its teeth, but to other dental products as well. DLDS yielded to that pressure. The termination of Trinity Dental, which had previously sold Dentsply products other than teeth, was a similar instance. When Trinity wanted to add teeth to its line for the first time and chose a competitor, Dentsply refused to supply other dental products.

Dentsply also pressured Atlanta Dental, Marcus Dental, Thompson Dental, Patterson Dental and Pearson Dental Supply when they carried or considered adding competitive lines. In another incident, Dentsply recognized DTS as a dealer so as to "fully eliminate the competitive threat that [DTS locations] pose by representing Vita and Ivoclar in three of four regions."

The evidence demonstrated conclusively that Dentsply had supremacy over the dealer network and it was at that crucial point in the distribution chain that monopoly power over the market for artificial teeth was established. The reality in this case is that the firm that ties up the key dealers rules the market.

In concluding that Dentsply lacked the power to exclude competitors from the laboratories, "the ultimate consumers," the District Court overlooked the point that the relevant market was the "sale" of artificial teeth to both dealers and laboratories. Although some sales were made by manufacturers to the laboratories, overwhelming numbers were made to dealers. Thus, the Court's scrutiny should have been applied not to the "ultimate consumers" who used the teeth, but to the "customers" who purchased the teeth, the relevant category which included dealers as well as laboratories. This mis-focus led the District Court into clear error.

The factual pattern here is quite similar to that in *LePage's, Inc. v. 3M,* 324 F.3d 141 (3d Cir.2003). There, a manufacturer of transparent tape locked up high volume distribution channels by means of substantial discounts on a range of its other products. *LePage's,* 324 F.3d at 144, 160-62. We concluded that the use of exclusive dealing and bundled rebates to the detriment of the rival manufacturer violated Section 2. *See LePage's,* 324 F.3d at 159.

Similarly, in *Microsoft,* the Court of Appeals for the D.C. Circuit concluded that, through the use of exclusive contracts with key dealers, a manufacturer foreclosed competitors from a substantial percentage of the available opportunities for product distribution. *See Microsoft,* 253 F.3d at 70-71.

The evidence in this case demonstrates that for a considerable time, through the use of Dealer Criterion 6 Dentsply has been able to exclude competitors from the dealers' network, a narrow, but heavily traveled channel to the dental laboratories.

C. Pricing

An increase in pricing is another factor used in evaluating existence of market power. Although in this case the evidence of exclusion is stronger than that of Dentsply's control of prices, testimony about suspect pricing is also found in this record.

The District Court found that Dentsply had a reputation for aggressive price increases in the market. It is noteworthy that experts for both parties testified that were Dealer Criterion 6 abolished, prices would fall. A former sales manager for Dentsply agreed that the company's share of the market would diminish should Dealer Criterion 6 no longer be in effect. In 1993, Dentsply's regional sales manager complained, "[w]e need to moderate our increases -- twice a year for the last few years was not good." Large scale distributors observed that Dentsply's policy created a high price umbrella.

Although Dentsply's prices fall between those of Ivoclar and Vita's premium tooth lines, Dentsply did not reduce its prices when competitors elected not to follow its increases. Dentsply's profit margins have been growing over the years. The picture is one of a manufacturer that sets prices with little concern for its competitors, "something a firm without a monopoly would have been unable to do." *Microsoft,* 253 F.3d at 58. The results have been favorable to Dentsply, but of no benefit to consumers.

Moreover, even "if monopoly power has been acquired or maintained through improper means, the fact that the power has not been used to extract [a monopoly price] provides no succor to the monopolist." *Microsoft*, 253 F.3d at 57 (quoting *Berkey Photo, Inc. v. Eastman Kodak, Co.,* 603 F.2d 263, 274 (2d Cir.1979)). The record of long duration of the exclusionary tactics and anecdotal evidence of their efficacy make it clear that power existed and was used effectively. The District Court erred in concluding that Dentsply lacked market power.

IV. ANTI-COMPETITIVE EFFECTS

Having demonstrated that Dentsply possessed market power, the Government must also establish the second element of a Section 2 claim, that the power was used "to foreclose competition." *United States v. Griffith,* 334 U.S. 100, 107 (1948). Assessing anti-competitive effect is important in evaluating a challenge to a violation of Section 2. Under that Section of the Sherman Act, it is not necessary that all competition be removed from the market. The test is not total foreclosure, but whether the challenged practices bar a substantial number of rivals or severely restrict the market's ambit. *LePage's*, 324 F.3d at 159-60; *Microsoft,* 253 F.3d at 69.

> A leading treatise explains,
> A set of strategically planned exclusive dealing contracts may slow the rival's expansion by requiring it to develop alternative outlets for its products or rely at least temporarily on inferior or more expensive outlets. Consumer injury results from the delay that the dominant firm imposes on the smaller rival's growth. Herbert Hovenkamp, *Antitrust Law* ¶ 1802c, at 64 (2d ed.2002).

By ensuring that the key dealers offer Dentsply teeth either as the only or dominant choice, Dealer Criterion 6 has a significant effect in preserving Dentsply's monopoly. It helps keep sales of competing teeth below the critical level necessary for any rival to pose a real threat to Dentsply's market share. As such, Dealer Criterion 6 is a solid pillar of harm to competition. *See LePage's.* 324 F.3d 141, 159 (3d Cir.2003) ("When a monopolist's actions are designed to prevent one or more new or potential competitors from gaining a foothold in the market by exclusionary, i.e. predatory, conduct, its success in that goal is not only injurious to the potential competitor but also to competition in general.").

148

A. Benefits of Dealers

Dentsply has always sold its teeth through dealers. Vita sells through Vident, its exclusive distributor and domestic affiliate, but has a mere 3% of the market. Ivoclar had some relationship with dealers in the past, but its direct relationship with laboratories yields only a 5% share.

A number of factors are at work here. For a great number of dental laboratories, the dealer is the preferred source for artificial teeth. Although the District Court observed that "labs prefer to buy direct because of potential cost savings attributable to the elimination of the dealer middleman [,]" in fact, laboratories are driven by the realities of the marketplace to buy far more heavily from dealers than manufacturers. This may be largely attributed to the beneficial services, credit function, economies of scale and convenience that dealers provide to laboratories, benefits which are otherwise unavailable to them when they buy direct.

The record is replete with evidence of benefits provided by dealers. For example, they provide laboratories the benefit of "one stop-shopping" and extensive credit services. Because dealers typically carry the products of multiple manufacturers, a laboratory can order, with a single phone call to a dealer, products from multiple sources. Without dealers, in most instances laboratories would have to place individual calls to each manufacturer, expend the time, and pay multiple shipping charges to fill the same orders.

The dealer-provided reduction in transaction costs and time represents a substantial benefit, one that the District Court minimized when it characterized "one stop shopping" as merely the ability to order from a single manufacturer all the materials necessary for crown, bridge and denture construction. Although a laboratory can call a manufacturer directly and purchase any product made by it, the laboratory is unable to procure from that source products made by its competitors. Thus, purchasing through dealers, which as a class traditionally carries the products of multiple vendors, surmounts this shortcoming, as well as offers other advantages.

Buying through dealers also enables laboratories to take advantage of obtaining discounts. Because they engage in price competition to gain laboratories' business, dealers often discount manufacturers' suggested laboratory price for artificial teeth. There is no finding on this record that manufacturers offer similar discounts.

Another service dealers perform is taking back tooth returns. Artificial teeth and denture returns are quite common in dentistry. Approximately 30% of all laboratory tooth purchases are returned for exchange or credit. The District Court disregarded this benefit on the ground that all manufacturers except Vita accept tooth returns. However, in equating dealer and manufacturer returns, the District Court overlooked the fact that using dealers, rather than manufacturers, enables laboratories to consolidate their returns. In a single shipment to a dealer, a laboratory can return the products of a number of manufacturers, and so economize on shipping, time, and transaction costs.

Conversely, when returning products directly to manufacturers, a laboratory must ship each vendor's product separately and must track each exchange individually. Consolidating returns yields savings of time, effort, and costs.

Dealers also provide benefits to manufacturers, perhaps the most obvious of which is efficiency of scale. Using select high-volume dealers, as opposed to directly selling to hundreds if not thousands of laboratories, greatly reduces the manufacturer's distribution costs and credit risks. Dentsply, for example, currently sells to twenty three dealers. If it were instead to sell directly to individual laboratories, Dentsply would incur significantly higher transaction costs, extension of credit burdens, and credit risks.

Although a laboratory that buys directly from a manufacturer may be able to avoid the marginal costs associated with "middleman" dealers, any savings must be weighed against the benefits, savings, and convenience offered by dealers.

In addition, dealers provide manufacturers more marketplace exposure and sales representative coverage than manufacturers are able to generate on their own. Increased exposure and sales coverage traditionally lead to greater sales.

B. "Viability" of Direct Sales

The benefits that dealers provide manufacturers help make dealers the preferred distribution channels -- in effect, the "gateways" -- to the artificial teeth market. Nonetheless, the District Court found that selling direct is a "viable" method of distributing artificial teeth. But we are convinced that it is "viable" only in the sense that it is "possible," not that it is practical or feasible in the market as it exists and functions. The District Court's conclusion of "viability" runs counter to the facts and is clearly erroneous. On the entire evidence, we are "left with the definite and firm conviction that a mistake has been committed." *United States v. Igbonwa,* 120 F.3d 437, 440 (3d Cir.1997).

It is true that Dentsply's competitors can sell directly to the dental laboratories and an insignificant number do. The undeniable reality, however, is that dealers have a controlling degree of access to the laboratories. The long-entrenched Dentsply dealer network with its ties to the laboratories makes it impracticable for a manufacturer to rely on direct distribution to the laboratories in any significant amount. *See United States v. Visa U.S.A.,* 344 F.3d 229, 240 (2d Cir.2003).

That some manufacturers resort to direct sales and are even able to stay in business by selling directly is insufficient proof that direct selling is an effective means of competition. The proper inquiry is not whether direct sales enable a competitor to "survive" but rather whether direct selling "poses a real threat" to defendant's monopoly. *See Microsoft,* 253 F.3d at 71. The minuscule 5% and 3% market shares eked out by direct-selling manufacturers Ivoclar and Vita, Dentsply's "primary competitors," reveal that direct selling poses little threat to Dentsply.

C. Efficacy of Dealer Criterion 6

Although the parties to the sales transactions consider the exclusionary arrangements to be agreements, they are technically only a series of independent sales. Dentsply sells teeth to the dealers on an individual transaction basis and essentially the arrangement is "at-will." Nevertheless, the economic elements involved -- the large share of the market held by Dentsply and its conduct excluding competing manufacturers - realistically make the arrangements here as effective as those in written contracts. *See Monsanto Co. v. Spray-Rite Serv. Corp.,* 465 U.S. 752, 764 n. 9 (1984).

Given the circumstances present in this case, there is no ground to doubt the effectiveness of the exclusive dealing arrangement. In *LePage's,* 324 F.3d at 162, we concluded that 3M's aggressive rebate program damaged LePage's ability to compete and thereby harmed competition itself. LePage's simply could not match the discounts that 3M provided. *LePage's,* 324 F.3d at 161. Similarly, in this case, in spite of the legal ease with which the relationship can be terminated, the dealers have a strong economic incentive to continue carrying Dentsply's teeth. Dealer Criterion 6 is not edentulous.[20]

D. Limitation of Choice

An additional anti-competitive effect is seen in the exclusionary practice here that limits the choices of products open to dental laboratories, the ultimate users. A dealer locked into the Dentsply line is unable to heed a request for a different manufacturers' product and, from the standpoint of convenience, that

---

[20] In some cases which we find distinguishable, courts have indicated that exclusive dealing contracts of short duration are not violations of the antitrust laws. *See, e.g., CDC Techs., Inc. v. IDEXX Labs., Inc..* 186 F.3d 74, 81 (2d Cir.1999) ("distributors" only provided sales leads and sales increased after competitor imposed exclusive dealing arrangements); *Omega Envtl., Inc. v. Gilbarco. Inc.,* 127 F.3d 1157. 1163 (9th Cir.1997) (manufacturer with 55% market share sold both to consumers and distributors, market showed decreasing prices and fluctuating shares); *Rvko Mfg., Co. v. Eden Servs.,* 823 F.2d 1215 (8th Cir.1987) (manufacturer sold its products through direct sales and distributors); *Roland Mach. Co. v. Dresser Indus., Inc.,* 749 F.2d 380 (7th Cir.1984) (contract between dealer and manufacturer did not contain exclusive dealing provision).

inability to some extent impairs the laboratory's choice in the marketplace.

As an example, current and potential customers requested Atlanta Dental to carry Vita teeth. Although these customers could have ordered the Vita teeth from Vident in California, Atlanta Dental's tooth department manager believed that they were interested in a local source. Atlanta Dental chose not to add the Vita line after being advised that doing so would cut off access to Dentsply teeth, which constituted over 90% ° of its tooth sales revenue.

Similarly, DLDS added Universal and Vita teeth to meet customers' requests, but dropped them after Dentsply threatened to stop supplying its product. Marcus Dental began selling another brand of teeth at one point because of customer demand in response to supply problems with Dentsply. After Dentsply threatened to enforce Dealer Criterion 6, Marcus dropped the other line.

E. Barriers to Entry

Entrants into the marketplace must confront Dentsply's power over the dealers. The District Court's theory that any new or existing manufacturer may "steal" a Dentsply dealer by offering a superior product at a lower price, *see Omega Environmental. Inc. v. Gilbarco.* 127 F.3d 1157 (9th Cir.1997), simply has not proved to be realistic. To the contrary, purloining efforts have been thwarted by Dentsply's longtime, vigorous and successful enforcement actions. The paltry penetration in the market by competitors over the years has been a refutation of theory by tangible and measurable results in the real world.

The levels of sales that competitors could project in wooing dealers were minuscule compared to Dentsply's, whose long-standing relationships with these dealers included sales of other dental products. For example, Dentsply threatened Zahn with termination if it started selling Ivoclar teeth. At the time, Ivoclar's projected $1.2 million in sales were 85% lower than Zahn's $8 million in Dentsply's sales.

When approached by Leach & Dillon and Heraeus Kulzer, Zahn's sales of Dentsply teeth had increased to $22-$23 million per year. In comparison, the president of Zahn expected that Leach & Dillon would add up to $200,000 (or less than 1% of its Dentsply's sales) and Heraeus Kulzer would contribute "maybe hundreds of thousands." Similarly, Vident's $1 million in projected sales amounted to 5.5% of its $18 million in annual Dentsply's sales.

The dominant position of Dentsply dealers as a gateway to the laboratories was confirmed by potential entrants to the market. The president of Ivoclar testified that his company was unsuccessful in its approach to the two large national dealers and other regional dealers. He pointed out that it is more efficient to sell through dealers and, in addition, they offered an entre to future customers by promotions in the dental schools.

Further evidence was provided by a Vident executive, who testified about failed attempts to distribute teeth through ten identified dealers. He attributed the lack of success to their fear of losing the right to sell Dentsply teeth.

Another witness, the president of Dillon Company, advised Davis, Schottlander & Davis, a tooth manufacturer, "to go through the dealer network because anything else is futile. . . . Dealers control the tooth industry. If you don't have distribution with the dealer network, you don't have distribution." Some idea of the comparative size of the dealer network was illustrated by the Dillon testimony: "Zahn does $2 billion, I do a million-seven. Patterson does over a billion dollars, I do a million-seven. I have ten employees, they have 6,000."

Dealer Criterion 6 created a strong economic incentive for dealers to reject competing lines in favor of Dentsply's teeth. As in *LePage*'s, the rivals simply could not provide dealers with a comparable economic incentive to switch. Moreover, the record demonstrates that Dentsply added Darby as a dealer "to block Vita from a key competitive distribution point." According to a Dentsply executive, the "key issue" was "Vita's potential distribution system." He explained that Vita was "having a tough time getting teeth out to customers. One of their key weaknesses is their distribution system."

Teeth are an important part of a denture, but they are but one component. The dealers are dependent on serving all of the laboratories' needs and must carry as many components as practicable. The artificial teeth business cannot realistically be evaluated in isolation from the rest of the dental fabrication industry.

> A leading treatise provides a helpful analogy to this situation: [S]uppose that mens's bow ties cannot efficiently be sold in stores that deal exclusively in bow ties or even ties generally; rather, they must be sold in department stores where clerics can spread their efforts over numerous products and the ties can be sold in conjunction with shirts and suits. Suppose further that a dominant bow tie manufacturer should impose exclusive dealing on a town's only three department stores. In this case the rival bow tie maker cannot easily enter. Setting up another department store is an unneeded and a very large investment in proportion to its own production, which we assume is only bow ties, but any store that offers less will be an inefficient and costly seller of bow ties. As a result, such exclusive dealing could either exclude the nondominant bow tie maker or else raise its costs in comparison to the costs of the dominant firm. While the department stores might prefer to sell the ties of multiple manufacturers, if faced with an "all-or-nothing" choice they may accede to the dominant firm's wish for exclusive dealing. Herbert Hovenkamp, *Antitrust Law* ¶ 1802e3, at 78-79 (2d ed.2002).

Criterion 6 imposes an "all-or-nothing" choice on the dealers. The fact that dealers have chosen not to drop Dentsply teeth in favor of a rival's brand demonstrates that they have acceded to heavy economic pressure.

This case does not involve a dynamic, volatile market like that in *Microsoft,* 253 F.3d at 70, or a proven alternative distribution channel. The mere existence of other avenues of distribution is insufficient without an assessment of their overall significance to the market. The economic impact of an exclusive dealing arrangement is amplified in the stagnant, no growth context of the artificial tooth field.

155

Dentsply's authorized dealers are analogous to the high volume retailers at issue in *LePage's*. Although the dealers are distributors and the stores in *LePage's*, such as K-Mart and Staples, are retailers, this is a distinction in name without a substantive difference. *LePage's*, 324 F.3d at 144. Selling to a few prominent retailers provided "substantially reduced distribution costs" and "cheap, high volume supply lines." *Id.* at 160 n. 14. The manufacturer sold to a few high volume businesses and benefitted from the widespread locations and strong customer goodwill that prominent retailers provided as opposed to selling directly to end-user consumers or to a multitude of smaller retailers. There are other ways across the "river" to consumers, but high volume retailers provided the most effective bridge.

The same is true here. The dealers provide the same advantages to Dentsply, widespread locations and long-standing relationships with dental labs, that the high volume retailers provided to 3M. Even orders that are drop-shipped directly from Dentsply to a dental lab originate through the dealers. This underscores that Dentsply's dealers provide a critical link to end-users.

Although the District Court attributed some of the lack of competition to Ivoclar's and Vident's bad business decisions, that weakness was not ascribed to other manufacturers. Logically, Dealer Criterion 6 cannot be both a cause of the competitors' lower promotional expenditures which hurt their market positions, and at the same time, be unrelated to their exclusion from the marketplace. Moreover, in *Microsoft*, in spite of the competitors' self-imposed problems, the Court of Appeals held that Microsoft possessed monopoly power because it benefitted from a significant barrier to entry. *Microsoft*, 253 F.3d at 55.

Dentsply's grip on its 23 authorized dealers effectively choked off the market for artificial teeth, leaving only a small sliver for competitors. The District Court erred when it minimized that situation and focused on a theoretical feasibility of success through direct access to the dental labs. While we may assume that Dentsply won its preeminent position by fair competition, that fact does not permit maintenance of its monopoly by unfair practices. We conclude that on this record, the Government established that Dentsply's

156

exclusionary policies and particularly Dealer Criterion 6 violated Section 2.

V. BUSINESS JUSTIFICATION

As noted earlier, even if a company exerts monopoly power, it may defend its practices by establishing a business justification. The Government, having demonstrated harm to competition, the burden shifts to Dentsply to show that Dealer Criterion 6 promotes a sufficiently pro-competitive objective. *United States v. Brown Univ.,* 5 F.3d 658, 669 (3d Cir.1993). Significantly, Dentsply has not done so. The District Court found that "Dentsply's asserted justifications for its exclusionary policies are inconsistent with its announced reason for the exclusionary policies, its conduct enforcing the policy, its rival suppliers' actions, and dealers' behavior in the marketplace."

Some of the dealers opposed Dentsply's policy as exerting too much control over the products they may sell, but the grandfathered dealers were no less efficient than the exclusive ones, nor was there any difference in promotional support. Nor was there any evidence of existence of any substantial variation in the level of service provided by exclusive and grandfathered dealers to the laboratories.

The record amply supports the District Court's conclusion that Dentsply's alleged justification was pretextual and did not excuse its exclusionary practices.

VI. AVAILABILITY OF SHERMAN ACT SECTION 2 RELIEF

One point remains. Relying on *dicta* in *Tampa Electric Co. v. Nashville Coal Co.,* 365 U.S. 320 (1961), the District Court said that because it had found no liability under the stricter standards of Section 3 of the Clayton Act, it followed that there was no violation of Section 2 of the Sherman Act. However, as we explained in *LePage's* v. 3M, 324 F.3d at 157 n. 10, a finding in favor of the defendant under Section 1 of the Sherman Act and Section 3 of the Clayton Act, did not "preclude the application of evidence of . . . exclusive dealing to support the [Section 2 claim." All of the evidence in the record here applies to the Section 2 claim and, as in

LePage's, a finding of liability under Section 2 supports a judgment against defendant. . . . Here, the Government can obtain all the relief to which it is entitled under Section 2 and has chosen to follow that path without reference to Section 1 of the Sherman Act or Section 3 of the Clayton Act. We find no obstacle to that procedure.

CHAPTER 9: MERGERS

Insert after *Heinz*, page 1080.

NOTE

United States v. *Oracle Corp.*, 331 F. Supp. 2d 1098 (D.C. Cal. 2004). In 2004, the Department of Justice and 10 states sought a preliminary injunction to block Oracle Corporation from acquiring People Soft, Inc., two companies that manufactured and sold a type of application software that automated business data processing ("EAS"). Programs that provide EAS functions include human relations management ("HRM"), financial management systems ("FMS"), customer relations management, supply chain management, product life cycle management, and business intelligence, among many others. The government claimed that the combination of the HRM and FMS functions, and then only at the high end of those two application systems, constituted a relevant market. One other large company - SAP - (like Oracle and People Soft) offered a comprehensive set of software, and many other companies offered specific sets of software to the market.

The case depended largely on relevant product market definition, and that issue in turn depended upon what various witnesses testified about the ability of the combined firms to raise price after the proposed merger.

In support of their proposed product market definition, the government presented at trial or through depositions 10 customer witnesses, five industry witnesses, two systems integration witnesses, three expert witnesses, and a few others who according to the court appeared mostly to fill a gap or two in the evidence or to supply "spice" for the record. Typically, competitor testimony has been regarded as suspect because rivals may be comfortable with the idea of a merger that leads to higher prices, which would lead to higher profits for all competitors in the market. On the other hand, customer evidence has in the past been regarded as fairly persuasive. The District Court, in denying a preliminary injunction, took a different view of the customer evidence in this particular case. After summarizing witness testimony, the Court concluded:

159

Plaintiffs' Evidence of a High Function HRM & FMS
Market

. . . The court will not attempt to recount or even summarize the entire evidentiary record. Given the quantity of evidence, that would be unduly time-consuming and is unnecessary. It suffices to note that the laboring oar of the plaintiffs' case was pulled by the customer witnesses (whom plaintiffs' counsel described as their strongest witnesses), by some of the systems integrator and industry witnesses and by the experts.

[Gorriz of Daimler testified]: Daimler has about 365,000 employees worldwide in about 100 manufacturing facilities. Since 1996, Daimler has used SAP as its financial management software. Daimler requires highly functional HRM to accommodate its large number of employees and to comply with the differing labor laws and union agreements in different countries. For its HRM needs, Daimler currently uses PeopleSoft. Daimler chose PeopleSoft based upon its reputation and the fact that companies of comparable size to Daimler have had success with PeopleSoft HRM. But when Daimler was first searching for an HRM vendor in 1996, Gorriz stated that "only SAP, PeopleSoft or Oracle could serve [Daimler's] needs for the HR management." Gorriz stated that Daimler considered no other vendors. Daimler's legacy system was "too old" for the company seriously to consider upgrading. Daimler did not consider outsourcing to be an option because Daimler's HRM requirements were, Gorriz testified, "too complex." Further, if Oracle, SAP or PeopleSoft were to increase their price for HRM by 10 percent, Gorriz stated that Daimler "would not consider any offer" from any other vendors.

Bob Bullock, Senior Vice President and Chief Information Officer of CH2M Hill, testified about the ERP needs of that civil and environmental engineering firm. CH2M Hill has 14,000 employees, 200 worldwide offices and over $2 billion in annual revenue. CH2M Hill has used Oracle FMS since 1993, but in 2002 the company decided to replace its legacy HRM software. Bullock stated that through consultation with the Gartner Group, CH2M Hill was given a list of HRM vendors. CH2M Hill did not seriously consider SAP, as it "was a very complex product" and had a "reputation for being a costly product." In Bullock's opinion, there were only two candidates, Oracle and PeopleSoft. CH2M Hill never considered outsourcing, Lawson or remaining on its legacy system. Oracle and PeopleSoft both offered initial bids between $1.5 and 41.6 million. Bullock stated that if this price had been 10 percent higher, CH2M Hill would not walked away from the deal with Oracle or PeopleSoft.

Curtis Wolfe, CIO for the State of North Dakota, testified about the state's process of picking an ERP vendor. North Dakota has approximately 10,000 full and part-time employees, 58 state agencies and a budget of $5 billion. In 2002, the state decided to buy a full ERP program that included FMS and HRM. North Dakota had a unique need in that it required that its ERP serve the state's higher education facilities as well. *Id.* North Dakota had six vendors submit proposals: Oracle, PeopleSoft, SAP, SCT, Jenzabar (a partner of Lawson) and Microsoft's Great Plains. The state eliminated SAP, Great Plains and Jenzabar almost immediately. SAP was too expensive, while Jenzabar and Great Plains did not have the required functionality. SCT did not make the final round; while SCT met the functionality for the higher education area, it could not do so with state agency needs. Oracle and PeopleSoft were in head to head competition and Wolfe testified that he believes that this caused the state to get a $6 to $8 million lower final bid from each vendor. If these final offers had been 10 percent higher, Wolfe stated that North Dakota would not have turned to Lawson, Microsoft, SCT, outsourcing or writing its own software.

Kenneth Johnsen, Chief of Technology for Pepsi Americas, testified as to his concerns about the Oracle/PeopleSoft merger. Pepsi Americas is the second largest bottler of Pepsi-brand soft drinks within the Pepsi system and the third largest bottler worldwide. Pepsi Americas has over 15,000 employees and annual revenues of about $3.2 billion. Pepsi Americas uses PeopleSoft ERP in its North America operations and SAP ERP in its European operations. Johnsen testified that he has "a concern" about the impact of this merger on the long-term effectiveness of the PeopleSoft ERP. Johnsen is concerned that a post-merger Oracle, while agreeing to maintain the PeopleSoft ERP, will not provide enhancements to the functionality of the software (i.e., upgrades). To Johnsen this leaves

161

Pepsi Americas with two options: constantly upgrade with point solutions (not his desired choice) or buy ERP from a new vendor. When asked, what vendors he could turn to meet his ERP needs, Johnsen claims there are no options outside of Oracle, PeopleSoft and SAP.

Scott Wesson, Senior Vice President and Chief Information Officer of AIMCO, discussed the company's choices for FMS and HRM software. AIMCO is the largest owner and operator of apartment buildings in the United States. The company owns approximately 2000 complexes in 47 states and the District of Columbia. AIMCO has over 6,500 employees and an annual revenue of about $1.5 billion. For its FMS, AIMCO uses PeopleSoft's financial suite. For its HR payroll systems, AIMCO currently uses Lawson. In 2002, AIMCO began to reevaluate its HRM options and it hired Towers Perrin consult in this process. Towers Perrin told AIMCO that only three vendors could meet AIMCO's HRM needs: PeopleSoft, Oracle and SAP. (There was no objection to the question that elicited this response). Wesson stated that AIMCO decided not to upgrade to the latest version of Lawson because it would have cost AIMCO "about the same * * * as it would to go with a new system" and also, Lawson "[was] lacking some key features" that AIMCO was looking for. AIMCO was deciding between Oracle and PeopleSoft when Oracle first made its tender offer to PeopleSoft. Wesson stated that because of this proposed merger, he believes PeopleSoft gave him a "very good deal" on the HRM. Wesson testified that Oracle agreed to match any price offered by PeopleSoft. Wesson said AIMCO ultimately chose PeopleSoft because PeopleSoft had guaranteed to pay AIMCO three times the contract price should there be a "change of ownership" at PeopleSoft. AIMCO is expecting to implement the PeopleSoft system in late 2004 or early 2005. Moreover, Wesson stated, AIMCO does not consider outsourcing to be a viable option because it is not quick to respond to "last minute changes," such as new benefits programs. Best of breed solutions are too expensive for AIMCO to consider.

Richard Cichanowicz, Vice President of Systems Integration of Nextel, testified about the wireless services company's ERP needs. Nextel has 13 million subscribers, over $8 billion in annual revenue 17,000 [transcript incorrect] employees. Before 2002, Nextel had been using PeopleSoft HRM, Oracle FMS and Ariba SCM. In 2002, however, Nextel determined that using one integrated solution would provide more operational efficiency. Nextel received advice from six consulting firms, which informed Nextel that Oracle, SAP and PeopleSoft could meet those software needs. Nextel then sent RFPs to Oracle and Peoplesoft. Nextel did not seriously consider SAP because it was already using Oracle for FMS and PeopleSoft for HRM and believed that conversion costs and risks for those two vendors would be lower. Nextel ultimately chose Peoplesoft, based on its scoring of vendor criteria such as functionality, ease of integration, scalability, audits, costs and relationship confidence. Even after it had chosen PeopleSoft, however, Nextel continued to negotiate with Oracle for leverage purposes until the signing of the December 2002 contract with PeopleSoft. Cichanowicz stated that if the price of the Oracle or PeopleSoft licenses had been 10 percent higher, Nextel would not have considered a best of breed approach, writing or building its own ERP software, outsourcing, staying with its previous system or using SAP or any other United States vendor.

Mary Elizabeth Glover, Vice President of Information Technology at Greyhound Lines, testified about her company's foray into the market for HRM software. Greyhound is in the bus transportation business in both the United States and Canada. The company employees some 16,000 people and has annual revenues of around $1.2 billion. For its FMS, Greyhound uses Oracle in the United States and J D Edwards in Canada. For its HRM, Greyhound uses a product called HR1 in the United States and HR2000 in Canada. The company outsources its payroll to ADP. Glover stated that the HR incumbent systems are "very old" and no longer meet the needs of the company. Further, she testified that outsourcing is too expensive for Greyhound. For these reasons, in 2001, Greyhound began a potential procurement process for new HRM software. The company hired CDG & Associates to match Greyhound with potential vendors who met their HRM needs. The firm narrowed the selection down to only four vendors: Oracle, PeopleSoft, Lawson and Ultimate Software. Greyhound never considered SAP because the consulting firm believed they were too costly. Ultimate Software was eliminated soon thereafter because of lack of functionality. Greyhound eliminated PeopleSoft as being too costly. Between Oracle and Lawson, Greyhound found that Oracle had more functionality;

therefore, Lawson was eliminated. But before Greyhound made a final choice, Glover stated that the company decided to give PeopleSoft a second look. Upon reexamination, Greyhound determined that both Oracle and PeopleSoft could meet the company's needs, with the company preferring PeopleSoft over Oracle. Unfortunately, the events of September 11, 2001, a new CEO and a decrease in profits caused Greyhound to lose the funds necessary to purchase the software. But Glover stated that should Greyhound ever decide to purchase HRM software, this proposed merger would make the purchase more costly, as Greyhound's only choices were Oracle and PeopleSoft. Without the competition between the two, Glover foresees prices increasing.

Phillip Maxwell, Senior Vice President and Chief Information Officer of the Neiman Marcus Group (NMG), testified about the ERP needs of the specialty retailer. NMG has properties located throughout the country, approximately 15,000 employees and $3 billion in annual sales. NMG formerly had used FMS software that was originally from MSA, a vendor purchased by Dun & Bradstreet and then GEAC subsequent to NMG's installation of the software. In 2002, NMG decided to replace its FMS software and began conferring with individuals in its business and technology units, three consulting firms and the Gartner Group. After examining vendors' functionality, experience in retail, price and size/stability, NMG narrowed its choices to Oracle and PeopleSoft. NMG did not consider SAP because of SAP's lack of strong presence in the retail vertical and Maxwell's opinion that SAP is "very expensive to implement." Had the cost of Oracle or PeopleSoft FMS software been 10 to 20 percent higher, NMG would not have considered SAP, any other FMS vendor, legacy software or internally developed software. Based on price, a high level comparison and detailed GAP analysis, NMG eventually selected Oracle to provide it with FMS software.

NMG also began licensing HRM software from Oracle in 2003, though it has not yet begun to implement that software. NMG went through a similar process in evaluating HRM software as it did in evaluating FMS software. As with the FMS software, NMG concluded that Oracle and PeopleSoft were its only viable alternatives. NMG did not believe that SAP suited its needs as a retailer. Had the cost of the Oracle or PeopleSoft HRM software been 10 to 20 percent higher, NMG would not have considered other HRM vendors, legacy software, internally developed software or outsourcing. NMG eventually selected the Oracle HRM software, but based on a 70 to 80 percent higher target price than previously predicted, NMG has delayed implementation of the Oracle HRM software to look for cost-reducing options. But Maxwell testified that, even with the 80 percent price increase, NMG has not abandoned the Oracle HRM.

Laurette Bradley, Senior Vice President of Information Technology at Verizon, testified about Verizon's current procurement of new HRM software. Verizon is a telecommunications company with a "majority holding in four of five different countries." Verizon has minor investments in over 30 countries worldwide with an annual revenue of approximately $66 billion. *Id.* Bradley testified that 49 percent of Verizon's labor is unionized worldwide, which places "significant demands upon [the] ERP systems, particularly [the] HR and payroll systems" because each union contract, from each jurisdiction, must be reflected and managed regarding payroll, vacation, absences, and personal days. Prior to October 2003, Verizon had used two different HRM programs, one from PeopleSoft and one from SAP. The PeopleSoft HRM was used to manage the former BellAtlantic part of the company and SAP HRM was used to manage the former GTE part of the company. The same is true of Verizon's FMS. But in October 2003, Verizon decided to consolidate the two systems as far as HRM software. Verizon chose PeopleSoft HRM for the entire company and as of the date of the trial, the new software was being implemented. *Id.* Bradley testified that a merger between Oracle and PeopleSoft makes her very concerned that Oracle will not be interested in upgrading or further "developing" current PeopleSoft software.

In the main, and contrary to the characterization of plaintiffs' counsel before trial, the court found the testimony of the customer witnesses largely unhelpful to plaintiffs' effort to define a narrow market of high function FMS and HRM. Each of these witnesses had an impressive background in the field of information technology. They appeared knowledgeable and well informed about their employers' ERP needs and resources. And the court does not doubt

165

the sincerity of these witnesses' beliefs in the testimony that they gave. What the court questions is the grounds upon which these witnesses offered their opinions on the definition of the product market and competition within that market.

The test of market definition turns on reasonable substitutability. *E. I. du Pont,* 351 U.S. 377, 76 S.Ct. 994, 100 L.Ed. 1264. This requires the court to determine whether or not products have "reasonable interchangeability" based upon "price, use and qualities * * *." What, instead, these witnesses testified to was, largely, their preferences.

Customer preferences towards one product over another do not negate interchangeability. See *R R Donnelley & Sons Co.,* 120 FTC 36, 54 n. 65 (1995) (citing Robert Pitofsky, *New Definitions of the Relevant Market and the Assault on Antitrust,* 90 Colum. L. Rev. 1805, 1816 (1990) ("There will almost always be classes of customers with strong preferences * * * but to reason from the existence of such classes to a conclusion that each is entitled to * * * a separate narrow market definition grossly overstates the market power of the sellers.")). The preferences of these customer witnesses for the functional features of PeopleSoft or Oracle products was evident. But the issue is not what solutions the customers would *like* or *prefer* for their data processing needs; the issue is what they *could* do in the event of an anticompetitive price increase by a post-merger Oracle. Although these witnesses speculated on that subject, their speculation was not backed up by serious analysis that they had themselves performed or evidence they presented. There was little, if any, testimony by these witnesses about what they would or could do or not do to avoid a price increase from a post-merger Oracle. To be sure, each testified, with a kind of rote, that they would have no choice but to accept a ten percent price increase by a merged Oracle/PeopleSoft. But none gave testimony about the cost of alternatives to the hypothetical price increase a post-merger Oracle would charge: e.g., how much outsourcing would actually cost, or how much it would cost to adapt other vendors' products to the same functionality that the Oracle and PeopleSoft products afford.

If backed by credible and convincing testimony of this kind or testimony presented by economic experts, customer testimony of the kind plaintiffs offered can put a human perspective or face on the injury to competition that plaintiffs allege. But unsubstantiated customer apprehensions do not substitute for hard evidence.

While listening to the testimony of these customer witnesses, it became clear to the court that these witnesses represent a group of extremely sophisticated buyers and users of information technology; they have decades of experience in negotiating in this field. This made more evident the failure of these witnesses to present cost/benefit analyses of the type that surely they employ and would employ in assessing an ERP purchase. The evidence at trial established that ERP customers have choices outside the integrated suites of Oracle, PeopleSoft and SAP. Indeed, Glover's testimony showed that - as Oracle contends - customers have some leverage by virtue of their existing installed base "to do nothing" and thereby resist anticompetitive price increases by ERP vendors. Although the court is not convinced that this is a long-term option due to the ever changing business and legal environment in which enterprises operate, this option does afford ERP customers some limited protection and leverage. At any rate, plaintiffs' customer witnesses did not, in their testimony, provide the court with data from actual or probable ERP purchases and installations to demonstrate that the witnesses' employers would have had no choice but to submit to a SSNIP imposed by a post-merger Oracle.

The court, therefore, finds that these witnesses did not establish by a preponderance of the evidence that the products offered by Oracle, PeopleSoft and SAP are in a distinct line of commerce or product market from those offered by other ERP vendors. The court finds that these witnesses did not establish that it was more likely than not that customers of a post-merger Oracle would have no choice but to submit to a small but significant non-transitory price increase by the merged entity. These findings do not rest alone on the court's skepticism about the testimony of plaintiffs' customer witnesses.

* * *

In the concluding sections of the opinion, the Court turned to questions of likely anticompetitive effects as the result of collusive behavior or unilateral effects. Largely on the basis of the

167

government's failure to establish relevant product market on the basis of consumer testimony or otherwise, the government's request for an injunction was denied.

CHAPTER 10: FOREIGN COMMERCE AND THE U.S. ANTITRUST LAWS

Insert as replacement to pages 1216-29.

F. HOFFMANN-LA ROCHE, LTD. v. *EMPAGRAN S.A.*

Supreme Court of the United States, 2004

542 U.S. 155, 124 S.Ct. 2359, 159 L. Ed. 2d 226

BREYER, J The Foreign Trade Antitrust Improvements Act of 1982 (FTAIA) excludes from the Sherman Act's reach much anticompetitive conduct that causes only foreign injury. It does so by setting forth a general rule stating that the Sherman Act "shall not apply to conduct involving trade or commerce . . . with foreign nations." It then creates exceptions to the general rule, applicable where (roughly speaking) that conduct significantly harms imports, domestic commerce, or American exporters.

We here focus upon anticompetitive price-fixing activity that is in significant part foreign, that causes some domestic antitrust injury, and that independently causes separate foreign injury. We ask two questions about the price-fixing conduct and the foreign injury that it causes. First, does that conduct fall within the FTAIA's general rule excluding the Sherman Act's application? That is to say, does the price-fixing activity constitute "conduct involving trade or commerce . . . with foreign nations"? We conclude that it does.

Second, we ask whether the conduct nonetheless falls within a domestic-injury exception to the general rule, an exception that applies (and makes the Sherman Act nonetheless applicable) where the conduct (1) has a "direct, substantial, and reasonably foreseeable effect" on domestic commerce, and (2) "such effect gives rise to a [Sherman Act] claim." §§a(1)(A), (2). We conclude that the exception does not apply where the plaintiff's claim rests solely on the independent foreign harm.

To clarify: The issue before us concerns (1) significant foreign anticompetitive conduct with (2) an adverse domestic effect and (3) an independent foreign effect giving rise to the claim. In more concrete terms, this case involves vitamin sellers around the world that agreed to fix prices, leading to higher vitamin prices in the United States and independently leading to higher vitamin prices in other countries such as Ecuador. We conclude that, in this scenario, a purchaser in the United States could bring a Sherman Act claim under FTAIA based on domestic injury, but a purchaser in Ecuador could not bring a Sherman Act claim based on foreign harm.

The plaintiffs in this case originally filed a class-action suit on behalf of foreign and domestic purchasers of vitamins under, *inter alia*, §1 of the Sherman Act, 26 Stat. 209, as amended, 15 U.S.C. §1 and §4 and 16 of the Clayton Act, 28 Stat. 731, 737, as amended, 15 U.S.C. §§15-26. Their complaint alleged that petitioners, foreign and domestic vitamin manufacturers and distributors, had engaged in a price-fixing conspiracy, raising the price of vitamin products to customers in the United States and to customers in foreign countries.

As relevant there, petitioners moved to dismiss the suit as to the *foreign* purchasers (the respondents here), five foreign vitamin distributors located in Ukraine, Australia, Ecuador, and Panama, each of which bought vitamins from petitioners for delivery outside the United States describing the relevant transactions as "wholly foreign"). Respondents have never asserted that they purchased any vitamins in the United States or in transactions in United States commerce, and the question presented assumes that the relevant "transactions occurr[ed] entirely outside U.S. commerce." The District Court dismissed their claims. *Ibid.* It applied the FTAIA and found none of the exceptions applicable. *Id.*, at *3-*4. Thereafter, the domestic purchasers transferred their claims to another pending suit and did not take part in the subsequent appeal.

A divided panel of the Court of Appeals reversed. 315 F. 3d 338. The panel concluded that the FTAJA's general exclusionary rule applied to the case, but that its domestic-injury exception also applied. It basically read the plaintiffs' complaint to allege that the vitamin manufacturers' price-fixing conspiracy (1) had "a direct, substantial, and reasonably foreseeable effect" on ordinary domestic trade or commerce, i.e., the conspiracy brought about higher domestic vitamin prices, and (2) "such effect" gave "rise to a [Sherman Act] claim," i.e., an injured domestic customer could have brought a Sherman Act

170

suit, 15 U.S.C. §§6a(1), (2). Those allegations, the court held, are sufficient to meet the exception's requirements. 315 F. 3d, at 341.

The court assumed that the foreign effect, i.e., higher prices in Ukraine, Panama, Australia, and Ecuador, was independent of the domestic effect, i.e., higher domestic prices. Ibid. But it concluded that, in light of the FTAIA's text, legislative history, and the policy goal of deterring harmful price-fixing activity, this lack of connection does not matter. Ibid. The District of Columbia Circuit denied rehearing *en banc* by a 4-to-3 vote.

We granted certiorari to resolve a split among the Courts of Appeals about the exception's application. Compare *Den Norske Stats Oljeselskap As* v. *HeereMac Vof,* 241 F. 3d 420, 427 (CA5 2001) (exception does not apply where foreign injury independent of domestic harm), with *Kruman* v. *Christie's Int'l PLC,* 284 F. 3d 384, 400 (CA2 2002) (exception does apply even where foreign injury independent); 315 F. 3d, at 341 (similar).

The FTAIA seeks to make clear to American exporters (and to firms doing business abroad) that the Sherman Act does not prevent them from entering into business arrangements (say, joint-selling arrangements), however anticompetitive, as long as those arrangements adversely affect only foreign markets. See H. R. Rep. No. 97-686, pp. 1-3, 9-10 (1982) (hereinafter House Report). It does so by removing from the Sherman Act's reach, (1) export activities and (2) other commercial activities taking place abroad, unless those activities adversely affect domestic commerce, imports to the United States, or exporting activities of one engaged in such activities within the United States.

The FTAIA says:

> "Sections 1 to 7 of this title [the Sherman Act] shall not apply to conduct involving trade or commerce (other than import trade or import commerce) with foreign nations unless—

171

"(1) such conduct has a direct, substantial, and reasonably foreseeable effect — "

(A) on trade or commerce which is not trade or commerce with foreign nations [i.e., domestic trade or commerce], or on import trade or import commerce with foreign nations; or

"(B) on export trade or export commerce with foreign nations, of a person engaged in such trade or commerce in the United States [i.e., on an American export competitor]; and

(2)   such effect gives rise to a claim under the provisions of sections 1 to 7 of this title, other than this section.

"If sections 1 to 7 of this title apply to such conduct only because of the operation of paragraph (1)(B), then sections 1 to 7 of this title shall apply to such conduct only for injury to export business in the United States."   15 U.S.C. §6a.

This technical language initially lays down a general rule placing *all* (non-import) activity involving foreign commerce outside the Sherman Act's reach. It then brings such conduct back within the Sherman Act's reach *provided that* the conduct *both* (1) sufficiently affects American commerce, i.e., it has a "direct, substantial, and reasonably foreseeable effect" on American domestic, import, or (certain) export commerce, and (2) has an effect of a kind that antitrust law considers harmful, i.e., the "effect" must "giv[e] rise to a [Sherman Act] claim." §§6a(1), (2).

We ask here how this language applies to price-fixing activity that is in significant part foreign, that has the requisite domestic

172

effect, and that also has independent foreign effects giving rise to the plaintiffs claim.

Respondents make a threshold argument. They say that the transactions here at issue fall outside the FTAIA because the FTAIA's general exclusionary rule applies only to conduct involving exports. The rule says that the Sherman Act "shall not apply to conduct involving trade or commerce (other than import trade or import commerce) *with* foreign nations." §6a (emphasis added). The word "with" means *between* the United States and foreign nations. And, they contend, commerce between the United States and foreign nations that is not import commerce must consist of export commerce - a kind of commerce irrelevant to the case at hand.

The difficulty with respondents' argument is that the FTAIA originated in a bill that initially referred only to "export trade or export commerce." H.R. 5235, 97th Cong., 1st Sess., §1 (1981). But the House Judiciary Committee subsequently changed that language to "trade or commerce (other than import trade or import commerce)." 15 U.S.C. §6a. And it did so deliberately to include commerce that did not involve American exports but which was wholly foreign.

The House Report says in relevant part:

> "The Subcommittee's 'export' commerce limitation appeared to make the amendments inapplicable to transactions that were neither import nor export, i.e., transactions within, between, or among other nations. . . Such foreign transactions should, for the purposes of this legislation, be treated in the same manner as export transactions - that is, there should be no American antitrust jurisdiction absent a direct, substantial and reasonably foreseeable effect on domestic commerce or a domestic competitor. The Committee Amendment therefore deletes references to 'export' trade, and

substitutes phrases such as 'other than
import' trade. It is thus clear that wholly
foreign transactions as well as export
transactions are covered by the
amendment, but that import transactions
are not." House Report 9-10 (emphases
added).

For those who find legislative history useful, the House
Report's account should end the matter. Others, by considering
carefully the amendment itself and the lack of any other plausible
purpose, may reach the same conclusion, namely that the FTAIA's
general rule applies where the anticompetitive conduct at issue is
foreign.

We turn now to the basic question presented, that of the
exception's application. Because the underlying antitrust action is
complex, potentially raising questions not directly at issue here, we
reemphasize that we base our decision upon the following: The price-
fixing conduct significantly and adversely affects both customers
outside the United States and customers within the United States, but
the adverse foreign effect is independent of any adverse domestic
effect. In these circumstances, we find that the FTAIA exception
does not apply (and thus the Sherman Act does not apply) for two
main reasons.

First, this Court ordinarily construes ambiguous statutes to
avoid unreasonable interference with the sovereign authority of other
nations. See, *e.g., McCulloch* v. *Sociedad Nacional de Marineros de
Honduras*, 372 U.S. 10, 20-22 (1963) (application of National Labor
Relations Act to foreign-flag vessels); *Romero* v. *International
Terminal Operating Co.*, 358 U.S. 354, 382-383 (1959) (application
of Jones Act in maritime case); *Lauritzen v. Larsen*, 345 U.S. 571,
578 (1953) (same). This rule of construction reflects principles of
customary international law - law that (we must assume) Congress
ordinarily seeks to follow. See Restatement (Third) of Foreign
Relations Law of the United States §§403(1), 403(2) (1986)
(hereinafter Restatement) (limiting the unreasonable exercise of
prescriptive jurisdiction with respect to a person or activity having
connections with another State); *Murray* v. *Schooner Charming*

Betsy, 2 Cranch 64, 118 (1804) ("[A]n act of Congress ought never to be construed to violate the law of nations if any other possible construction remains"); *Hartford Fire Insurance Co.* v. *California*, 509 U.S. 764, 817 (1993) (SCALIA, J., dissenting) (identifying rule of construction as derived from the principle of "prescriptive comity").

This rule of statutory construction cautions courts to assume that legislators take account of the legitimate sovereign interests of other nations when they write American laws. It thereby helps the potentially conflicting laws of different nations work together in harmony - a harmony particularly needed in today's highly interdependent commercial world.

No one denies that America's antitrust laws, when applied to foreign conduct, can interfere with a foreign nation's ability independently to regulate its own commercial affairs. But our courts have long held that application of our antitrust laws to foreign anticompetitive conduct is nonetheless reasonable, and hence consistent with principles of prescriptive comity, insofar as they reflect a legislative effort to redress domestic antitrust injury that foreign anticompetitive conduct has caused. See *United States* v. *Aluminum Co. of America*, 148 F. 2d 416, 443-444 (CA2 1945) (L. Hand, J.); 1 P. Areeda & D. Turner, Antitrust Law ¶236 (1978).

But why is it reasonable to apply those laws to foreign conduct *insofar as that conduct causes independent foreign harm and that foreign harm alone gives rise to the plaintiff's claim?* Like the former case, application of those laws creates a serious risk of interference with a foreign nation's ability independently to regulate its own commercial affairs. But, unlike the former case, the justification for that interference seems insubstantial. See Restatement §403(2) (determining reasonableness on basis of such factors as connections with regulating nation, harm to that nation's interests, extent to which other nations regulate, and the potential for conflict). Why should American law supplant, for example, Canada's or Great Britain's or Japan's own determination about how best to protect Canadian or British or Japanese customers from anticompetitive conduct engaged in significant part by Canadian or British or Japanese or other foreign companies?

We recognize that principles of comity provide Congress greater leeway when it seeks to control through legislation the actions of *American* companies, see Restatement §402; and some of the anticompetitive price-fixing conduct alleged here took place in *America*. But the higher foreign prices of which the foreign plaintiffs here complain are not the consequence of any domestic anticompetitive conduct *that Congress sought to forbid*, for Congress did not seek to forbid any such conduct insofar as it is here relevant, i.e., insofar as it is intertwined with foreign conduct that causes independent foreign harm. Rather Congress sought to release domestic (and foreign) anticompetitive conduct from Sherman Act constraints when that conduct causes foreign harm. Congress, of course, did make an exception where that conduct also causes domestic harm. See House Report 13 (concerns about American firms' participation in international cartels addressed through "domestic injury" exception). But any independent domestic harm the foreign conduct causes here has, by definition, little or nothing to do with the matter.

We thus repeat the basic question: Why is it reasonable to apply this law to conduct that is significantly foreign *insofar as that conduct causes independent foreign harm and that foreign harm alone gives rise to the plaintiff's claim*? We can find no good answer to the question.

The Areeda and Hovenkamp treatise notes that under the Court of Appeals' interpretation of the statute

> "a Malaysian customer could . . . maintain an action under United States law in a United States court against its own Malaysian supplier, another cartel member, simply by noting that unnamed third parties injured [in the United States] by the American [cartel member's] conduct would also have a cause of action.

> Effectively, the United States courts would provide worldwide subject

matter jurisdiction to any foreign suitor wishing to sue its own local supplier, but unhappy with its own sovereign's provisions for private antitrust enforcement, provided that a different plaintiff had a cause of action against a different firm for injuries that were within U.S. [other-than-import] commerce. It does not seem excessively rigid to infer that Congress would not have intended that result." P. Areeda & H. Hovenkamp, Antitrust Law ¶273, pp. 51-52 (Supp. 2003).

We agree with the comment. We can find no convincing justification for the extension of the Sherman Act's scope that it describes.

Respondents reply that many nations have adopted antitrust laws similar to our own, to the point where the practical likelihood of interference with the relevant interests of other nations is minimal. Leaving price fixing to the side, however, this Court has found to the contrary. See, *e.g.*, *Hartford Fire*, 509 U.S. at 797-799 (noting that the alleged conduct in the London reinsurance market, while illegal under United States antitrust laws, was assumed to be perfectly consistent with British law and policy); see also, *e.g.*, 2 W. Fugate, Foreign Commerce and the Antitrust Laws §16.6 (5th ed. 1996) (noting differences between European Union and United States law on vertical restraints).

Regardless, even where nations agree about primary conduct, say price fixing, they disagree dramatically about appropriate remedies. The application, for example, of American private treble-damages remedies to anticompetitive conduct taking place abroad has generated considerable controversy. See, *e.g.*, 2 ABA Section of Antitrust Law, Antitrust Law Developments 1208-1209 (5th ed. 2002). And several foreign nations have filed briefs here arguing that to apply our remedies would unjustifiably permit their citizens to bypass their own less generous remedial schemes, thereby upsetting a balance of competing considerations that their own domestic antitrust

177

laws embody. *E.g.*, Brief for Federal Republic of Germany et al. as *Amici Curiae* 2 (setting forth German interest "in seeing that German companies are not subject to the extraterritorial reach of the United States' antitrust laws by private foreign plaintiffs - whose injuries were sustained in transactions entirely outside United States commerce - seeking treble damages in private lawsuits against German companies"); Brief for Government of Canada as *Amicus Curiae* 14 ("treble damages remedy would supersede" Canada's "national policy decision"); Brief for Government of Japan as *Amicus Curiae* 10 (finding "particularly troublesome" the potential "interfere[nce] with Japanese governmental regulation of the Japanese market").

These briefs add that a decision permitting independently injured foreign plaintiffs to pursue private treble-damages remedies would undermine foreign nations' own antitrust enforcement policies by diminishing foreign firms' incentive to cooperate with antitrust authorities in return for prosecutorial amnesty. Brief for Federal Republic of Germany et al. as *Amici Curiae* 28-30; Brief for Government of Canada as *Amicus Curiae* 11-14. See also Brief for United States as *Amicus Curiae* 19-21 (arguing the same in respect to American antitrust enforcement).

Respondents alternatively argue that comity does not demand an interpretation of the FTAIA that would exclude independent foreign injury cases across the board. Rather, courts can take (and sometimes have taken) account of comity considerations case by case, abstaining where comity considerations so dictate. Cf., *e.g., Hartford Fire, supra*, at 797, n. 24; *United States* v. *Nippon Paper Industries Co.*, 109 F. 3d 1, 8 (CA1 1997); *Mannington Mills, Inc.* v. *Congoleum Corp.*, 595 F. 2d 1287, 1294-1295 (CA3 1979).

In our view, however, this approach is too complex to prove workable. The Sherman Act covers many different kinds of anticompetitive agreements. Courts would have to examine how foreign law, compared with American law, treats not only price fixing but also, say, information-sharing agreements, patent-licensing price conditions, territorial product resale limitations, and various forms of joint venture, in respect to both primary conduct and remedy. The legally and economically technical nature of that enterprise means lengthier proceedings, appeals, and more proceedings - to the point where procedural costs and delays could themselves threaten interference with a foreign nation's ability to maintain the integrity of its own antitrust enforcement system. Even in this relatively simple price-fixing case, for example, competing briefs tell us (1) that potential treble-damage liability would help enforce widespread anti-price-fixing norms (through added deterrence) and (2) the opposite, namely that such liability would hinder antitrust enforcement (by reducing incentives to enter amnesty programs). Compare, *e.g.*, Brief for Certain Professors of Economics as *Amici Curiae* 2-4 with Brief for United States as *Amicus Curiae* 19-21. How could a court seriously interested in resolving so empirical a matter - a matter potentially related to impact on foreign interests - do so simply and expeditiously?

We conclude that principles of prescriptive comity counsel against the Court of Appeals' interpretation of the FTAIA. Where foreign anticompetitive conduct plays a significant role and where foreign injury is independent of domestic effects, Congress might have hoped that America's antitrust laws, so fundamental a component of our own economic system, would commend themselves to other nations as well. But, if America's antitrust policies could not win their own way in the international marketplace for such ideas, Congress, we must assume, would not have tried to impose them, in an act of legal imperialism, through legislative fiat.

Second, the FTAIA's language and history suggest that Congress designed the FTAIA to clarify, perhaps to limit, but not to *expand* in any significant way, the Sherman Act's scope as applied, to foreign commerce. See House Report 2-3. And we have found no significant indication that at the time Congress wrote this statute courts would have thought the Sherman Act applicable in these circumstances.

The Solicitor General and petitioners tell us that they have found no case in which any court applied the Sherman Act to redress foreign injury in such circumstances. Tr. of Oral Arg. 21; Brief for United States as *Amicus Curiae* 13; Brief for Petitioners 13; see also *Den Norske*, 241 F. 3d, at 429 ("[W]e have found no case in which jurisdiction was found in a case like this - where a foreign plaintiff is

179

injured in a foreign market with no injuries arising from the anticompetitive effect on a United States market"). And respondents themselves apparently conceded as much at a May 23, 2001, hearing before the District Court below. 2001 WL 761360, at *4.

Nevertheless, respondents now have called to our attention six cases, three decided by this Court and three decided by lower courts. In the first three cases the defendants included both American companies and foreign companies jointly engaged in anticompetitive behavior having both foreign and domestic effects. See *Timken Roller Bearing Co.* v. *United States*, 341 U.S. 593, 595 (1951) (agreements among American, British, and French corporations to eliminate competition in the manufacture and sale of anti-friction bearings in world, including United States, markets); *United States* v. *National Lead Co.*, 332 U.S. 319, 325-328 (1947) (international cartels with American and foreign members, restraining international commerce, including United States commerce, in titanium pigments); *United States* v. *American Tobacco Co.*, 221 U.S. 106, 171-172 (1911) (American tobacco corporations agreed in England with British company to divide world markets). In all three cases the plaintiff sought relief, including relief that might have helped to protect those injured abroad.

In all three cases, however, the plaintiff was the Government of the United States. A Government plaintiff, unlike a private plaintiff, must seek to obtain the relief necessary to protect the public from further anticompetitive conduct and to redress anticompetitive harm. And a Government plaintiff has legal authority broad enough to allow it to carry out this mission. 15 U.S.C. §25; see also, *e.g.*, *United States* v. *E. I. du Pont de Nemours & Co.*, 366 U.S. 316, 334 (1961) ("[I]t is well settled that once the Government has successfully borne the considerable burden of establishing a violation of law, all doubts as to the remedy are to be resolved in its favor"). Private plaintiffs, by way of contrast, are far less likely to be able to secure broad relief. See *California* v. *American Stores Co.*, 495 U.S. 271, 295 (1990) ("Our conclusion that a district court has the power to order divestiture in appropriate cases brought [by private plaintiffs] does not, of course, mean that such power should be exercised in every situation in which the Government would be entitled to such relief"); 2 P. Areeda & H. Hovenkamp, Antitrust Law §§303d-303e,

180

pp. 40-45 (2d ed. 2000) (distinguishing between private and government suits in terms of availability, public interest motives, and remedial scope); Griffin, Extraterritoriality in U.S. and EU Antitrust Enforcement, 67 Antitrust L. J. 159, 194 (1999) ("[P]rivate plaintiffs often are unwilling to exercise the degree of self-restraint and consideration of foreign governmental sensibilities generally exercised by the U.S. Government"). This difference means that the Government's ability, in these three cases, to obtain relief helpful to those injured abroad tells us little or nothing about whether this Court would have awarded similar relief at the request of private plaintiffs.

Neither did the Court focus explicitly in its opinions on a claim that the remedies sought to cure only independently caused foreign harm. Thus the three cases tell us even less about whether this Court then thought that foreign private plaintiffs could have obtained foreign relief based solely upon such independently caused foreign injury.

Respondents also refer to three lower court cases brought by private plaintiffs. In the first, *Industria Siciliana Asfalti, Bitumi, S. p. A.* v. *Exxon Research & Engineering Co.*, 1977 WL 1353 (SDNY, Jan. 18, 1977), a District Court permitted an Italian firm to proceed against an American firm with a Sherman Act claim based upon a purely foreign injury, *i.e.*, an injury suffered in Italy. The court made clear, however, that the foreign injury was *"inextricably bound up with . . . domestic restraints of trade,"* and that the plaintiff *"was injured . . . by reason of an alleged restraint of our domestic trade,"* *id.*, at *11, *12 (emphasis added), *i.e.*, the foreign injury was dependent upon, *not independent of*, domestic harm. See Part VI, infra.

In the second case, *Dominicus Americana Bohio v. Gulf & Western Industries, Inc.*, 473 F. Supp. 680 (SDNY 1979), a District Court permitted Dominican and American firms to proceed against a competing American firm and the Dominican Tourist Information Center with a Sherman Act claim based upon injury apparently suffered in the Dominican Republic. The court, in finding the Sherman Act applicable, weighed several different factors, including the participation of American firms in the unlawful conduct, the partly domestic nature of both conduct and harm (to American tourists, a

181

kind of "export"), and the fact that the domestic harm depended in part upon the foreign injury. *Id.*, at 688. The court did not separately analyze the legal problem before it in terms of independently caused foreign injury. Its opinion simply does not discuss the matter. It consequently cannot be taken as significant support for application of the Sherman Act here.

The third case, *Hunt* v. *Mobil Oil Corp.*, 550 F. 2d 68, 72 (CA2 1977), involved a claim by Hunt, an independent oil producer with reserves in Libya, that other major oil producers in Libya and the Persian Gulf (the "seven majors") had conspired in New York and elsewhere to make it more difficult for Hunt to reach agreement with the Libyan government on production terms and thereby eliminate him as a competitor. The case can be seen as involving a primarily foreign conspiracy designed to bring about foreign injury in Libya. But, as in *Dominicus*, the court nowhere considered the problem of independently caused foreign harm. Rather, the case was about the "act of state" doctrine, and the sole discussion of Sherman Act applicability – one brief paragraph - refers to other matters. 550 F. 2d, at 72, and n. 2. We do not see how Congress could have taken this case as significant support for the proposition that the Sherman Act applies in present circumstances.

The upshot is that no pre-1982 case provides significant authority for application of the Sherman Act in the circumstances we here assume. Indeed, a leading contemporaneous lower court case contains language suggesting the contrary. See *Timberlane Lumber Co.* v. *Bank of America*, 549 F. 2d 597, 613 (CA9 1976) (insisting that the foreign conduct's domestic effect be "sufficiently large to present a cognizable injury to the plaintiffs" (emphasis added)).

Taken together, these two sets of considerations, the one derived from comity and the other reflecting history, convince us that Congress would not have intended the FTAIA's exception to bring independently caused foreign injury within the Sherman Act's reach.

V

Respondents point to several considerations that point the other way. For one thing, the FTAIA's language speaks in terms of

182

the Sherman Act's *applicability* to certain kinds of *conduct*. The FTAIA says that the Sherman Act applies to foreign "conduct" with a certain kind of harmful domestic effect. Why isn't that the end of the matter? How can the Sherman Act both *apply to the conduct* when one person sues but *not apply to the same conduct* when another person sues? The question of who can or cannot sue is a matter for other statutes (namely, the Clayton Act) to determine.

Moreover, the exception says that it applies if the conduct's domestic effect gives rise to "a claim," not to *"the plaintiff's claim"* or *"the* claim *at issue."* 15 U.S.C. §6a(2) (emphasis added). The alleged conduct here did have domestic effects, and those effects were harmful enough to give rise to "a" claim. Respondents concede that this claim is not their own claim; it is someone else's claim. But, linguistically speaking, they say, that is beside the point. Nor did Congress place the relevant words "gives rise to a claim" in the FTAIA to suggest any geographical limitation; rather it did so for a more neutral reason, namely, in order to make clear that the domestic effect must be an adverse (as opposed to a beneficial) effect. See House Report 11 (citing *National Bank of Canada* v. *Interbank Card Assn.*, 666 F. 2d 6, 8 (CA2 1981)).

Despite their linguistic logic, these arguments are not convincing. Linguistically speaking, a statute can apply and not apply to the same conduct, depending upon other circumstances; and those other circumstances may include the nature of the lawsuit (or of the related underlying harm). It also makes linguistic sense to read the words "a claim" as if they refer to the "plaintiffs claim" or "the claim at issue."

At most, respondents' linguistic arguments might show that respondents' reading is the more natural reading of the statutory language. But those arguments do not show that we *must* accept that reading. And that is the critical point. The considerations previously mentioned - those of comity and history - make clear that the respondents' reading is not consistent with the FTAIA's basic intent. If the statute's language reasonably permits an interpretation consistent with that intent, we should adopt it. And, for the reasons stated, we believe that the statute's language permits the reading that we give it.

Finally, respondents point to policy considerations that we have previously discussed, *supra*, at 11, namely, that application of the Sherman Act in present circumstances will (through increased deterrence) help protect Americans against foreign-caused anticompetitive injury. As we have explained, however, the plaintiffs and supporting enforcement-agency *amici* have made important experience-backed arguments (based upon amnesty-seeking incentives) to the contrary. We cannot say whether, on balance, respondents' side of this empirically based argument or the enforcement agencies' side is correct. But we can say that the answer to the dispute is neither clear enough, nor of such likely empirical significance, that it could overcome the considerations we have previously discussed and change our conclusion.

For these reasons, we conclude that petitioners' reading of the statute's language is correct. That reading furthers the statute's basic purposes, it properly reflects considerations of comity, and it is consistent with Sherman Act history.

VI

We have assumed that the anticompetitive conduct here independently caused foreign injury; that is, the conduct's domestic effects did not help to bring about that foreign injury. Respondents argue, in the alternative, that the foreign injury was not independent. Rather, they say, the anticompetitive conduct's domestic effects were linked to that foreign harm. Respondents contend that, because vitamins are fungible and readily transportable, without an adverse domestic effect (*i.e.*, higher prices in the United States), the sellers could not have maintained their international price-fixing arrangement and respondents would not have suffered their foreign injury. They add that this "but for" condition is sufficient to bring the price-fixing conduct within the scope of the FTAIA's exception.

The Court of Appeals, however, did not address this argument, 315 F. 3d, at 341, and, for that reason, neither shall we. Respondents remain free to ask the Court of Appeals to consider the claim. The Court of Appeals may determine whether respondents properly preserved the argument, and, if so, it may consider it and decide the related claim.

For these reasons, the judgment of the Court of Appeals is vacated, and the case is remanded for further proceedings consistent with this opinion.

O'CONNOR, J. took no part in the consideration or decision of this case.

SCALIA, J. with whom JUSTICE THOMAS J. concurring in the judgment.

I concur in the judgment of the Court because the language of the statute is readily susceptible of the interpretation the Court provides and because only that interpretation is consistent with the principle that statutes should be read in accord with the customary deference to the application of foreign countries' laws within their own territories.

Insert after Supreme Court's *Empagran* decision *supra*.

EMPAGRAN S.A. v. *F.HOFFMANN-LA ROCHE, LTD.*

United States Court of Appeals, D.C. Circuit, 2005

417 F.3d 1267

HENDERSON, J. The appellants, foreign corporations that purchased vitamin products outside of the United States for distribution in foreign countries from the appellee foreign manufacturers, brought this action asserting, *inter alia,* price fixing in violation of the Sherman Act. The district court dismissed the Sherman Act claim for lack of subject matter jurisdiction under the Foreign Trade Antitrust Improvements Act (FTAIA), which makes the Sherman Act inapplicable to conduct involving non-import foreign trade or commerce with one exception: when "such conduct has a direct, substantial, and reasonably foreseeable effect" on *domestic* trade or commerce and "such effect gives rise to a claim under [the Sherman Act]. This court in a divided opinion reversed the district court, reasoning that "where the anticompetitive conduct has the requisite harm on United States commerce, FTAIA permits suits by foreign plaintiffs who are injured solely by that conduct's effect on foreign commerce." The United States Supreme Court granted *certiorari* and vacated this court's decision concluding that under the FTAIA the Sherman Act does not apply where "price-fixing conduct significantly and adversely affects both customers outside the United States and customers within the United States, but the adverse foreign effect is independent of any adverse domestic effect." *F. Hoffman-La Roche, Ltd. v. Empagran S.A.,* 124 S.Ct. 2359, 2366 (2004). The Supreme Court remanded to this court, however, to assess the appellants' alternate theory for Sherman Act liability, namely, that "because vitamins are fungible and readily transportable, without an adverse domestic effect (*i.e.,* higher prices in the United States), the sellers could not have maintained their international price-fixing arrangement and respondents would not have suffered their foreign injury." 124 S.Ct. at 2372. We reject the appellants' alternate theory and conclude that we are without subject-matter jurisdiction under the FTAIA.

While the FTAIA excludes from the Sherman Act's reach most anti-competitive conduct that causes only foreign injury, it creates exceptions for conduct that "significantly harms imports, domestic commerce, or American exporters." *Empagran,* 124 S.Ct. at 2363. At issue is the "domestic-injury exception" of section 6a(2), which we conclude, as counsel for the United States argued, applies in only limited circumstances.

The appellees suggest that the exception applies only to injuries that arise in U.S. commerce, thus describing its reach by the situs of the transaction and resulting injuries rather than by the situs of the effects of the allegedly anti-competitive conduct giving rise to the appellants' claims. This interpretation has no support from the text of the statute, which expressly covers conduct involving "trade or commerce with foreign nations." In addition, the legislative history makes clear that the FTAIA's "domestic effects" requirement "does not exclude all persons injured abroad from recovering under the antitrust laws of the United States." The appellants need only demonstrate therefore that the U.S. effects of the appellees' allegedly anti-competitive conduct "g[a]ve rise to" their claims.

During oral argument, counsel for the United States identified three decisions with factual scenarios that, in its view, satisfy the narrow "domestic-injury exception": *Pfizer, Inc. v. Gov't of India,* 434 U.S. 308 (1978); *Industria Siciliana Asfalti, Bitumi, S.p.A. v. Exxon Research & Eng'g Co.,* 1977 WL 1353 (S.D.N.Y.1977); and *Caribbean Broad. Sys. v. Cable & Wireless PLC,* 148 F.3d 1080 (D.C.Cir.1998). Counsel nonetheless argued, and we agree, that each of these cases is distinguishable. For example, in *Pfizer,* which involved a conspiracy that operated both domestically and internationally, the Supreme Court held "only that a foreign nation otherwise entitled to sue in our courts is entitled to sue for treble damages under the antitrust laws to the same extent as any other plaintiff," without addressing the requisite causal relationship between domestic effect and foreign injury. In *Industria,* the foreign injury was "inextricably bound up with the domestic restraints of trade," because a reciprocal tying agreement effected the exclusion of the American rival of one defendant, resulting in higher consumer prices. Finally, in *Caribbean* this court expressly found the FTAIA permitted a Sherman Act claim that involved solely foreign injury.

There the plaintiff broadcaster, Caribbean, which operated an FM radio station based in the British Virgin Islands, filed an antitrust action against a competing FM radio station and its joint venturer, alleging that the defendants had violated the Sherman Act by preserving the defendant station's radio broadcast monopoly in the eastern Caribbean region through, *inter alia,* misrepresentations to its advertisers regarding the station's broadcasting reach. While the court expressly addressed only how Caribbean's allegations satisfied subsection 1 of the FTAIA (finding the requisite effect of the defendants' conduct on domestic trade or commerce), it is clear from the court's opinion that Caribbean's allegations satisfied subsection 2 as well. The domestic effect the court found was that U.S. advertisers paid the defendant station excessive prices for advertising. It was this effect of the defendants' monopolizing conduct -- forcing U.S. businesses to pay for advertising on the defendant station - that caused Caribbean to lose revenue because it was unable to sell advertising to the same U.S. businesses. *See* 148 F.3d at 1087.

> The appellants' theory in a nutshell is as follows:
> Because the appellees' product (vitamins) was fungible and globally marketed, they were able to sustain super-competitive prices abroad only by maintaining super-competitive prices in the United States as well.[1] Otherwise, overseas purchasers would have purchased bulk vitamins at lower prices either directly from U.S. sellers or from arbitrageurs selling vitamins imported from the United States, thereby preventing the appellees from selling abroad at the inflated prices. Thus, the super-competitive pricing in the United States "gives rise to" the foreign super-competitive prices from which the appellants claim injury.

The appellants paint a plausible scenario under which maintaining super-competitive prices in the United States might well have been a "but-for" cause of the appellants' foreign injury. As the appellants acknowledged at oral argument, however, "but-for" causation

---

[1] The appellants assert the appellees accomplished this equipoise both by fixing a single global price for the vitamins and by creating barriers to international vitamin commerce in the form of market division agreements that prevented bulk vitamins from being traded between North America and other regions.

between the domestic effects and the foreign injury claim is simply not sufficient to bring anti-competitive conduct within the FTAIA exception. The statutory language - "gives rise to" - indicates a direct causal relationship, that is, proximate causation, and is not satisfied by the mere but-for "nexus" the appellants advanced in their brief. *See* Appellants Br. at 22-23. This interpretation of the statutory language accords with principles of "prescriptive comity" - "the respect sovereign nations afford each other by limiting the reach of their laws," *Hartford Fire Ins. Co. v. California,* 509 U.S. 764, 817 (1993) (Scalia, J., dissenting) - which require that we "ordinarily construe[] ambiguous statutes to avoid unreasonable interference with the sovereign authority of other nations." *F. Hoffman-La Roche, Ltd.,* 124 S.Ct. at 2366. To read the FTAIA broadly to permit a more flexible, less direct standard than proximate cause would open the door to just such interference with other nations' prerogative to safeguard their own citizens from anti-competitive activity within their own borders. *See id.* at 2367 ("Why should American law supplant, for example, Canada's or Great Britain's or Japan's own determination about how best to protect Canadian or British or Japanese customers from anticompetitive conduct engaged in [in] significant part by Canadian or British or Japanese or other foreign companies?").

Applying the proximate cause standard, we conclude the domestic effects the appellants cite did not give rise to their claimed injuries so as to bring their Sherman Act claim within the FTAIA exception. While maintaining super-competitive prices in the United States may have facilitated the appellees' scheme to charge comparable prices abroad, this fact demonstrates at most but-for causation. It does not establish, as in the cases the United States cites, that the U.S. effects of the appellees' conduct - i.e., increased prices in the United States - proximately caused the foreign appellants' injuries. Nor do the appellants otherwise identify the kind of direct tie to U.S. commerce found in the cited cases. Although the appellants argue that the vitamin market is a single, global market facilitated by market division agreements so that their injuries arose from the higher prices charged by the global conspiracy (rather than from super-competitive prices in one particular market), they still must satisfy the FTAIA's requirement that the U.S. effects of the conduct give rise to their claims. The but-for causation the appellants proffer establishes only an indirect connection between the U.S. prices and the prices they paid when they purchased vitamins abroad. *Cf. Sniado v. Bank Austria AG,* 378 F.3d 210, 213 (2d. Cir.2004). Under the appellants' theory, it was the foreign effects of price-fixing outside of the United States that directly caused, or "g[a]ve rise to," their losses when they purchased vitamins abroad at super-competitive prices. That the appellees knew or could foresee the effect of their allegedly anti-competitive activities in the United States on the appellants' injuries abroad or had as a purpose to manipulate United States trade does not establish that "U.S. effects" proximately caused the appellants' harm. The foreign injury caused by the appellees' conduct, then, was not "inextricably bound up with . . . domestic restraints of trade," as in *Industria* and *Caribbean Broadcasting. See Empagran,* 124 S.Ct. at 2370. It was the foreign effects of price-fixing outside of the United States that directly caused or "g[a]ve rise to" the appellants' losses when they purchased vitamins abroad at super-competitive prices.

For the foregoing reasons, the judgment of the district court is affirmed.

Insert after the D.C. Circuits *Empagran decision supra.*

The Supreme Court's *Empagran* decision leaves one significant issue unresolved: whether the foreign injuries alleged were independent of the domestic effects of the conduct at issue. A high threshold for proving linkage would be consistent with the Court's general message of restraint in the remainder of the *Empagran* decision; conversely, if linkage could be proven easily, because of factors like fungibility, ease of transport, and world-market pricing, then this final point in the opinion might have taken away with the left hand much of what the right hand gave. In the two years following *Empagran,* the lower courts have adopted the former approach, generally imposing a stringent test for plaintiffs who are trying to bring foreign conduct within the reach of the U.S. antitrust laws.

The Second Circuit was the first to address the issue, in a case involving a conspiracy by foreign banks to fix the exchange rates for the Euro. *Sniado v. Bank Austria*, 378 F.3d 210 (2d Cir. 2004). There, the plaintiff alleged in his complaint that the "domestic component of the conspiracy was necessary...for the conspiracy's overall success." *Sniado*, 378 F.3d at 213. Notably, the plaintiff refrained from asserting "that currency exchange fees in the United States reached supra-competitive levels, [or] that but for the European conspiracy's effect on United States commerce, he would not have been injured in Europe." The Second Circuit concluded that the allegation of a "necessary" link was too conclusory, and thus found that the conduct was outside the reach of the U.S. antitrust laws. *Id.* at 213.

When *Empagran* returned to the D.C. Circuit on remand, see decision *supra,* the Court found, as a preliminary matter, that "the statutory language – "gives rise to" – indicates a direct causal relationship, that is, proximate causation, and is not satisfied by the mere but-for 'nexus' the appellants advanced...." *Empagran S.A. v. F. Hoffmann-La Roche*, Ltd., 417 F.3d 1267, 1271 (D.C. Cir. 2005). The appellants countered that because the product (vitamins) was fungible and marketed globally, the only way to sustain supra-competitive prices outside the United States was to maintain such prices within the United States, to the detriment of U.S. consumers. Otherwise, they continued, foreign high prices would collapse as a result of arbitrage. The D.C. Circuit was unpersuaded, noting that this theory "demonstrates at most but-for causation." *Id.* at 1271. In general, later courts have followed this approach.

Prior to the D.C. Circuit's decision on remand, a district court in Minnesota had refused to dismiss the claims of a foreign plaintiff in an international MSG price-fixing case. *In re Monosodium Glutamate Antitrust Litigation*, No. 00-MDL-1328, 2005 WL 1080790 (D. Minn. May 2, 2005). The court declared that "[i]n *Empagran*, the Supreme Court recognized that a claim based on foreign injury that depends on the domestic effect of the defendant's anti-competitive conduct involves but-for causation." *Id.* at *3. The court went on to find that the plaintiffs had successfully pleaded the alternative theory presented in *Empagran. Id.* at *8. Upon reconsideration, however, the court dismissed the case, explicitly following the D.C. Circuit's reasoning. *In Re Monosodium Glutamate*, No. 00-MDL-1328, 2005 WL 2810682 at *3 (D. Minn. Oct. 26, 2005).

The global marketplace theory also failed in three other cases involving fungible commodities. In a magnesium oxide case, the court declared that allowing the theory would "effectively nullify the Supreme Court's ruling in *Empagran*." *eMAG Solutions LLC v. Toda Kogyo Corp.*, No. C 02-1611 PJH, 2005 WL 1712084 at *8 (N.D. Cal. July 20, 2005). Plaintiffs claiming that the adverse effects on U.S. commerce were "necessary for the success of [a food additive price-fixing] conspiracy" were told that their theory had been "explicitly rejected in *Sniado*." *Latino Quimica-Amtex v. Akzo Nobel Chemicals B.V.*, No. 03-Civ-10312(HBDF), 2005 WL 2207017 at *11 (S.D.N.Y. Sept. 7, 2005). Finally, in a case alleging global price fixing of DRAM chips, the court dismissed the claims, stating "[t]here is simply no persuasive authority that plaintiff can muster to support an argument that … [a] global price-fixing conspiracy sufficiently alleges causation…post *Empagran I* and *II*." *In re: Dynamic Random Access Memory Antitrust Litigation*, Nos. C 02-1486 PJH & C 05-3026 PJH, 2006 WL 515629 at *5 (N.D. Cal. March 1, 2006.)

One case stands out from this trend: *MM Global Services v. Dow Chemical Co.*, 329 F. Supp. 2d 337 (D. Conn. 2004). There, the plaintiff foreign distributors alleged that they had been forced to participate in a resale-price-maintenance conspiracy. That conspiracy, they claimed, decreased competition in the primary sales market and directly injured plaintiffs when they purchased the products for resale. *MM Global*, 329 F. Supp. 2d at 342. The court held that there was a sufficient causal link between this domestic effect and the plaintiff's injury. *Id.* at 342. The decision was not changed after *Empagran*, but the fact that it involved a vertical arrangement makes it distinguishable from the other cases.

Empagran has not yet affected the general tendency of courts to speak of the FTAIA rule as one concerning subject matter jurisdiction, rather than coverage of the statute, despite the fact that Justice Breyer's opinion (without discussing the point) takes the latter approach. This question may return, however, given the fact that the Supreme Court continues to caution against confusing a missing element of a claim with a jurisdictional defect. *Arbaugh v. Y &H Corp.*, 126 S. Ct. 1235 (2006). In that decision, the Court emphasized that judges should not presume that a limitation on a statute's scope is jurisdictional unless Congress clearly indicates that this is what it meant. *Id.* at 1245.

Some post-*Empagran* decisions have used the language of subject matter jurisdiction with little analysis. Thus, the Second Circuit's *Sniado* decision affirmed a dismissal for lack of subject matter jurisdiction "[i]n light of the Supreme Court's decision in *Empagran*" without any subsequent commentary. *Sniado, supra,* 378 F.3d 210. The *MM Global Services* court adopted a similar approach in addressing a defendant's motion under Fed. R. Civ. P. 12(b)(1). *MM Global Services, supra,* 329 F. Supp. 2d at 342. Finally, when the district court in Minnesota dismissed the *MSG* case, it did so with scant analysis of the jurisdictional question. *In re Monosodium Glutamate, supra,* 2005 WL 2810682. The court used jurisdictional terminology in the body of its opinion, see *id.* at *2, but (confusingly) concluded finally that "Plaintiffs cannot state a claim under the Sherman Act." *Id.* at *3.

Other courts have simply followed pre-*Empagran* decisions that characterize the FTAIA as a rule of subject-matter jurisdiction, without considering whether *Empagran* itself or *Arbaugh* requires another look at the question. The district court in New Jersey cited cases from the Seventh, Ninth and Third Circuits as authority for the proposition that "the FTAIA establishes *jurisdictional* prerequisites for foreign antitrust claims, and does not merely impose additional substantive elements." *CSR Limited v. CIGNA Corporation*, 405 F. Supp. 2d 526 (D.N.J. 2005). The Southern District of New York likewise held that any claim that could not allege proximate causation failed on its face to allege subject-matter jurisdiction. *Latino Quimica*, 2005 WL 2207017 at *13. Additionally, the court in *EMAG Solutions* agreed with the defendants that the Supreme Court's admonition to keep the test simple meant to keep the *jurisdictional* test simple. *EMAG Solutions*, 2005 WL 1712084 at *8. The court dismissed the claims under Fed. R. Civ. P. 12(b)(1) and found it unnecessary to address the defendant's motion to dismiss for lack of antitrust standing. *Id.* at *12.

Insert Note on *General Electric/Honeywell* before Problem 27, page 1267.

Comity and cooperation sometimes cannot paper over significant differences of perspective that remain between the major competition regimes in the world. A notable example of such a difference of perspective occurred when the European Commission decided to block the merger of two U.S. companies, General Electric ("GE") and Honeywell. On December 14, 2005, the European Court of First Instance ("CFI") issued its opinion rejecting the efforts of GE and Honeywell to have the Commission's decision annulled.

Under the European Merger Control Regulation then in force, a merger "creating or strengthening a dominant position as a result of which effective competition would be significantly impeded" may not proceed. Articles 2(2)-(3) Council Regulation 4064/89, 1990. The Commission had emphasized four key factors that would lead to the creation or strengthening of dominant positions: the vertical integration of Honeywell's engine starters with GE's manufacturing; the extension of GE Capital and GECAS's influence into Honeywell's markets; the risk of bundling practices; and diminished competition as a result of horizontal overlaps. Case T-201/01, *General Elect. v. Comm'n*, OJ C48 25.02.2006, p. 26 paras.15-16. The CFI agreed that these grounds were legally sufficient reasons to block a merger. *Id.* at para. 47. The court also upheld the Commission's finding that GE had a dominant position. *Id.* at para.179. Thirdly, the court said that the Commission was justified in relying on the "strategic use" of GE Capital and GECAS as evidence of GE's dominant position. *Id.* at para. 242. Finally, it agreed with the Commission that the limited number of suppliers of engine starters meant that GE could disrupt the supply to its competitors. *Id.* at para. 298.

Even though it rejected the companies' challenge to the Commission decision, the CFI was quite critical about some of the Commission's reasoning. In particular, it noted that the Commission had committed "manifest errors of assessment" with regard to the effects of the transaction on particular markets. Citing Case T-5/02, *Tetra Laval BV v. Comm'n*, the court agreed with GE that the Commission had failed to take proper account of the deterrent effects of EU competition law. *Id.* at para. 312. Ultimately, however, the

Commission convinced the court that its horizontal overlap argument was strong enough to sustain its decision, and it thus avoided a reversal. *Id.* at para. 553.

The CFI's approach to the Commission's conglomerate effects arguments suggests that, in the future, the EC will be less likely to find anti-competitive effects in such arrangements. Again citing *Tetra Laval*, the court declared that *convincing* evidence was required to show that GE would attempt to use its aircraft leasing services and financial clout to force airlines to accept Honeywell products and drive out competitors. *Id.* at para. 327. Furthermore, the Commission would also have to establish that those practices would have created a dominating position in the *relatively near future*. *Id.* at para. 327. In order to meet this somewhat demanding standard, the Commission first had to demonstrate that the practices were in the parties' commercial interests. *Id.* at para. 333. By neglecting the role of airline preferences in calculating the costs to GE of pursuing such a strategy, the Commission failed to meet its burden. *Id.* at para. 353. The Commission also had neglected to analyze the market for small regional aircraft, raising doubts about its claim that the merger would create a dominant position in this market. *Id.* at para. 355. These errors were serious enough to cause the court to set aside these parts of the Commission's judgment. *Id.* at para. 364. This part of the decision is notable for the court's heavy emphasis on the lack of economic evidence supporting the alleged anticompetitive conglomerate effects of the merger.

The CFI's handling of the bundling issue also reflects a more rigorous and economically-based approach. The Commission had raised concerns that GE and Honeywell would use a bundling strategy to eliminate rivals. The court noted that because purchasers of avionics and engines are often not the same individual, pure bundling would be difficult to achieve. *Id.* at para. 410. Again, the court was troubled by the lack of a detailed economic analysis of the individual platform packages to determine which ones were actually capable of being bundled. *Id.* at para. 418. The most important part of the discussion, however, relates to the new evidentiary threshold for conglomerate merger cases. The Court reemphasized that the *Tetra Laval* test could be met only by proving "on the basis of convincing evidence and with a sufficient degree of probability" that the alleged anticompetitive conduct will lead to or strengthen a dominant position in the relatively near future. *Id.* at para. 429. Finding that the Commission had merely described the economic conditions necessary to bring about it a certain market result, the Court held that the Commission had not met its burden. *Id.* at para. 462.

Much has changed in the EU's approach to merger enforcement. By continuing to rely on *Tetra Laval*, the CFI appears to have accepted that conglomerate mergers are generally considered competitively neutral. Stefan Schmintz, *The European Commission's Decision in GE/Honeywell and the Goals of Antitrust Law*, 23 U. Pa. J. Int'l Econ. L. 539, 592 (2002). Thus, while not adopting the "hard line Chicago School approach," the court made it clear that nothing less than rigorous economic analysis will do, when anticompetitive effects must be proven. Id. at 593. Also, as noted above [2005 Supp. at 10], in 2004 the Commission adopted a new Merger Regulation that shifted the focus away from "creating a dominant position" to "significantly impeding effective competition." Ilene Knable et al. *Nature vs. Nurture and Reaching the Age of Reason: The U.S./E.U Treatment of Transatlantic Mergers*, 61 N.Y.U. Ann. Surv. Am. L. 453, 491-492 (2005). In addition, the EU's new Horizontal Guidelines specifically provide for the consideration of efficiencies that may benefit consumers. *Id.* at 491-492. It is still the case, however, that European competition law places relatively greater stress on the role of individual competitors than does U.S. law. Former Competition Commissioner Monti remarked that Europe strives to protect "the conditions of Darwinian competition just as our American friends, provided that it is Darwinian competition on the merit." Knalbe, *supra* at 493. It remains to be seen how much distance still separates American and European merger enforcement.

Note on *IMS Health* and the European Approach to Essential Facilities

On April 29, 2004, the European Court of Justice issued its ruling in *IMS Health GmbH & Co. OHG v. NDC Health GmbH & Co. KG*, Case C-418/01, OJ C 118.30.04.2004, p. 14. The opinion provides both clarification of the EU's application of the "essential facilities" doctrine and an interesting contrast to the U.S. Supreme Court's decision in *Verizon Communications Inc. v. Law Office of Curtis V. Trinko*, 540 U.S. 398 (2004).

As *Trinko* illustrated most recently, the U.S. Supreme Court has not expressly accepted or rejected the doctrine in the United States; its language there was, however, skeptical. See 540 U.S. at 410-11. Lower courts have generally held that a party seeking to apply the doctrine must prove: 1) control of the essential facility by a monopolist; 2) the competitor's inability practically or reasonably to duplicate the essential facility; 3) denial of use of the facility to a competitor; and 4) feasibility of providing access. *See, e.g., MCI Communications v. AT&T Co.*, 708 F.2d 1081, 1132-33 (7th Cir. 1983). The European approach is not quite so strict. Citing an earlier decision, the Court of Justice held that "to determine whether a product or service is indispensable...it must be determined whether there are products or services which constitute alternative solutions...even if less advantageous ... and whether there are technical, legal or economic obstacles ... making it impossible or at least unreasonably difficult ... to create ... alternative products or services. *IMS Health, supra,* at para. 28. The Court concluded that a refusal to grant access to a copyright that meets this test would violate EU competition law when the refusal "prevent[s] the emergence of a new product for which there is potential consumer demand, [the refusal] is unjustified and...exclude[s] any competition on a secondary market." *Id.* at para. 38. The Court emphasized that these conditions are *cumulative*, which resolved an earlier debate about whether all three were necessary. *Id.* at para. 38.

At this point, the Court of Justice's concept of indispensability closely resembles the U.S. definition of "essential." The European court has moved from an emphasis on the dominant position of the supplier to a position that rejects the idea that dominance alone demonstrates that the service or product is indispensable. See Sebastien J. Evrard, *Essential Facilitates in the European Union: Bronner and Beyond*, 10 Colum. J. Eur. L. 491, 509 (2004). U.S. courts have likewise refused to apply the doctrine where the plaintiff had a clear opportunity to use a substitute input, such as a sales force. *See Olympia Equipment Leasing Co. v Western Union*, 797 F.2d 370, 377. (7th Cir. 1986). Difficult questions remain, however. Commentators have criticized the lack of guidance with respect to the question whether a refusal to license hinders the development of a new product. For example, the Court did not say whether the new product could exist on the same market as the original product in question and what attributes made it "new." Donna M. Gitter, *Strong Medicine for Competition Ills: The Judgment of the European Court of Justice in the IMS Health Action and Its Implications for Microsoft Corporation*, 15 Duke J. Comp. & Int'l L. 153, 185 (2005) *citing* Estelle Derclaye, *The IMS Health Decision: A Triple Victory*, 27 World Competition 397, 404 (2004).

The Court of Justice, like the U.S. courts, rejected in *IMS Health* the notion that the essential facilities doctrine contains an explicit requirement of two existing, vertically integrated markets. The Court held that the only requirement was to identify "a potential or even hypothetical market." C-418/01 at para. 44 of Court's Reply. Thus, as long as "two different stages of production may be identified and are interconnected, the upstream product is indispensable." *Id.* at para. 44. Compare Robert Pitofsky *et al. The Essential Facilities Doctrine under U.S. Antitrust Law*, 70 Antitrust L.J. 443, 458 (2002).

The requirement in *IMS Health* that there be a risk of all competition being eliminated underscores a lingering ambiguity in the application of the doctrine in the United States. The European Court of Justice left it to the national court to decide whether IMS's refusal to grant a license for its copyrighted "brick structure" (used for providing sales data for pharmaceutical products) would result in the elimination of all competition on the secondary market. C-418/01 at R38. This aspect of the opinion calls to mind two conflicting interpretations of the essential facilities doctrine: under one, the facility is essential only if control carries with it the power utterly to eliminate competition, and under the other, something less than the ability to achieve total annihilation will suffice. On balance, the *IMS Health* decision appears to have moved the European Union toward the position that the United States had maintained for several years. But, as *Trinko* illustrates, the situation in the United States is a moving target. At present, this is another area in which important, though nuanced, differences remain between these two major systems of competition law.

CHAPTER 11: PRICE DISCRIMINATION AND THE
ROBINSON-PATMAN ACT

Insert as Note after *Morton Salt,* page 1307.

Volvo Trucks North American v. *Reeder-Simco,* 546 U.S. 164 (2006). Reeder-Simco was one of many franchised dealers selling new and used heavy-duty Volvo trucks to government and industrial purchasers. The sales process involved competitive bidding. The customer described its product specifications and invited bids from particular dealers based on existing relationships with the dealer, the dealers' reputation, geographic location and other factors. When a dealer received an invitation to bid, it turned to Volvo and requested a discount on the wholesale price, and that discount affected the dealer's bid to the customer.

With two exceptions, Reeder-Simco never bid for a sale to a particular customer against another Volvo dealer. It learned, however, that Volvo had granted greater concessions to other Volvo dealers competing for sales to other customers greater than the concessions granted to Reeder-Simco. A jury found discrimination that violated the Robinson-Patman Act and the Court of Appeals affirmed, concluding that Reeder-Simco and the favored dealers were competing purchasers at the "same functional level."

The Supreme Court reversed, concluding that the Robinson-Patman Act only applied to discrimination between dealers competing to sell products to the same customer at about the same time. When the allegedly favored dealer received a better concession to sell to a different purchaser, it was rarely a "competitor" of Reeder-Simco at the same time. As to the two instances where Reeder-Simco did compete head-to-head with another Volvo dealer, the majority found that the discrimination had not been shown to be substantial.

In a concluding statement of policy, Justice Ginsburg offered the following:

"Even if the Act's text could be construed in
the manner urged by Reeder and embraced by the
Court of Appeals, we would resist an

interpretation geared more to the protection of existing <u>competitors</u> than to the stimulation of <u>competition</u>. . . . By declining to extend Robinson-Patman's governance [to cases like this], we continue to construe the Act 'consistently with broader policies of the antitrust laws.' . . . *See Automatic Canteen Co. of America* v. *FTC* (cautioning against Robinson-Patman constructions that 'extend beyond the prohibitions of the Act and, in doing so, help give rise to a price uniformity and rigidity in open conflict with the purposes of other antitrust legislation')."

Justices Stevens and Thomas dissented.